Harlots, Hussies,
& Poor Unfortunate Women

ATLANTIC CROSSINGS
Rafe Blaufarb, Series Editor

Harlots, Hussies, & Poor Unfortunate Women

Crime, Transportation & the Servitude of Female Convicts 1718–1783

EDITH M. ZIEGLER

THE UNIVERSITY OF ALABAMA PRESS
Tuscaloosa

Typeface: Garamond Premier Pro

Cover photograph: *A St. Giles's Beauty*; courtesy of the Lewis Walpole Library
Cover design: Michele Myatt Quinn

∞
The paper on which this book is printed meets the minimum requirements of American National Standard for Information Sciences—Permanence of Paper for Printed Library Materials, ANSI Z39.48–1984.

Library of Congress Cataloging-in-Publication Data

Ziegler, Edith Miriam, 1944–
    Harlots, hussies, and poor unfortunate women : crime, transportation, and the servitude of female convicts, 1718–1783 / Edith M. Ziegler.
        pages cm. — (Atlantic crossings)
    Includes bibliographical references and index.
    ISBN 978-0-8173-1826-0 (trade cloth : alk. paper) — ISBN 978-0-8173-8749-5 (e book) 1. Women prisoners—Great Britain—History—18th century. 2. Penal transportation—Maryland—History—18th century. I. Title.
    HV9644.Z54 2014
    364.3′74097309033—dc23

                                                    2013035417

*In memory of my father, Idrisyn F. Jones, whose
great interest in America's history seeded my own.*

Contents

Illustrations

Acknowledgments

As an Australian with an interest in the history of my own country as well as that of the United States, I have long been curious about the British penal policy of transportation. I learned early that the War of Independence curtailed the shipment of convicts to the American colonies and provided the catalyst for the British government's decision to establish a penal colony in New South Wales, but I wanted to know more. My questioning eventually led to my researching the topic of the convicted British women who were transported to Maryland in the eighteenth century.

During my research I have had reason to be grateful to many people and organizations, particularly to associate professor Jennifer Clark of the University of New England who supported this project and my ongoing historical interests and investigations.

My research has been aided by the assistance of many marvelous librarians, museum curators, and archivists. I would like to thank the staffs of the Enoch Pratt Free Library of Baltimore, the London Metropolitan Archives, the Maryland Historical Society, the Maryland State Archives, the Public Record Office at Kew in the United Kingdom, the State Library of New South Wales, the State Library of Victoria, the Surrey History Centre at Woking in the United Kingdom, the University of New England's Dixson Library, the University of Sydney's Fisher Library, the library of the University of New South Wales, and the Virginia State Library.

I am also grateful for the advice and assistance I have received from the employees of numerous image repositories: the Baltimore Museum of Art (Rachel Sanchez), the Birmingham Assay Office in England (Sally Hoban), the Colonial Williamsburg Foundation (Marianne Martin), the Lewis Walpole Library at Yale University (Susan Walker), the National Portrait Gallery in London (Alexandra Ault), the Maryland Historical Society (James Singewald), and the Oxford Museum, Maryland (Ellen Anderson).

A number of individuals have made a special and highly valued contribution to my research, investigating overseas archives when I was not able to do so myself. In July 2012 Libby and Alex Jones took time out from a vacation in the United

Kingdom to undertake research on my behalf in various (and widely flung) record offices in London. Dr. Allender Sybert, president of the Maryland Genealogical Society, provided me with data regarding eighteenth-century convictions of British women in Charles and Kent counties in Maryland. Rebecca Crago, research center coordinator of the Historical Society of Frederick County, Maryland, conducted an extensive search of that county's archives and turned up information and details that I would never have been able to find or include without her help.

I also benefited greatly from the hugely generous assistance of Robert Barnes. Bob has an encyclopedic knowledge of Maryland's colonial history and its archival records, and he has written several books on Maryland's early settlers. He not only located family and court records for me in the Maryland State Archives but also afforded me his advice on court processes and personnel. I cannot thank him enough for his interest in and enthusiasm for my research. Our association has been a privilege for me.

Donna Cox Baker of the University of Alabama Press has been the very best kind of editor. Thanks to her initial enthusiasm for my project and her tireless support, the process of turning my manuscript into a book has been stimulating, thought provoking, and very enjoyable. In addition I am most grateful to Dan Waterman, the editor in chief and humanities editor of the University of Alabama Press, and to all members and associates of the press involved in the many stages of the book's production.

Thanks are also due to members of my extended family and to those many friends who were intrigued by the subject, encouraged my research, and suggested I write this book to reach a wider audience.

Introduction

This book is about eighteenth-century women—women from England, Ireland, Scotland, and Wales—who committed crimes or otherwise broke the law. After their indictment, trial, and conviction, these women were punished by being transported to the American colonies, often to Maryland. The fate of these women has been largely overlooked by historians. Although their story forms only a small part of the overall narrative of American immigration, it contributes to the larger picture of unfree labor in the colonial Chesapeake. Moreover, the story of these women provides an alternative narrative to other accounts that explore the behaviors, attitudes, and beliefs of the majority population—the free and the bound—and throws these behaviors, attitudes, and beliefs into sharper relief.

In recent decades historical inquiries have paid heed to the lives of everyday, nonelite people, and this book is in keeping with that approach. It seeks to increase what is known about the backgrounds and the experiences of the transported convict women who, together with their male colleagues, were referred to in Maryland as "His Majesty's Seven-year Passengers" or by similar epithets indicative of derision and disdain.[1]

In exploring its subject, *Harlots, Hussies, and Poor Unfortunate Women* places Maryland in a transatlantic context. It shows the impact that Britain's penal policies and mercantile trading arrangements had on one of its American possessions over a period of more than sixty years, between 1718 and 1783. It also considers white servitude in the economy of a society that was in the process of consolidating a slave-based plantation system while at the same time becoming more diversified economically. It was a society that, as it grew in diversity and complexity, was beginning to chafe at restrictions on the range of its economic activity, on its legislative independence, and ultimately on its political autonomy. Convict transportation was a prime feature and symptom of all that was odious to Americans about imperial hegemony and colonial subordination.

In 1718 the idea of exiling British criminals, including women, from their native land so they might "eat the bitter bread of banishment under foreign clouds" was not new.[2] It had first been floated in 1584 by Richard Hakluyt, an idealistic

English clergyman, in *A Discourse of Western Planting*. Hakluyt stated there were "many thousands of idle persons within this realm" who, having no work, were "mutinous or very burdensome" and often fell "to pilfering and thieving and other lewdness." He claimed the prisons were full of such people, who "pitifully pine away, or else at length are miserably hanged." He proposed that these idle persons and thieves be "condemned for certain years in the western parts" (principally in Newfoundland) where they could be kept usefully occupied in producing various commodities.[3] In 1597 an act of Parliament established the legal authority to allow deportation "beyond the seas" in order to rid the community of those who would not "be reformed of their roguish kind of life."[4] Several schemes were proposed without much result because there was not then a sufficiently appropriate destination.

In August 1611 Governor Thomas Dale of Virginia wrote to Robert Cecil, Earl of Salisbury, about that new colony's critical labor shortage and suggested a solution that echoed the earlier proposals: "On account of the difficulty of procuring men in so short a time, all offenders out of the common gaols condemned to die should be sent for three years to the colony: so do the Spaniards people the Indies."[5] Dale's position as governor meant he was more likely to be able to influence those who had the power to do something with the idea. Moreover, there was now an actual place to which "rogues" could be deported.

Whether or not it was acting on Dale's recommendation, just over three years later, on January 23, 1615, the Privy Council made the first order enabling prisoners to be reprieved from capital punishment in order that they might "yeald a proffitable service to the commonwealth in partes abroad, where it shal be found fitt to employ them" (see appendix 3).[6] By the time of the Declaration of Independence in 1776, when the white population of America had reached approximately two million, more than fifty thousand male and female convicts had been transported to the North American colonies from Britain and Ireland.[7] The trade ceased conclusively only after the Continental Congress resolved in 1788 "that it be recommended to the several states to pass laws for preventing the transportation of convicted malefactors from foreign countries into the United States."[8]

For all the advantages that transportation (or banishment and exile) seemed to possess—it was a relatively inexpensive means of disposing of unwanted felons, a source of colonial labor, a visible deterrent to would-be offenders, and a chance of redemption to those already under sentence—it was employed somewhat irregularly in the period before the onset of the English Civil War in 1641. However, the reforming Parliament of 1649 disposed of several thousand Irish and Royalist prisoners of war by sending them to America and, in 1656, the Council of State ordered the apprehending of "lewd and dangerous persons who have no way of livelihood . . . and treating with merchants for transporting them to the English plantations in America."[9] After the Restoration of the Stuart monarchy in 1660, King Charles II appointed a Council for Foreign Plantations for the better governance of the colonies. On June 3, 1661, this council established a committee "to consider the best way of encouraging and furnishing people for the plantations and how felons condemned to death for small offenses and single persons, men and women found to be sturdy beggars, may be disposed of for that use and to consider an office of registry for same and for the preventing of stealing of men, women and children."[10] Soon after the establishment of this committee, transportation was being regularly employed as a punishment. Between 1661 and 1717, approximately forty-five hundred felons were pardoned for transportation, though actually getting them to the colonies posed a persistent problem. Jailers were reluctant to release felons to shippers because they would then lose the fees earned and moneys derived from their charges. Shippers felt the sureties they were obliged to pay were too steep, and the zeal of the government for spending money to "people the colonies" was never consistent. Moreover, colonists in America and the West Indies began to demonstrate an unwillingness to receive "persons of bad character," merchants were reluctant to transport anyone without saleable skills (especially women), and war made the trade risky and unreliable anyway.[11]

In the early years of the eighteenth century, those who were actually involved in the administration of justice—the courts and the British Parliament—were keen to find a usable secondary punishment to stiffen the penalties following a successful plea of "benefit of clergy," which was a mitigating practice with origins in the deference paid by secular authorities to the medieval church.[12] By the end of the seventeenth century, any person convicted of a felony could "call for the book" and, if able to demonstrate the ability to read, was deemed to be clergy, based upon the ancient theory that all who could read were in holy orders. In 1705 Parliament made this manifestly absurd fiction even more bizarre by providing that those who wished to plead benefit of clergy did not actually need to demonstrate literacy. At the same time it set forth a list of felonies that were "nonclergyable," including petty treason, piracy, murder, arson, rape, witchcraft, burglary, stealing goods with a value of more than a shilling, and highway robbery. Those convicted of "clergyable" offenses were often branded on their thumb or, if convicted of petty larceny, subjected to a public whipping, but then went free—often to commit further offenses.

In December 1717, Parliament considered a bill for "the further preventing of Robberies, Burglaries, and other felonies and for the more effectual Transportation of Felons."[13] The bill provided an alternative to the binary punishment regime of death or freedom and proposed a means of differentiating better the penalties to be meted out respectively to serious criminals (those tried mainly at the assizes— the higher courts presided over by circuit judges appointed by the Crown) and to less menacing lawbreakers, including women and children, who were normally dealt with by county justices at the courts of quarter sessions. The bill offered hope, too, for the reestablishment of societal order, which appeared to be under threat, as indicated by the extremely high crime rate in metropolitan London and other urban centers. Crime had risen sharply in 1714–15 following the end of the War of the Spanish Succession and the accession of the Hanoverian King George I—which had sparked rioting from pro-Jacobites.[14] The bill was developed by a committee headed by Sir William Thomson, recorder of London and solicitor general. Its members represented the counties of Surrey and Middlesex and the City of London.[15] It was shortly enacted as 4 Geo. I, c. 11 and became effective in March 1718 (see appendix 4).[16] Thomson continued to be involved with the implementation and operation of the Transportation Act and its further refinement until his death in 1739.[17]

From 1718, although all colonies received convicts, only a few went to New England. Approximately 97 percent of transported felons went to Virginia or Maryland, where there was a continual demand for cheap, white bonded labor for skilled and semiskilled farming tasks and for domestic work.[18] The best-known female convicts were actually fictional—Moll Flanders, the creation of the novelist Daniel Defoe, and Polly Haycock, the creation of the anonymous "A Creole."[19] Yet possibly around fifteen thousand real women were transported after 1718. Around half of these were sold as servants in Maryland, a colony whose economic circumstances made convict labor particularly attractive.[20] Yet, in comparison to the larger number of female British convicts (approximately twenty-five thousand) who were transported to Australia after 1788 and who have been regarded (even if equivocally) as legitimate contributors to that country's foundation, the convict women who were transported to Maryland seem to have been of little interest to scholars of the colonial period, as discussed below.

Actually, American historians took a long time to show any interest at all in convicts (let alone women convicts). This is despite the fact that, between 1718 and 1776, more than six hundred convicts were transported each year from England and Wales alone. It has been estimated that, over this same period, a further sixteen thousand Irish and eight hundred Scottish convicts were transported as well. By midcentury convicts comprised at least one-quarter of all British immigrants received by the American colonies and one-half of all English immigrants.[21] A census taken in Maryland in 1755 showed that in four counties where the convict component of the workforce was largest, approximately 12 percent of bound laborers over the age of sixteen were convicts.[22]

Despite these numbers, when George Bancroft wrote his epic and influential *History of the United States*, which was published in several volumes between 1834 and 1874, he said (in relation to transported convicts) that he had been economi-

The Fortunate Transport, English, 1760–80, black and white line engraving. (The Colonial Williamsburg Foundation, Museum Purchase.)

cal in dispensing the truths he had discovered. Having "a handful, he only opened his little finger."[23] Bancroft was thus knowingly deceptive when he alleged that most of the convicts were guilty of crimes that were "chiefly political" and that the number transported for social crimes was "never considerable."[24] In his history about the American mission—the ingathering of people seeking liberty of religious expression and those who were imbued with a vision of advancing the cause of human freedom—convicts could have no place.

By the end of the nineteenth century, probing investigation had replaced lofty disdain and several historians had attempted to quantify the actual numbers involved in transportation and the significance to the colonies of this importation. In his 1879 *History of Maryland—From the Earliest Period to the Present Day*, John Thomas Scharf stated (with what sounded like some surprise) that "the numbers imported into Maryland before the revolution of 1776 must have amounted to at least twenty thousand."[25] In 1907 Basil Sollers went beyond a concern with quantification and described the way in which convicts met Maryland's labor shortage from the seventeenth century until the Revolution. He also described the early hostility to convict women and the sustained hostility to transportation overall. In his monograph he provided an account of an attempt in 1697 by the lord justices of

England to dispose of fifty female prisoners who were incarcerated in Newgate—London's principal prison. Agents for Massachusetts, New York, Maryland, Virginia, Carolina, Barbados, Jamaica, and the Leeward Islands were all approached and asked whether their colonies would accept the prisoners; all said no. The agents were of the opinion that the women would contaminate colonial society, that their only value would be as field laborers (for which they had no experience), and that, "being altogether useless," they would be rejected as house servants. Similar objections would be heard again in the ensuing eighty years.[26]

In 1946 Richard B. Morris published *Government and Labor in Early America*, which made extensive use of colonial court records to establish the legal basis of different types of indentured servitude. The following year Abbot Emerson Smith published *Colonists in Bondage: White Servitude and Convict Labor in America*.[27] Both books, but particularly Smith's, were concerned with the phenomenon of bound labor as a fundamental feature of the colonial period. During this period all colonies (including those of the Caribbean) sustained chronic labor shortages until slavery started making a significant impact. Smith mentioned women briefly in conjunction with indentured servitude and the conditions of life for bonded servants.

After the appearance of *Colonists in Bondage*, nearly forty years elapsed before A. Roger Ekirch started bringing out precursor articles for the comprehensive and significant work he published in 1987, *Bound for America: The Transportation of British Convicts to the Colonies, 1718–1775*.[28] This wide-ranging and thoroughly researched account described the role transportation played in Britain's criminal justice system and the colonial economy. However, although Ekirch showed that significant numbers of women were transported and provided some examples of their crimes and subsequent treatment, he touched only lightly on issues of gender as a factor in British justice or on female convicts' assignment within a specific economic environment, such as Maryland's. Sixteen years later Edmund Morgan published *American Slavery, American Freedom*, a groundbreaking book on servitude and its impact.[29]

Bound for America seemed to spark the interest of a new generation of historians, including Kenneth Morgan, Farley Grubb, Gwenda Morgan, and Peter Rushton. The research of these last two historians into crime and punishment in Britain's provincial jurisdictions—especially the punishment of women in Newcastle, Durham, and Northumberland—has particular relevance for the topic being explored in this book.[30]

Maryland's convict women "contributed to a complex world of the free and the unfree occupying different conditions of liberty and bondage, some tied to masters for relatively short periods of time and many more doomed by their race to servitude for life with no rights of their own." All were interwoven into "a hierarchy of ranks and degrees of dependency that was simultaneously a pluralistic world of peoples from Europe, Africa and the Americas."[31] The convict women were regarded as outcasts—justly condemned to forced labor for their crimes.

While the actual experiences of the convict women may not have differed to any great extent from the experiences of other bound laborers or those members of society who lacked much acknowledged economic status—the "lower sort"—they are nonetheless deserving of separate attention. It is a historiographical truism that, if women are not dealt with directly in accounts of the past, their experiences tend to be overlooked and the particularities of gender ignored. This is largely true of the (growing) body of literature concerning convict transportation to the American colonies; female convicts have been incorporated into frameworks set up to examine the experiences of male convicts.[32] Similarly, those histories that have examined questions associated with other types of white female labor such as (for example) indentured servants overlook the implications of forced exile and (even though it was quite legal) the completely involuntary aspect of the convict women's presence in America.

In the last two decades or so, much of the historical writing that has focused specifically on the colonial Chesapeake—especially Maryland and Virginia—has been concerned with revealing the societal complexity and diversity mentioned above. Major studies, such as those by Kathleen M. Brown, Lois Green Carr, Rhys Isaacs, Allan Kulikoff, Gloria Main, Debra Meyers, and Lorena S. Walsh, to name just a few historians, have shown how issues of class, ethnicity, gender, and race were intertwined and how a small cadre of elite white men came to assert a confident authority over their realm.[33] This authority systematically relegated slaves, servants, and women to an inferior status, their principal role to be concerned with production and reproduction—subject always to white male control by husband, fathers, lawmakers, masters, judges, vestrymen, and so on. After their arrival in Maryland, the convict women were greatly affected by all these issues—by class, ethnicity, gender, and race and by the patriarchal assumptions that governed every aspect of their lives. This study therefore reflects the larger concerns of historians of the colonial Chesapeake generally and of Maryland in particular.[34]

In an electronic bulletin published some years ago by the Maryland State Archives, an unnamed historian is quoted as having asserted in relation to transported British convicts that "modern Marylanders need not worry, these 'undesirables' could not possibly have been ancestors of people living today."[35] Taking a cue from this comment, *Harlots, Hussies, and Poor Unfortunate Women* will go beyond the derogatory labels that were often attached to convicts in order to develop a clearer profile of just who Maryland's convict women were and whether, and to what extent, they were "undesirables."

Factoring gender and feminism into what is known about convict transportation to Maryland and post-arrival servitude is no easy task because of the limitations of the source material. Because transportation was a private business activity, the principal data relating to the shipping of convicts are British Treasury Money-Books (ledgers), extant ships' landing certificates (which are incomplete), the records of various legal disputes, and the letterbooks of a few of the merchants and factors involved in the convict trade. There is no record depository in either Britain or Maryland that holds anything comparable to the convict "indents" that arrived with every transport vessel carrying convicts to Australia in the nineteenth century. By the 1830s these indents listed each of the convicts on board plus his or her age, educational level (literacy), religion, conjugal status, children, place of origin, occupation, crime, place and date of sentence, sentence length, and any former convictions. In addition, these indents provided personal information—height, complexion, eye color, distinguishing characteristics, and so on.

In conducting the research for this book, an attempt has been made to create a sort of skeleton indent for just over twelve hundred of the female convicts transported to Maryland—approximately two hundred women in each decade between 1718 and the 1770s. This has been done by marrying trial information—largely, but certainly not exclusively, drawn from the records of the Old Bailey—to the surviving passenger lists of transport vessels known to have landed their convict cargoes in Annapolis and other Maryland ports. These passenger lists have been examined to establish their gender composition and the geographic origins of a significant proportion of the women who were transported from England and Wales (but not Ireland or Scotland). These data have allowed some analysis and tabular presentation to explain or enlarge the text. Additionally, as a means of identifying regional patterns of English crime, *all* the transported women whose names are available in the extensive listings developed from English court records by Peter Wilson Coldham have been counted and their counties of origin recorded (see appendix 1, table 1).[36]

Information about the women in the post-arrival period has had to be scratched together from wherever it could be found—merchant letterbooks, newspaper items, runaway advertisements, contemporary estate inventories, and Maryland's county court records. All these sources provide data to develop some minor narratives for individual women—usually women whose behavior drew adverse attention for some reason. These records give the occasional glimpse of a servant's circumstances, albeit mediated by others.

A certain amount of creativity has been necessary to reconstruct the lives of people who left no written documents of their own and rarely rated a mention in the diaries, letters, and business papers of others. Besides the documentary sources mentioned above, the discovery process has involved assessing information drawn from archaeological investigations of places where the women may have lived and worked. It has also involved checking museum holdings for the farming implements, tools, and utensils they are likely to have used. The houses of the affluent planters that still exist may or may not have been home to convict women but, in any case, they typically tell the visitor more about the lives of their owners than the cooks, kitchen hands, housemaids, laundresses, seamstresses, and other servants on whose labor their functioning depended. Where house museums do attempt to present "belowstairs" life, it is usually to acquaint visitors with the realities of black slavery rather than unfree white servitude, though a certain amount of general information about domestic service can be inferred.

Despite the fragmentary, incomplete, and inconsistent source material, *Harlots, Hussies, and Poor Unfortunate Women* presents new, or at least more detailed, information about where Maryland's convict women came from, the types of crimes they committed (and the seriousness of these), their marital and family status, their occupational skills and whether these were suited to the colonial economy, their personal characteristics, and so on. As well, it builds on the work of previous historians of transportation and white servitude in colonial America to envision and explore the experiences of the women in their geographic, economic, social, and cultural worlds—the turbulent world of eighteenth-century England, Scotland, Ireland, and Wales that they inhabited before they were sentenced and the world to which they were subsequently transported. The two worlds of the convict women were, of course, not static throughout the six transportation decades. Any major statutory, regulatory, and/or policy changes that took place in those decades and that might have affected the women have been noted, as have shifts in the political and economic environment—particularly the American Revolution, which ended the convict trade. The book also looks at issues of gender and sexuality and considers the ways in which the female convict's experience might have differed from the male convict's and whether (and how) being a convict may have affected—even altered—the reality of being female or gendered notions of that reality.

The topic of the book is developed through a linear account. The first chapter outlines the economic and technological changes of the eighteenth century in Britain and Ireland and the nature of legislative responses to what was perceived to be a sharp increase in the incidence of crime—chiefly property crime. The second chapter describes the implications of the Transportation Act for the lives of women who were convicted under its provisions. It contains trial testimony and the text of several convict petitions—some of the only sources in which the women's own words are on record—and the reaction of women to the prospect of exile. The actual operation of the convict trade is covered in the third chapter. It shows how the trade was essentially a branch of the slave trade and how shipping merchants were able to derive very healthy profits from a publicly subsidized business. It also gives readers an idea of the conditions experienced by women on their often-dangerous voyage to Maryland. The fourth chapter covers the hostility or ambivalence demonstrated toward convicts by Maryland's colonial authorities and the attempts by these authorities to restrict and control the influx of felons. It also describes arrival, sale, and purchase procedures and offers thumbnail sketches of some of the people who were in the business of buying convict women regularly. The fifth chapter deals at some length with the post-arrival lives of the convicts—the sort of work to which they were assigned, their isolation, their physical privations, their friendships and relationships, the restrictions on their personal behavior, the punishments they bore—particularly those they bore for having illegitimate children—and their opportunities for relief and recreation. The sixth chapter examines newspaper advertisements placed by owners when women escaped their servitude, using them as a vehicle to establish further details about the convict women's lives—their clothing, their appearance, and their behaviors, especially those that did not accord with gendered notions of appropriate female conduct. The seventh chapter explores what happened to the convict women after they completed their servitude. It shows that although some returned to Britain, there really was no "going home" for these women. The final chapter examines the impact of the American Revolution on the convict trade and how this offended ideals of freedom and a republic consciously built on a rhetoric of rights and civic virtue. It discusses the significance of the Revolution for women generally and for the convict women in particular. It suggests several reasons explaining why—Chesapeake historians aside—the story of the convict women, their lives and circumstances, is so little known to the American public today.

1
Social Change, Crime, and the Law

The women who were transported to Maryland between 1718 and 1783 were the products of a society in a state of greater than usual flux.[1] In fact, for the (nearly) sixty years of the transportation period, the world the women inhabited before their deportation was undergoing major cultural, demographic, economic, and social changes.[2] These changes, particularly those affecting agriculture and home-based industrial production, had a significant impact on the lives of women. The changes helped to create the conditions for rising crime in England, Ireland, and Wales and (to a lesser extent) in Scotland. Though women were less likely than men to face prosecution in the courts, they were significant contributors to the increased incidence of crime—particularly theft.

In 1718 Britain was still primarily rural and, although towns of size and substance were beginning to develop in Lancashire, the West Riding of Yorkshire, and the West Midlands, the majority of the population was still located in the south of England. By midcentury this had started to change. Aided by an ongoing and accelerating rural exodus and (in the northwest) by an influx of Irish immigrants, Bristol, Manchester, Liverpool, Sheffield, Leeds, Halifax, Birmingham, and Coventry all ceased to be sprawling villages and expanded into major towns. By 1781 the population of England and Wales had grown to approximately seven million (up by 40 percent since 1700) and, despite emigration and a devastating midcentury famine, the population of Ireland had reached approximately four million.[3] This increase in population had a marked effect on the British economy. It enlarged both the labor supply and the home market for goods and services. It also helped to enable the start of the industrial revolution, which, over time, would see many of the institutions and practices of a traditional rural society disturbed, eroded, or replaced by those more suited to urban capitalism and a developing consumer economy.[4]

From about the middle of the century, innovations in iron production, as well as water and steam power, contributed to the early stages of what was actually not so much a revolution as an ongoing, though quickening, process of technological innovation applied to manufacturing. Multiple innovations started putting at risk the artisan-based fabrication of textiles. Spinning and weaving gradually moved from the cottage to the manufacturing mill and from the country to the town.[5] As towns and commercial service hubs grew rapidly, these provided new opportunities for middle-class enterprise and advancement but they also increased the circulation of money and acted as magnets for a range of criminal activity.

Adding to the societal turbulence was the incidence of periodic large-scale unemployment. Between 1701 and 1763 Britain was involved in four major European wars, and those whose war-based employment ended with the cessation of hostilities (chiefly men) sometimes turned to crime as a means of economic survival for themselves and their families. There was certainly a noticeable spike in the crime rate at the end of each of these wars.[6]

Others who turned to crime included displaced agricultural workers. Although the enclosure of fields and common grazing land had been going on for centuries, in the fifty years between 1720 and 1770, Parliament passed no fewer than 686 enclosure acts, and these significantly eroded the access rights of local people to land on which they had (for example) previously grazed sheep or cows or grown crops. Moreover, enclosures often led to the destruction of the cottages in which agricultural workers lived.

The supersession of open by enclosed fields and of collective by individual ownership meant that enterprising farmers could undertake improvements in crop selection and animal breeding and could experiment with other agricultural innovations without worrying too much that their efforts would be wasted. It also meant, however, that yeomen producers who were neither sufficiently ambitious to apply new knowledge nor in possession of the requisite capital to invest in new or improved technologies lost out in the agricultural revolution. Single women were particularly hard hit by the enclosure of commons and were left with few remaining options to earn a livelihood other than casual field labor or odd jobs in their village. Landless farmers, farm laborers, and their wives were others who often had to become wage laborers in towns or in the multiplying mills, where they worked long hours for minimal pay.[7]

In order for the displaced to survive in this unfamiliar and arduous environment, they needed to become attuned to hierarchy, obedient to direction, and willing to comply with a fixed routine.[8] To some of those averse to the consequences of rural change or resentful of their progressive impoverishment, crime offered a means of claiming back age-old privileges or recovering a sense of autonomy by hitting back at the system—a system of rule that depended on deference and patronage.[9]

As towns grew, so too did the system of roads and waterways that linked them. Along these unpoliced thoroughfares there was constant movement of people and of all sorts of valuable goods. This traffic furnished lucrative opportunities

for the highwaymen and organized gangs of robbers, sometimes armed and sometimes female, who terrified travelers and communities. In April 1770 four young
women—Sarah Page, Catharine Goodwin, Mary Allaway, and Elizabeth Talbot—
concealed themselves in a roadside field waiting for passersby to rob. When Diana
Sawbridge came along, they pounced. Goodwin cursed Sawbridge and knocked
her down with a closed fist, putting her "in corporal fear and danger of her life"
while the others stole her money and clothes. Apprehended shortly thereafter, the
gang members were convicted and sentenced to death but, owing to their youth,
were reprieved to be transported to Maryland for fourteen years. In July 1770
their fellow transportees on the *Scarsdale* included two women and a male con-
federate who had been similarly convicted (and reprieved) for a robbery "on the
King's Highway."[10] These women provide examples of a type of criminality that
was markedly at odds with the notion (and the statistics) that women were rarely
involved in violent crime.

The apparent growth in the crime rate was deeply unsettling to the British ruling and mercantile classes and a source of fear and suspicion for all owners of property, employers, and the masters and mistresses of households. Perpetrators were
regarded with loathing and, while men were the chief culprits, women who offended were viewed similarly as a threat to civil order, authority, and social certainty.[11] Yet some women, especially those in rural areas, through want or necessity often felt they had no other option.

Although there were regional and local differences throughout Britain in both
the rate of change in conventional farming practices and the jobs available in provincial industry, many aspects of the upheaval in country life were widespread and
challenged traditional roles and assumptions—though nowhere were notions such
as "traditional" and "customary" defined or codified or even consistent. Nevertheless, it was generally held that rural women would make a significant contribution
to family income—by spinning yarn for payment, growing crops, raising chick-
ens, and keeping a cow or some other animal. All of these activities were commonly supplemented with field work at harvest time. Rural women also engaged
in time-honored practices once considered more or less legitimate by both land-
owners and rural laborers alike, such as trapping game on common land, collecting harvest gleanings, picking up underwood from the forest floor, and gathering
chips of coal for fuel.[12] Common-right usages differed from locality to locality and
from parish to parish according to innumerable variables. They altered over time
and were the subject of expectations that were always under negotiation because
of the many interested parties competing for advantage.[13]

Although customary rural practices may often have been contested in the past,
because of the eighteenth century's expansion and institutionalization of a tougher
criminal code, they started to become punishable as crimes.[14] In 1722 Hannah

Bartlett of Hampshire was convicted for stealing a gamecock—a rooster that could be trained for cock fighting. More than fifty years later, in 1774, Ann Bragg was convicted in Durham for stealing coal from one of Sir James Lowther's collieries. Lowther was the developer of both the port of Whitehaven and the Cumberland coal fields and one of the richest men in eighteenth-century England. Both Bartlett and Bragg were transported and, although the records lack the detail needed to be certain, they were possibly victims of the greater legal stringency.[15] If this was the case, they were more likely to be "lawbreakers"—transgressors of socially constructed laws designed to protect the sanctity of property—rather than full-time criminals who lived from the proceeds of crime and whose actions were both illegal and not legitimized by public opinion.[16] The numbers of "lawbreakers" never comprised a very large segment of property criminals (or those who were transported for such crimes), and there were regional differences in the types of crimes committed. Yet many women were responsible for actions that the law defined as crimes but were not regarded as much more than misdemeanors (if even that) by non–property holders or the poor.

When no longer able to rely on traditional methods of supplementing their subsistence, some rural women fought back. Upon apprehension for "stealing faggot wood" or "breaking a hedge and cutting," some asserted they had committed no crime. Such a one was Ann Osborn of the parish of Egham in Surrey, who was arrested two days before Christmas in 1762. Hauled before the justice of the peace, Edward Cooper, she confessed to him that on Saturday, December 18, she had taken "some dry wood from the grounds belonging to Stephen Tenent yeoman of the parish of Egham, his property." Osborn was either truly mystified by her arrest or simply attempting to justify herself, but she asserted she "did not know that there was any harm in it."[17] In the same parish in the same year Judith Marshe and Diana Hudson were indicted for "feloniously stealing and taking away from the top grounds of Nicholas Hogsflesh some parcels of oak wood cut from his property." They apparently had nothing to burn at home.[18] Here were examples of laws made and enforced by those with vested interests that were not always acceptable to the moral opinion of those who were most directly affected by them.[19]

In Scotland, women were fiercely protective of traditional practices and felt morally justified in defending what they believed to be their traditional rights through protest and direct action. Throughout the century, they resisted the clearance of people from the Highlands, an economic policy designed to convert whole regions to farming and sheep grazing at the expense of traditional crofting.[20]

At a time when members of the working class spent most of any cash income they received on food (and most of that on bread), possibly the most important area of resistance and protest for women was associated with bread production and distribution. Markets and prices were frequently manipulated during the eighteenth century, and this often provoked a strong reaction from members of the community who, in the face of rising prices, sometimes physically attacked millers and bakers. Bread riots occurred in every decade from the 1720s to the 1780s.[21]

Women not only took part in food protests but often instigated and led them—probably because the price and availability of food so immediately touched the interests of their families. In 1740 there were serious riots in Norwich and Newcastle-upon-Tyne, and these were graphically reported in the influential *Gentleman's Magazine*.[22] In the Northumberland town of Stockton, which lies approximately thirty-two miles south of Newcastle, women boarded vessels laden with corn and forced the crew to off-load the grain to a crowd waiting on the quay. For their part in this insurgence, Hannah Crone and Anne Withy were sentenced at the Durham assizes to transportation for seven years. These women were likely carried to America on a vessel captained by Matthias Giles or John Hodgson, partners from the Tyneside area in a regular trade with Maryland.[23]

In both 1740 and 1741, the high price of bread, coupled with a shortage of harvest work, was catastrophic for farm families. When women stole food, their family's privation was sometimes mentioned at their trials as a means of seeking some mitigation of their sentence.[24] However, in 1767, when Elizabeth Lloyd from Wiltshire stole bread and bacon, much of the population of southwestern England was still recovering from famine conditions and the judge was thus singularly unsympathetic. He sentenced Lloyd to hang, though she later received a conditional pardon—transportation for fourteen years. Elizabeth Foster and Hannah Lawrence—both from Ealing, then a separate town west of London—stole poultry. Although they were convicted of "animal theft," the small scale of their theft suggests the birds were for their table. In June 1768 a London widow named Mary Rock was sentenced to transportation for "stealing cheese at St. Botolph's, Bishopsgate." Elizabeth Giles from Staffordshire also stole cheese.[25]

Despite the difficulties of the rural economy, women who remained in the country were able to derive support from their family and neighbors in times of hardship. Also, because the "justice system" was still the province of the church parish and highly personalized, rural lawbreakers might expect to appear before the local justice of the peace (usually a district landowner), and this might work to their benefit if they had previously been well regarded and had community support. Unmarried women who had no parental home to shield and buffer them against want and could not subsist without such support had little option but to move away from home.

Some women who moved to towns and cities looked for work as domestic servants or for employment in the needle trades as milliners, seamstresses, tailors, coat makers, and embroiderers. A large number took seasonal jobs in market gardens or in the dairies that supplied the city with milk, cream, butter, and cheese.[26]

Women living in towns had the freedom to participate in a larger range of social pursuits, but their wages, while higher than those paid elsewhere in Britain, were still half the wages of men.[27]

~

London was the city to which perhaps one-sixth of the total population of England was drawn at some time in their lives, and mobility was especially high among young single women.[28] Approximately two-thirds of the women who were transported to Maryland and Virginia between 1718 and the outbreak of the War of Independence were convicted in London and its environs (see appendix 1, table 1).[29]

By midcentury London was not only the largest city in Britain but also the largest in Europe. It was a center of consumption for the rest of the country's produce and products. For those in regular employment in the city, wages provided purchasing power. From a population estimated to be around 575,000 in 1700, the city grew to 675,000 in 1750 (up 17.4 percent), when it was home to approximately 11 percent of England's total population.[30] It consisted of roughly ninety-seven parishes within the old walls of the city, plus another thirty or so parishes in Middlesex, Surrey, and Westminster and sixteen wards or dependencies in the borough of Southwark and Blackfriars, overseen by the lord mayor of London.[31] A parish had both ecclesiastical and civil dimensions; parish officials were responsible, among other things, for maintaining records of births and deaths and for the administration of the Poor Law and the Laws of Settlement.[32] Unmarried women, widows, and children who were indigent paupers in the care of the parish were often placed as servants with mistresses who received a small subsidy from Poor Law officials in order to relieve the parish of its responsibilities.[33]

The women and girls who moved into London from the country were much in demand as domestic servants, but if they were not able to find work, they did not usually qualify for charity from their new parish. Cut loose from the safety and restraint of a familiar community, they often became prostitutes. Many became addicted to alcohol (usually gin), especially in the principal years of the "gin craze" (1720s–1740s), when Britain's eighteenth-century grain surplus was being used to produce huge volumes of the beverage.

According to the novelist and magistrate Henry Fielding (1707–54), gin became "the principal sustenance of more than 100,000 people in this Metropolis." Fielding believed that the death-dealing drink was sold below cost in bawdy houses as an aid to drunken promiscuousness between strangers.[34] Gin was also used as a sort of currency with which to pay for goods. When Elizabeth Stavenaugh, alias Howell, was on trial for theft, one of the prosecution witnesses was described in court as a pawnbroker who "takes in pawns for a halfpenny worth of gin." After Elizabeth Wallis discovered that Anne Groves, a laundress she had engaged "out of charity," had stolen household linen and clothing with a value of 24 shillings, she knew where to find her. Wallis said, "I took her in a Gin Shop." Groves was wearing some of the missing clothes and had pawned others.[35]

Gin was not the only culprit in public drunkenness and its link to crime. Both the victims and the perpetrators of theft were frequently under the influence of alcohol. Some of those bringing prosecutions shamelessly described how they had lost their valuables after nighttime peregrinations from public house to tavern to alehouse for "a dram" of spirits, "a bottle of cherry brandy," "a bowl of liquor," "a half pint of brandy," "a quart of beer," a "pot of flip," or "a tiff of punch." Cider, negus (a hot drink of fortified wine), port, purl (a flavored ale), shrub (a cocktail of fruit juice, spice, sugar, and rum), Madeira, mountain wine, and so on were other alcoholic drinks mentioned in trial evidence. Alehouses and brandy taverns were often established specifically to cater for the needs of criminals—as places for receiving stolen goods and providing entertainment for those on the wrong side of the law.

New arrivals in London who succumbed to criminal temptation were more likely to be prosecuted than in their rural parishes, where social bonds were tighter and community sanctions and censure might be used in place of legal prosecution and punishment. There was also a great deal more to be tempted by in London, in terms of material goods, than in the countryside. Before industrialization and mass production took hold, all goods were hand-made by highly skilled craftsmen. At the end of the seventeenth century there had been an influx of foreign immigrants who helped to add to the range and quality of the goods available. For example, the making of guns, watches, clocks, precious metalware, glass, lenses, paper, tapestry, printed cotton, wigs, fans, hats, woven silk, and shoes all benefited from the arrival of French Huguenots from the 1680s.[36]

A transformation of retailing in the seventeenth and eighteenth centuries meant that goods such as these were often displayed in shop windows or on the pavement outside, thus allowing passersby to inspect "the thousands of inventions and ideas" that were available for sale. Such displays not only increased the temptation to steal but also the opportunity to do so. Instead of shoplifting being the furtive snatching of small objects, it became more purposeful. Often forays were planned by two or more women to obtain specific items of high value. One woman would distract the shopkeeper while the other did the stealing. They hid the items under their skirts and petticoats or inside their sleeves.[37]

The growth of consumerism affected all members of eighteenth-century society and fueled an increase in the numbers of receivers, pawnbrokers, and dealers in secondhand goods. Receivers sometimes worked directly with shoplifters, pickpockets, prostitutes, and common thieves to ensure an adequate supply of saleable products.[38]

While much of the clothing, fabrics, and personal items stolen by the transported women was of a utilitarian nature—a linen shirt or shift was the single most frequently stolen item—occasionally their trial records give glimpses of the exquisite products, clothes, and fabrics of the era. Eleanor Ogle, who was shipped to Maryland on the eve of the Revolution in 1776, had been sentenced to fourteen years' transportation for receiving stolen goods. At her trial in September 1775, it was alleged that she had been found in possession of two cloth coats embroidered with gold, a scarlet cloth waistcoat laced with gold, a pair of silk breeches, a silk waistcoat, a pair of silver buckles inlaid with gold, two pairs of men's lace ruffles, and a red morocco pocketbook with two silver locks.[39]

Trial evidence was more frequently a reminder of the seamy underbelly of urban centers, especially London—the nocturnal city of drunkenness and carnality where brothels proliferated. The trials of pickpockets often involved prostitutes who had fleeced clients when they (the clients) were drunk and/or asleep. On January 4, 1734, after soliciting Evan Edwards in Temple Bar and taking him to her cellar lodgings in St. Giles, Grace Long managed to remove from his apparently capacious breeches a silver watch with two seals, a gold seal, a pair of silver shoe buckles, a pair of silver knee buckles, a pair of crystal buttons, a gold ring, a mother-of-pearl snuffbox, and 8 guineas. At her trial for pocket picking just a fortnight later, despite the worth of the items stolen, the jury found Long guilty of theft to the value of only 10 pence—thus ensuring she would be transported rather than hanged.[40] Female pickpockets often worked together—one might entice a man into a sexual encounter, and when he had removed his breeches in her room, another woman might steal from them a watch or money. In May 1737 Ann Wilson worked such a scam with Mary Solomon when they jointly robbed William Glasspool of his watch in her Whitechapel lodgings. Only Wilson was found guilty and transported.[41]

The artist William Hogarth was acutely aware of the perils awaiting young women who moved to the city and depicted these in satiric but didactic engravings.[42] In his 1732 series A Harlot's Progress he traced the story of Moll Hackabout, a country girl who arrives in London and is brought to ruin through vanity, the follies and miseries of vice, and a society whose laws, customs, and members are predisposed against women and exploit their vulnerability.[43] Though Hogarth's moral tale depended on exaggeration—Moll's dissolution is shown as happening very quickly in just six pictures—it was true that life in the complex environment of the city was of a different order for women than life in the countryside or a village or market town. Its greater freedom carried greater risks.

Of the ninety-two women hanged at Tyburn between 1703 and 1772, most were single and only one-third were born in London.[44] Mary Stanford, before going to the gallows in August 1726, told the ordinary of Newgate—a sort of chaplain who later published the condemned prisoners' stories—that she had been brought

The Harlot's Progress: Moll Hackabout in Bridewell by William Hogarth. (Hogarth, *The Complete Works of William Hogarth*.)

up in a Christian family but once she was old enough to go into service, she had left home and traveled to London, where she soon began associating with "the worst of company." These associates "proved her utter ruin for she followed the trade of street-walking, and addicted herself to all manner of lewdness and wickedness, whoring, drinking, &c." Her childhood "knowledge and practice of religion . . . was almost wholly obliterated."[45] In a sample of 456 women who were convicted at the Old Bailey and transported to Maryland between 1718 and 1776, 241 (52.9 percent) were described as single, or "spinsters," and a further 80 (17.5 percent) were widows (see appendix 1, table 6). It has been estimated that from the end of the seventeenth century, there was a trend toward more women—particularly widows—heading households because of the premature death of a spouse. In the laboring classes the possibility of remarriage was much less likely than for middle-class women.[46] The fact that about 70 percent of the convict women were not married may be tied to their involvement in crime. With declining employment opportunities in traditional sectors such as agriculture, often the only means for a woman to survive was through marriage, going into service, prostitution, or crime. There was an important economic dimension to being married and having a family from which the unmarried could not benefit.[47]

~

In the twenty-first century, the term "Georgian London" conjures up an image of supreme style and societal sophistication in architecture and landscaping, in furniture and artifacts, in music and in literature. Yet, in the first half of the eighteenth century, as the rich built their aesthetically pleasing and well-appointed houses around newly laid out green squares in the city's West End, the poor remained in the older parts of Westminster, such as Covent Garden, Seven Dials, and the Strand, or in the decaying East End. These areas were the center of trade and commerce—and also of crime.[48] These two Londons—the one of luxury and the other of abject poverty—had an uneasy coexistence and regularly collided. In 1723, Sarah Wilbourn was transported for stealing silver from the household of Sir Robert Walpole, the hugely influential Whig statesman and first lord of the Treasury—generally recognized as having been Britain's first prime minister. In 1731 and 1736 respectively, Elizabeth Deacon and Catherine Pollard were convicted for grand larceny, having stolen valuable silver from the royal household— "the property of our Sovereign Lord King George [II]." Pollard's prosecutor was a page to the king's daughter, Princess Mary.[49]

In the decrepit and decaying parts of London there were areas containing warrens of narrow lanes with ancient or evocative names and unsavory reputations— Black Boy Alley, Fox Lane, Petticoat Lane, Pudding Lane, Shoe Lane, Thieving Lane, and so on. Here too were fetid slums of crowded tenements and disintegrating houses that had been subdivided and rented out as lodgings. These would later be termed *rookeries*, places where "criminals, prostitutes, alcoholics and ragged reprobates roosted noisily, ghettoized away from the rest of society."[50] Most infamously, the central London parish of St. Giles in the Fields (immortalized in the outrage and despair of William Hogarth's 1750 engraving *Gin Lane*) was home to a relentless tide of immigrants, coiners (counterfeiters), sex workers, thieves, and addicts of varying kinds.

In the five years following the implementation of the Transportation Act, there were no fewer than 166 trials at the Old Bailey involving residents from St. Giles in the Fields. Thirty of the women sentenced at these trials were subsequently transported to Maryland. One of them was Margaret Ford who, her prosecutor alleged, had stolen a scarlet riding hood and some other things from her master, Richard Moreland, who kept the Crown Tavern in Drury Lane. This street was renowned for its theaters and cockfighting arenas. Ford denied the theft. She said the items could have been taken by anybody because her master kept a very disorderly house and, if she were guilty of anything, it was of helping him find whores for gentlemen.[51] Alcohol, prostitution, nightlife, crime, and disorder—Ford's evidence encapsulated the character of St. Giles.

In these wretched London slums, the poor preyed not only on the rich and "middling people" but also on each other. In July 1742, a man named Adrian Hannor was a prisoner in the Poultry Compter, a small debtors' prison run by a sheriff and his staff according to their own rules. They charged inmates for everything essential to survival: food, drink, clothes, bedding, and medicine. Many prisoners in the Poultry Compter—by definition already in severe financial difficulties—often found themselves in a downward spiral of increasing poverty and squalor. Disease was rife and there was a significant mortality rate.[52] When Hannor became very ill, a fellow inmate, Mary Donoho, alias Davison, undertook to nurse him. While so doing, she stole money that Hannor had hidden under his mattress. A fellow prisoner asked Donoho, "How could you be so barbarous as to rob Hannor when he was sick, in distressed circumstances, and had a wife and four children to maintain?" Donoho had no answer—what answer was there to make? She was transported two months later.[53]

The wife of William Ashworth was an unfortunate woman who had been incarcerated in Newgate but later discharged to her home in Bowl-yard, St. Giles, where also lived a widow, Jane Knight, and an unmarried woman, Ann Clements. One night, Mrs. Ashworth suffered a fit (which may have been gin-induced delirium tremens), and her candle (her only night-light) went out. Rather than relighting the candle, her husband held on to her while she was convulsing—and the two lodgers took advantage of the dark to steal clothing, household items, and money. Clements was convicted and transported.[54]

Even the very poorest of the poor—those dependent on parish charity—could be both victims and perpetrators. In February 1770 Mary Harwood was an inmate of Blackfriars workhouse. John Powell, the master of the workhouse, assigned her to do the laundry for the other inmates. Given this opportunity, Harwood stole and then pawned workhouse-issued shirts, aprons, handkerchiefs, and other items. The pawnbroker cannot have been under any misapprehension regarding the origin of the items offered. By an act of Parliament in 1697—which remained in force until 1810—clothing supplied by the parish had to be clearly marked at the top of the shoulder of the right sleeve with a large "P" together with the first letter of the name of the parish. This was required so as to deny paupers any grounds for pride and "to discourage those who could work from claiming the funds intended for the relief of the indigent poor." At her trial Harwood "said nothing in her defence"— she would have been hard put to do so. She was convicted and transported.[55]

Nor were some shopkeepers safe from each other. In 1725 Martha Blaithwaite or Braithwait of Wapping had a shop or stall at Rag Fair, the London market for

Sir John Fielding (1721–80) by Nathaniel Hone. (Copyright © National Portrait Gallery, London.)

used clothes on Rosemary Lane near Tower Hill. Separated by a deal partition was another shop or stall operated by Elizabeth Mitchell. One night Blaithwaite removed the dividing partition and stole from Mitchell's shop, two gowns, a petticoat, three scarves, three hoods, thirty yards of lace, and some other goods. The combined value of the items stolen was 9 pounds and 10 shillings, but Blaithwaite was found guilty of theft to the value of 4 shillings and 10 pence—just under the amount for which a capital sentence would apply. She was sentenced to transportation.[56]

Henry Fielding and his blind half brother, Sir John Fielding (1722–80)—also a magistrate—were fully knowledgeable about St. Giles and its denizens as well as the rest of the city's thriving criminal milieu. They lobbied continually for regulatory legislation and sought to convince the powerful Duke of Newcastle that there was an urgent and compelling need for a police force.[57] Yet, noting how often crime was nurtured in poverty, Sir John Fielding was also interested in preventive measures. He was especially sympathetic to the plight of poor urban women, such as widows who had been left to provide for dependent children. In 1751 he wrote *A Plan for Reserving Those Deserted Girls Who Become Prostitutes from Necessity*, in which he stated: "Infinite are the number . . . in this town whose families are generally too large to receive even maintenance, much less education from the labour

A St. Giles's Beauty, a London prostitute in her St Giles's lodgings, 1784. (Engraving from Lewis Walpole Library, Yale University, Connecticut.)

of their parents; and the lives of their fathers being often shortened by their intemperance, a mother is often left with many helpless children to be supplied by her industry whose resources for maintenance is either the washtub, green stall or barrow. What must then become of the daughters of such women where poverty and illiterateness conspire to expose them to every temptation?"[58]

The answer to Fielding's question seems clear enough. What he did not say, however, was that while poverty may have destined many young women to become prostitutes or criminals, these labels neither delimited other roles nor implied full-time or professional engagement. Women could be prostitutes and thieves while also being skilled cooks, needlewomen, servants, and so on. They could also have a primary or supplementary occupation. For example, as well as being a prostitute and pickpocket, the aforementioned Grace Long was an "oyster-woman"—she sold the shellfish from trays to passersby in Temple Bar. Perhaps there was an occupational congruence in street selling; other women who were apparently prostitutes were also street vendors of bottles, coal, flint-glass, fruit and vegetables, rat traps, hare skins, kitchen supplies, old clothes, washing lines, and almost anything else. They alerted potential customers with distinctive cries. The pickpocket Ann Wilson was said to "cry currants and gooseberries about the street."[59]

Fielding implied strongly that poverty and illiteracy made victims of women, not appearing to allow that some might have had agency in their occupational choice. In fact, the pay of workers such as milliners, mantua makers, and stay makers was so low that many women and girls engaged in these trades resorted regularly to prostitution to supplement their earnings. An observer in 1747 wrote that milliners' premises were little more than brothels.[60] The elaborate hat worn by the smiling, buxom young woman in the illustration *A St. Giles's Beauty* may suggest she was a milliner. She was certainly a prostitute, as is made clear by the manner in which she exposes her breast. Her accommodation appears decrepit and contingent—the pull-down bed behind the curtain, the sparse furnishings, and the makeshift decorative effect of the flowers in the chamber pot.

Many of Maryland's transportees worked more or less professionally in the sex trade where, according to James Boswell, the famous chronicler of mid-eighteenth-century London, a splendid madam could earn 50 guineas a night while "the civil nymph with white thread stockings who tramps along the Strand would resign her engaging person to your honour for a pint of wine and a shilling."[61] Margaret King was a prostitute who was indicted in 1752 for stealing clothing from the owners of the Greyhound Inn in Drury Lane. At her trial she stated that she regularly took clients to the inn, actually a well-known bawdy house. Appropriately, the vessel on which she was later transported was called the *Greyhound.* Catherine Haines and her husband, who were transported in April 1763 after convictions for pocket picking and receiving, were said at their trial to be to be "people of very bad character" and well known for operating "a bawdy-house in Fleet Lane."[62]

Britain's growing provincial cities were not unlike London but with less wealth, more poverty, a higher incidence of disease, and greater lawlessness. Newcastle-upon-Tyne, according to Daniel Defoe, had "a prodigious number" of poor people and greater distinctions of weath and status than did many other towns with "very considerable Merchants" and "numerous" laborers.[63] Provincial cities too were having to deal with a rise in criminal activity in which quite large numbers of women were involved. In the twenty-five years before the American War of Independence, women accounted for over half the number of transportees sentenced in Newcastle-upon-Tyne. In Bristol (although the data are incomplete) approximately one-third of all transportees sentenced in the courts were women.[64]

~

Whether in a metropolis such as London, a smaller city, a town, or a country village, it was not hard to transgress. In 1722, in an overreaction to some minor agrarian disturbances, Parliament passed the unprecedented and draconian Waltham Black Act (9 Geo. I, c. 22), which in itself constituted a complete and severe criminal code. It prescribed the gallows for a huge number of offenses without taking into account the circumstances of the offense or the offender.[65] In fact, in every decade of the eighteenth century there was a further statutory shift toward harsher punishments.[66] Lawmakers believed these punishments would have a deterrent value, thus assisting to uphold the social order and protect the privileged status of the propertied. Throughout the century there were many who thought the severity of punishments should be increased to include greater agony and torture.[67] However, despite the ever-escalating harshness of statutory punishment, juries and judges often acted with mercy and discretion when determining both guilt and an appropriate sentence. After 1750, although capital convictions increased, a constantly declining number of death sentences were actually carried out in London, although in the home counties the proportion of condemned who were executed remained steady.[68]

In the sample of approximately twelve hundred women who were transported between 1718 and 1783, it can be seen that as a percentage of all the types of crimes committed by Maryland's convict women, comparatively few involved acts of violence. This accords with the findings of J. M. Beattie, Peter King, and others who have researched eighteenth-century crime. These have established that when women were violent they were mostly violent against members of their own household—husbands, children, and servants.[69] They were, however, prominently represented in indictments for property crime owing to their occupations and opportunities—particularly as apprentices, servants, and day laborers. In fact, some laws were framed with women in mind—particularly servants—and "theft from a dwelling house of goods over the value of 40 shillings" became a capital offense in 1713.[70]

The crime about which householders were most apprehensive was the sort committed by Mary Hewson in November 1718. Hewson, from the London parish of St. Dunstan's in Stepney, was hired as a live-in servant by a woman called Mary Kemp and had gone to live at Kemp's house on Thursday, November 6. Just two days later Hewson decamped, taking with her Mrs. Kemp's silver spoons and a great many items of clothing. When arrested, Hewson was wearing a gown belonging to Kemp's daughter; she claimed—rather lamely—that she had bought it from a secondhand clothes dealer. Less than a month later she was on trial at the Old Bailey, where she was found guilty and sentenced to transportation; hers was an oft-told tale.[71] Householders had good reason to be concerned about their servants. They knew of the household's valuables, they knew when the owners would be out, and they had some knowledge of the local neighborhood and where they might be able to dispose of stolen goods.

The largest category of crime for which the women transported to Maryland were convicted at the Old Bailey was "Grand Larceny," followed by "Theft from a Specified Place," "Theft—Other," "Theft—Shoplifting," and "Theft—Pocket-picking," though these categories weren't really discrete and it seems prosecutors and/or court recorders used their own assessment in deciding the indictment category. Women who stole from a specified place as well as pickpockets and shoplifters were often charged with grand larceny.

Shoplifting and pocket picking—often regarded as "women's crimes"—were both capital offenses if the sums stolen exceeded 5 shillings or 1 shilling respectively.[72] During the period 1730–60, however, many women who were sentenced to death at the Old Bailey for high-value theft were subsequently reprieved, their sentence commuted to transportation either for life or for fourteen years, and many others convicted of similar crimes were sentenced initially to transportation for fourteen years. This occurred even when they were described at their trials as "notorious offenders," as were Sarah Kingman and Margaret Newel.[73] In the twenty-five years between 1718 and 1743, 233 women were sentenced to death at the Old Bailey. Of these, 47 (20.2 percent) had their sentences respited for pregnancy and another 97 (41.6 percent) were conditionally pardoned—mostly to be transported. Of those originally sentenced to death, 76 were transported to Maryland—mostly for fourteen years unless the original sentence had been for murder or infanticide. In such cases transportation was usually for "life"—though their actual servitude never seems to have been longer than fourteen years.[74]

In the provincial courts, which appear to have developed their own judicial culture, sentencing practices reflected local priorities and relationships. At Newcastle-upon-Tyne, women indicted for theft were not usually tried at the assizes because the local authorities seemed to want to keep the outcomes of these trials under their own control. Most thefts in that jurisdiction were thus treated as minor (regardless of the value of the stolen goods) and were prosecuted in the quarter sessions. Women constituted the majority of thieves tried at the Newcastle quarter sessions during the eighteenth century, and they dominated the court lists in the 1750s and 1760s. At Exeter in Devon all thefts were treated as grand larceny (a transportable offense), with only the most shocking cases classed as capital crimes. Yet an Exeter woman named Thomasine Hall (or Hose), who did receive a capital sentence for housebreaking in 1764, was eventually reprieved for transportation.[75]

Even when women were tried in the assizes, some judges seemed to prefer a lesser sentence (if appropriate) rather than have women travel the route from capital sentence to petition to the Crown to conditional pardon. Only one-fifth of the female transportees sentenced at the assizes in Durham, Northumberland, and Newcastle-on-Tyne had been conditionally pardoned, compared with a majority of the male transportees.[76]

There was a relentless sameness in the types of thefts for which women—especially servants—were convicted throughout the transportation period. At the

Old Bailey more than 35 percent of female convictions for theft involved clothing—aprons, capes (or "cardinals"), cloaks, coats, gowns, handkerchiefs, hats, mantuas, riding hoods, shifts, shirts, shoes, stays, and stockings (see appendix 1, table 5 for a breakdown of items stolen mentioned in the convictions of 1,174 women transported to Maryland).[77] This is explained by the fact that, in the new consuming spirit of the eighteenth century, clothing was at the heart of the aspirations of men and women, who were very attentive to their outward appearance. Friedrich August Wendeborn, who lived in London for more than twenty years as the minister of a German congregation, wrote in the 1780s that "all the city's poor and common people do their best to wear fine clothes, and those who cannot afford to purchase them buy the old at second hand that they may at least have the appearance of finery."[78] Although there was quite a deal of regional variation, it appears from the comments of other contemporary observers that working people everywhere were clothes conscious and had different items of apparel for everyday wear and for "Sunday Best."[79]

Clothing was stolen either to satisfy the individual aspirations noted by Wendeborn or to convert to cash. Good clothing could be the equivalent of a savings account. The scale of clothing thefts in London created a thriving secondhand market—in which women were directly involved—and expanded vastly the opportunities for pawnbrokers and receivers. One exasperated judge exclaimed: "You pawnbrokers are the bane of society. It is a question but if you were to be indicted for receiving those goods, knowing them to have been stolen, but that this worthy jury would find you guilty."[80]

Indictment records provide an encyclopedic guide to the broad range of clothing fabrics available—brocade, buckskin, calamanco, camblet, cambric, chambray, check, cheney, damask, dimity, dowlas, duffle, fustian, gauze, grogram, holland, huckaback, kersey, linsey-woolsey, muslin, oznabrig (or osnaburg), sarcenet, silk, soosey, wincey, and more besides. Some shoplifters made off with whole bolts of fabric as well as impressive quantities of ribbon and lace. In July 1718 Mary Wade from the parish of St. Dunstan's in the west was sentenced to transportation for stealing 93 yards of lace (valued at 10 pounds) from Joseph Pomfret's shop. In May 1761 Eleanor Middleditch stole 10 yards of "blond lace." In December 1765 Catherine Wilks and her husband stole 320 yards of gauze (a lightweight, open-weave, muslinlike fabric), 48 gauze handkerchiefs and 30 gauze caps, 6 yards of Scotch lawn, 50 linen handkerchiefs, 50 yards of thread lace, 5 yards of silk lace, 5 yards of silk ribbon, 1 duffle cardinal, and several other items.[81] These women's thefts reflect the importance attached to trimmings. By the second half of the century trimmings made of ribbons, lace, gauze, silk flowers, and fringes were more the focus of a fashionable gown than its fabric. Around the Strand there were spe-

Engraved advertising notice for John Flude's business. He was a pawnbroker and silversmith in Grace Church Street, East London. The upper two levels of the shop window display secondhand clothes, including stays. (Courtesy of the Birmingham Assay Office, England.)

cialist dealers in lace—the costly gold and silver lace used on both men's and women's clothing as well as imported Brussels and Mechlin lace and the "Bone Lace" made in Buckinghamshire.[82]

A further 21 percent of female thefts described in the trials of twelve hundred women at the Old Bailey involved household items (see appendix 1, table 5). In trial after trial the evidence mentioned the theft (often by a lodger or servant) of linen or "flaxen" sheets, pillowbiers or pillowcases, clouts (diapers or napkins), table linen, blankets, feather bolsters, quilts, and similar items, and also silver spoons, pewter plates, copper kettles, boiling pots and porridge pots, saucepans, candlesticks, and books.[83] Household items were taken because servants had ready access to them and they were easy to pawn or sell. Slightly fewer than 20 percent of thefts involved jewelry, watches, and/or money.[84]

Patterns of theft in other major cities such as Bristol and Newcastle-on-Tyne were similar to those in London, though Bristol, being bigger and richer, probably offered better opportunities for would-be thieves than Newcastle.[85] At the Newcastle quarter sessions, 36.4 percent of female thefts involved clothing, and the theft of household items also featured prominently.[86] In urban areas, at least, it was not difficult to find buyers for almost anything and thus nothing that was potentially saleable was overlooked, no matter how humble the object—in 1725 Margaret Fitchett was exiled for seven years for stealing a chamber pot.[87]

A crime that was specifically committed by young unmarried women (who were often household servants or daily staff who lived out, such as charwomen) was infanticide. The law establishing infanticide as a crime, enacted in the reign of King James I, stated: "Whereas many lewd women, that have been delivered of bastard children, to avoid their shame, and to escape punishment, do secretly bury or conceal the death of their children and after, if the child be found dead, the said women do allege, . . . that the said child was born dead [it will be regarded] that the said child or children were murdered by the said women, their lewd mothers, or by their assent or procurement."[88] In other words, whenever a "bastard baby" was found dead, the concealment of its birth was, in itself, prima facie evidence of murder. The court had to decide on the basis of graphic and harrowing evidence whether babies had actually been stillborn. Married women who killed their children were usually charged with homicide rather than infanticide.[89]

Pregnancy was a disaster for women who went into service. Although being a servant offered a certain amount of economic independence, it was a precarious occupation that becoming pregnant put at risk. Most employers insisted on their servants being celibate because pregnancy and the resultant birth of the child were very inconvenient and upset the household for an uncertain period of time. Servants who broke this requirement could not expect to keep both job and child.[90] Their stark choices were usually either to have an abortion, to pay their parish 10 pounds to take on full responsibility for the baby (knowing it would be unlikely to survive for long and that if it did live, it would be apprenticed to work by age seven), or to kill it immediately after birth—though after 1741 some London women could leave unwanted children at Thomas Coram's Foundlings' Hospital. Between January 1718 and December 1737, fifty-six women and one man were tried at the Old Bailey for infanticide. Twenty-three of the indictments involved servants.[91]

Most women indicted for infanticide were acquitted, with juries inclined to extend the benefit of the doubt—especially if the woman had acquired baby clothes and linen in preparation for the birth. Yet, over the whole transportation period, twenty women were sentenced to death for infanticide. Six of these were reprieved and transported. Such a one was Ann Terry, a woman in her late thirties who, after a painful labor, delivered a baby girl in April 1744. Not long after the birth she threw the baby out of an upper-story window, killing it. She was put on trial the following month. Witnesses testified that for six years Terry had worked reliably for a London cobbler fixing uppers to the soles of shoes. She was described as being quiet and honest—if rather dim. She apparently found it hard to take care of herself. One witness said that Terry's barbarous act resulted from her wanting "to hide her shame" but that she was delirious and not making any sense. Another said Terry was non compos mentis—that is, "deranged, imbecile, lunatic, or not of sound mind." There may have been truth to this because Terry was reprieved—to be transported for life in October 1744.[92]

Not all lawbreakers were light-fingered servants, strayed innocents, or the struggling poor. London had plenty of full-time criminals who had their own customs, language, and hierarchy. Women were involved as receivers of stolen goods, as burglars, as forgers and fraudsters, as coiners and counterfeiters, as thieves, as shoplifters, and as pickpockets. All these occupations were represented in Maryland's transportees. Some women were repeat offenders. At the 1718 trial of Elizabeth Burton, or Black Bess, of the parish of St. Sepulchre, she was described as a "well-known receiver of stolen goods." Similarly, when Sarah McCabe, alias Flood, alias Ridgely, alias Clarke, alias Brewit, appeared in the Surrey assize court in 1764, she faced multiple prosecutors because she had "for upwards of twenty years carried on the practice of shoplifting."[93]

Some very alarming women inhabited the criminal underworld. Sarah Bibby was a sort of female Fagin who helped recruit waifs and strays off the streets of London for a den of thieves in which children were trained for a life of crime. At Bibby's trial for stealing in December 1745 it was noted that although she was only twenty-four years of age, she was "an old thief." When it suited her—and it seemed to suit her fairly frequently—Bibby gave evidence against her accomplices, including the little boys she had been grooming. At an earlier trial in 1745 it was claimed that by giving evidence against people who crossed her, Bibby had "hanged five or six last sessions" and "would hang a great many more." In the event, she would not. In February 1745 the vessel on which Bibby was being transported to Maryland—the *Plain Dealer*—was overpowered by a French man-of-war (the *Zephyre*). After a pitched battle, Captain Dobbins, most of his crew, and some of the convicts were taken onto the French ship. With thirty-five male and forty-five female convicts still on board, the *Plain Dealer* was then dispatched to "any port in France." The vessel was lost off the coast of France near Brest, and all perished except for seven French sailors. The whole incident was related by Captain Dobbins in a letter he wrote to William Parks on March 7, 1745/46, and this was published in Park's *Virginia Gazette*.[94]

Mary Morgan was a transportee from Surrey whose activities were undoubtedly thuggish. Usually when a woman was indicted for "housebreaking," it meant she had, in daylight hours, simply gone through the open door of a house to snatch something espied from the street. But there was nothing opportunistic about Morgan's housebreaking activities. In 1752 she smashed her way into a house in Southwark by knocking a large hole through an outside wall. Caught and convicted, she was sentenced to death but was reprieved and transported for fourteen years.[95]

Some women had underworld nicknames such as Scamp (a highwaywoman), Sparrow (a pickpocket), Cutpurse (also a pickpocket), and so on. The names of the infamous Jenny Diver and Mary Cut and Come Again derived from their habitual pocket picking, which eventually led both of them to the gallows.[96] A few women were fraudsters who plied their avocation with colorful audacity and outrageous gall. In 1755 Mary Smith, a widow, was sentenced to death for having stolen 24 guineas from Samuel Meadwell at Snowhill (near Newgate) in January 1749. At that time Meadwell was a very young and gullible country boy from Northamptonshire and was completely taken in by Smith when she told him she could make him very rich because she was an astrologer. She had, she said, demonstrated her astrological arts "before very great people, princes, and the like." Meadwell was persuaded by Smith to put all the money he owned into a handkerchief and then to tie this up with two peppercorns and a little salt. Smith said she would add some mold to the peppercorns and by means of alchemy (and a mysterious incantation) his few guineas would become a great fortune in gold, which he would find the next day in his master's cellar. Smith evaded prosecution for five years until Meadwell—by now older and much wiser—finally caught up with her. Smith was conditionally pardoned upon transportation for life and was deported on the *Tryal* in 1755.[97]

The women transported to Maryland came from the society and the judicial environment described above. They included insurgent bread rioters and aggrieved rural women greatly affected by enclosure and the loss of what they regarded as their customary rights. They included unmarried and widowed women without family support who had suffered from the decline in home-based industry such as spinning, and servants who had pilfered small items from their masters and mistresses or had made off with valuable items on a fairly significant scale. They also included pickpockets (who were frequently prostitutes), shoplifters, and receivers of stolen goods. A tiny number of them were guilty of infanticide—an occasional consequence of the punitive treatment of unwed mothers and the stigma of illegitimacy. Still others were professional criminals who thrived on the century's turbulence and lax policing—particularly in urban areas—and were involved in various nefarious enterprises (see appendix 1, table 3 for a summary of categories of crimes committed by 1,229 women sentenced at the Old Bailey between 1718 and 1776).[98] Some were active perpetrators in wrongdoing and others were victims of misfortune. Their conviction and the court trial process extinguished somewhat the differences between the women. The experience of transportation and colonial servitude would be new to them all.

2
Punishment, Pleas,
and the Prospect of Exile

The final text of the Transportation Act of 1718 implies that it was intended to achieve multiple objectives: to serve as a deterrent to crime, to offer the chance of rehabilitation to those already convicted, and to confer an economic benefit on the colonies through its provision of labor and population (see appendix 4). Yet its principal objective was to rid the mother country of wrongdoers who, as described in the previous chapter, appeared to offer a rising threat to the very stability of civil society. The exile of offenders was an infinitely preferable option to wholesale capital punishment and offered the further advantage of not being visible to those citizens whose sensibilities might be affronted by the sight of freeborn Englishmen and women in chains or undertaking forced labor.

The act had an immediate effect on sentencing practices. Those convicted at the Old Bailey in London started receiving the sentence soon after the act became effective. It was a similar case in the home counties and in other areas such as Bristol, Devon, Lancashire, and Newcastle-upon-Tyne. In fact, just one month after passage of the act, the justices at the Easter quarter sessions in Devon sentenced Ann Osby, alias Asby, to transportation.[1] Nevertheless, whereas all counties were required to transport those convicts sentenced at or reprieved from cases determined at the assizes, a degree of judicial discretion determined whether the penalty would be used for cases tried at the county quarter sessions. In some counties the new direction in penal practice was ignored for several decades before first being employed as a punishment. Isobel Martin (a pickpocket) and Margaret, wife of Samuel Likard (who had been involved in a robbery with assault) were sentenced to transportation at Cumberland's quarter sessions in 1741—the first so sentenced by that county's justices. It was not until the 1750s that Durham's justices adopted the penalty at the quarter sessions.[2] However, it should be pointed out that in some counties, although there was an early judicial enthusiasm for transportation, this was not always matched (at least initially) with adequate arrangements for actually shipping the convicts to America, and convicts languished in jail for long periods before departure.

Offenders who were tried at the quarter sessions had the advantage that these courts met at least four times a year in the relevant county. Those whose more serious crimes required a trial at the assizes might have to wait six or seven months or even longer. These courts were presided over by circuit judges appointed by the Crown who visited each part of the country only twice a year—or sometimes much less frequently.

Everything to do with the assizes involved elaborate rituals whose intention was to demonstrate the majesty of the law and the power of the state. When the judges arrived in a town, this was announced with a pealing of bells and trumpet fanfares. The sheriff would ride out to greet the judicial visitors personally, and the most important and influential citizens would send richly liveried carriages to provide an escort. In court the judges were dressed in scarlet robes lined with ermine and wore full-bottomed wigs. They addressed the jury and announced their verdicts with eloquent, quasi-religious sermons that were intended to impress on their listeners the virtues of authority and the depravities of vice—and its often fatal consequences.[3] At Hull in Yorkshire, a town within the northern circuit, the assizes were sometimes held just once in seven years because of the huge expense of entertaining the judges and their retinues with the balls, dinners, and other celebratory functions that they and the residents of Hull considered appropriate. Those awaiting trial in Hull lingered in prison for all this time.[4]

Before the Transportation Act was passed, 60 percent of men convicted of clergyable offenses were branded on the thumb and discharged, but after 1718 that same proportion was sent to the American colonies.[5] Transportation also reduced the number of men who were whipped and then released. The change in the punishment of women was not quite so dramatic, in that a smaller percentage of women were sent to America and rather more were sentenced to a whipping and then discharged. Nevertheless, the effect on the treatment of women was significant for it ensured that the largest proportion of the women convicted of clergyable property offenses would be transported. Both men and women who previously would have had every expectation of immediate discharge (albeit after a whipping or branding) were now more likely to be returned to jail to await their shipment to one of the American colonies.[6]

The new regime also encouraged the transportation of those who were not actually criminals but unemployed youths between the ages of fifteen and twenty-one whose circumstances exposed them to the danger of criminality. These had to be willing to go and enter into a contract that would permit shippers to transport them. Later on, those who were regarded as vagrants, vagabonds, or "incorrigible rogues" could be transported (without trial) on the strength of a magistrate's order. In 1752 the female members of Northumberland's "gang of the Faws" (a Romany family of itinerant tinkers) were ordered out of the country. The county of

Devon exported a few of these vagabonds every decade between 1750 and 1776, including four women.[7] However, the practice of transporting vagrants and vagabonds was far more common in Ireland than it was in England. Irish courts banished large numbers of people who were associated in the public mind with begging, petty crime, and prostitution (often women).[8]

The initial Transportation Act was later made even more effective, with further acts (6 Geo. I, c. 23; 7 Geo. II, c. 218; and 8 Geo. III, c. 15) strengthening the arrangements by which convicts were delivered to shipping contractors, simplifying sentencing procedures, and enabling the speedy removal of capital offenders who had been pardoned by the king on condition of transportation.[9] Inevitably, throughout the century, additional offenses for which transportation was the punishment were added by statute.[10]

While eighteenth-century law was intended to be punitive, sentencing decisions could be mystifyingly unequal, even allowing for the widespread exercise of judicial discretion. In 1725 a young servant named Sarah Partridge was sentenced to transportation for seven years for stealing from her master one shirt (assessed as having a value of 10 pence). She was transported to Maryland on the *Forward* in September 1725. A fellow passenger was a burglar, Mary Matthews, who had received an identical sentence for breaking into a locked house at midnight when all inside were asleep. Matthews had stolen eight pewter plates, two porridge pots, a teakettle, two saucepans, four shirts, a gown, and other things—assessed at a value of 39 shillings (just under the value at which a capital sentence would apply) but probably worth a lot more. In September 1745, Mary Mclaughlin was sentenced to transportation for fourteen years for receiving stolen goods comprising a sheet and a pair of stockings. Less than a year and a half later, Anne Boswell was reprieved on condition of transportation for fourteen years for murder. She had, with malice aforethought, stuck a knife in her husband's back to a depth of four and a half inches, and he had taken quite some time to die.[11]

In reaching such disparate decisions, judges sought to weigh carefully the seriousness of a prisoner's offense, her character, and her standing in the community. In fact, such matters were often regarded as a crucial question for the court—sometimes just as crucial as questions of guilt or innocence. Character references given in court by friends and neighbors were important but carried little weight if the prisoner had no credibility. When Barbara Hensman (otherwise Harman) was tried for stealing several pieces of valuable silverware from her mistress, her two character witnesses claimed Hensman always "behaved herself well" and was "a sober honest woman"—which rather flew in the face of the facts of the case and of Hensman's own confession.[12] References of good character from employers, property owners, and local worthies were more highly regarded and might persuade a judge to pass a lighter sentence than he might otherwise have done or even to recommend a pardon. On the other hand, if someone of influence wanted to see a prisoner transported, then judges were unwilling to disoblige him.[13] When an offender was unable to produce character witnesses or was a repeat offender, then little mercy was shown. Women, having less status than men, were made vulnerable by the need to obtain references.[14]

All British law was administered within a framework of ideas about gender that assumed women should be virtuous, chaste, modest, compassionate, and pious—but were sometimes governed by emotion rather than intellect. When they were so governed they could be lustful, passionate, shrewish, and lazy. These traits were ascribed to Rebecca Stones, alias Frances Armstrong, spinster, of Edwalton, when she was sentenced at the Nottingham quarter sessions in January 1773. The trial record described her as "bad, loose and indolent," and there was thus no doubt about her punishment: she was transported.[15]

Sentencing might take into account mitigating factors such as age or illness. Additionally, if a woman was a widow or without a male breadwinner, a judge might weigh the costs to her parish of providing poor relief and of looking after her children until these were old enough to be apprenticed (usually at six or seven years of age).

In the eighteenth century laboring people (and rural people in particular) had a strongly developed sense of the place in which they lived, where they had probably been born. This place was intimately known and "richly associated with its own distinctive memories, relics, folklore, legends, and customary practices."[16] The implications for women of conviction and banishment—separation from this familiar place (home) and from husband, children, extended family, and community, were pitiable even in those cases where the punishment was richly deserved. At a time when female life expectancy was 39.5 years, even women in their early twenties might (and often did) die before completing their sentences.[17] Even if they lived, there was no certainty that, once transported, they would ever return. For the women who were sentenced to transportation for stealing an apron, a broom, or a ribbon worth a few pence, the punishment of what might be permanent exile was very harsh—even for repeat offenders. It was no less bleak for those who were guilty of more serious crimes.

In July 1735 a London prostitute named Ann Blackerby was sentenced to transportation for "theft from a specified place"—rooms over a brandy tavern. She had stolen from an exceedingly inebriated client (a "gentleman" named David Forrester) a silver-hilted sword, a silk waistcoat trimmed with gold lace, a stock (neckcloth) and stock buckle, and a pair of stockings. When she heard the verdict, the awful realization of what it meant seemed to hit her suddenly. She cried out to the judge and to all those in the courtroom, "My curse and God's curse go with ye, and the prayers of my children fall upon ye." But it was too late to be rueful, and neither angry imprecations nor tearful invocations cut any ice with the judge. Ann Blackerby was duly transported in December of that year.[18]

Beside the anguish of severing all ties with home, women are likely to have feared the idea of America itself. Few of them would have had the slightest knowledge of the colonies—though some may have heard stories—and may have imagined that they were going to be shipped to an isolated and inhospitable wilderness full of savage Indians and wild and dangerous beasts.[19]

Occasionally family members would be convicted and transported together, which may have lessened the fear of leaving all that was familiar and dear. In April 1732 a mother and daughter—Rose Curry and Elizabeth (Betty) Curry, alias Giles—were both carried to Maryland on the *Patapsco Merchant*. The two of them had been convicted for "theft from a specified place"—the house of Henry Peirson, where Betty was a servant. The court heard that while Peirson was at church on Sunday mornings, Betty would admit Rose to the house and allow her mother to take various goods that Rose would later try to sell. One day Rose Curry approached a dealer, Elizabeth Basingham, who knew Henry Peirson and recognized his property. Caught red-handed, Rose begged pardon and said she regretted having been "the ruin of her daughter."[20]

There were far more instances of unrelated women who had committed crimes together being transported on the same vessel. Mary Dew, alias Holloway, and Elizabeth Cole, alias Majesty Bess, were both passengers on the *Patapsco Merchant* in March 1729. In court the two had been described as "infamous characters." The witnesses for both the prosecution and the defense were widows of notorious criminals who had been recently hanged at Tyburn. Both Dew and Cole were convicted of stealing "a considerable quantity of money from the person of Isaac Stanton" which, noted the court, "may learn him a little wit." A couple of years later Elizabeth Deacon and Mary Watson, who were jointly convicted in February 1731 (for theft and receiving stolen goods), were also transported together on the *Patapsco Merchant*.[21] Whether the women were friends or just co-conspirators, their proximity may have eased the anxiety of the Atlantic crossing and exile.

Because of the relatively high numbers of prisoners convicted at the Old Bailey, it is likely that some of the London transportees discovered neighborhood friends or acquaintances as fellow passengers on their transport vessels. Among the convicts carried to Maryland on the *Worcester* in 1719, there were two women from the parish of Stepney, three from St. Sepulchre's, three from All Hallows on the Wall, four from St. Andrew's Holborn, and five from St. Botolphe's, Aldgate (as well as three male convicts from that parish). Ironically, perhaps, the rector of St. Botolphe's, Aldgate, at this time (1708 to 1730) was the Reverend Thomas Bray, who was heavily involved in the Society for the Propagation of the Gospel in Foreign Parts, an organization that supported missionary work in the American colonies. It is unlikely he considered his wayward and transported parishioners in connection with these endeavours.[22] Because so little information is extant about individual convict assignments in Maryland, it is not known whether the women mentioned in the paragraphs above—family members, co-conspirators, and/or fellow parishioners—served out their time together in America or were even in contact with each other after arrival so that they might maintain some link with home.

In both the period between their indictment and trial and the time between their conviction and departure for Maryland or Virginia, women were incarcerated in conditions of unimaginable filth and squalor. An anonymous account of Newgate Prison (probably written by Daniel Defoe) published in 1717, *The History of the Press Yard*, and a 1777 report on prisons by the reformer John Howard show that for the whole transportation period (and for most of the century) prisons were places of disease, depravity, and despair—made worse by the official indifference that extended to all "malefactors."[23] In 1753 an item in the *Gentleman's Magazine* reported that a prisoner awaiting trial at Newgate might be one of up to three hundred people crammed into two rooms whose dimensions were fourteen feet by eleven feet and only seven feet high (4.27 m by 3.35 m and 2.13 m high). Moreover, "these places had not been cleaned for some time. . . . The poisonous quality of the air was still further aggravated by the heat and closeness of the court, and by the perspirable matter of a great number of all sorts of people penned up for the most part of the day."[24] John Howard's report was even more revealing. He reported that some of those confined could be seen suffering from disease, sometimes dying in loathsome cells of pestilential fevers and smallpox. He believed them to be the victims of the cruelty and deliberate inattention of the sheriffs. "There are several Bridewells in which prisoners have no allowance of food at all. In some the keeper farms what little is allowed them: and when he engages to supply each prisoner with one or twopence worth a day, I have known this shrink to half." Howard also found that prisoners were not given an allowance of straw with which they might make up a bed. As a consequence, some lay upon rags and others upon the bare floors—usually stone. Some were abused by cruel jailers who loaded them with heavy irons that made lying down to sleep difficult and painful. He noted that women were not always spared from this severity.[25]

Within the prisons riots, drunkeness, and gambling were common. All the prisoners were "confined together: debtors and felons; men and women; the young beginner and the old offender: and with all these, in some counties, such are as guilty or misdemeanors only." Howard recorded that mentally ill prisoners were not separated from the sane.[26]

Women frequently mitigated their ordeal by prostituting themselves for favors to jailers (under turnkeys) and inmates alike. These favors might include the promise of help to escape from prison.[27] Many women became pregnant during

King George II (reigned 1727–60) by the studio of Charles Jervas. (Copyright © National Portrait Gallery, London.)

their incarceration—sometimes deliberately in order to support their pleas for pardons. Others were already pregnant when they entered prison and gave birth in these sordid conditions. In 1730 Ester Hampton, described as "wife of Sawbridgeworth and Great Hadham, Yeoman," was sentenced to death in Hertfordshire but "pleaded her belly" and was later reprieved. Her baby, Sarah, was born in Hertford Gaol, and Hampton was transported in December 1731. Ann Newbert was sentenced in Shropshire in 1759 for "stealing at Wellington" and was ordered to be transported "one month after her delivery." Mary Ryan was another who, after receiving a death sentence for burglary, successfully "pleaded her belly," but she had to linger on in prison for a whole year after giving birth before being transported. Mary Aspinall, who was sentenced in 1748, had her "lying-in and the cost of burying her child paid for by the House of Correction in Manchester." She was then transported.[28] The contractors who shipped convicts to America did not want women encumbered with babies on board their vessels. Moreover, it was extremely difficult to convince buyers who wanted domestic servants or field labor to accept women who could not or would not be separated from their newborns.

Upon learning that they were to be "cast for transportation," it is likely most women experienced distress and remorse for the consequences of their convictions— and for being found out for their crimes. Certainly these emotions can be detected in the petitions some of them addressed to the king, his ministers, or holders of high offices seeking a reprieve. The discrepancy in rank between the young women and these men of might and majesty only sometimes redounded to the women's benefit.[29] For example, in 1724 a farmer's daughter named Mary Earland who had been convicted at the assizes in July of that year addressed a pitiful entreaty to Thomas Pelham-Holles, the Duke of Newcastle, who had recently been appointed secretary of state for the south. Her petition, which was written while she was incarcerated in the County Gaol of Devon, stated that she was the victim of a "malicious prosecution" for a theft she had not committed and had been sentenced "for want of proper assistance having neither counsel nor Attorney to act for her." She described herself as "a young widow and the mother of a child not two years old" who would become a charge on the parish because her father, "being upwards of sixty years of age," was unable to care for it. Her distraught father "attended his Lordship from the remotest part of Devonshire on his daughter's behalf" because "her misfortune was heartbreaking to him." His Lordship appears to have been unmoved by her plea.[30]

On September 6, 1739, Catherine Floyd, alias Davis, alias wife of Henry Huggins, was sentenced to transportation for stealing a quantity of men's and women's stockings from a shop owned by one Sarah Hatt. Almost immediately she petitioned the king (George II) from Newgate, stating that she "came of very respectable parents and always acquired her bread in a very industrious and honest manner and was never guilty of any felonious crime whatsoever in her life before." She went on to say that she had three small children to support who depended entirely on her "personal industry and now laboured under the most miserable circumstances" because she was "pregnant with another and almost ready to lie in."[31] Floyd's petition was economical with the truth as she had been convicted (as Catherine Davison) in December 1737 for stealing household linen and other goods from Thomas Cramphorn and had been sentenced to a public whipping. On this 1739 occasion, her petition may have been persuasive, as there is no record of her transportation in the twelve months following the conviction to which her petition referred. She was, however, a serial offender and would be transported in 1741, 1742, and 1744. She will appear several more times in this book.[32]

In 1746 Mary Brown, a convicted Irishwoman who had been given a fourteen-year sentence for "a small theft under the value of thirty shillings," was also greatly fearful for the future of her five children. In her petition to the king she said they would be deprived "not only of Education but of the Common Necessarys of Life so as to be equall sufferers by her transportation as if she had actually been exe-

Thomas Pelham-Holles, first Duke of Newcastle-under-Lyne (1693–1768) by William Hoare. (Copyright © National Portrait Gallery, London.)

cuted." Eleanor Connor, a pickpocket, addressed her petition to the archbishop of Canterbury. Her entreaty was heartfelt and earnest as she was most anxious to impress on him that the prospect of never seeing her children again should she be transported into a strange country was "next to death itself."[33]

About 29.6 percent of 456 women who were sentenced to transportation at the Old Bailey between 1719 and 1776 (and whose marital status was noted) were married (see appendix 1, table 6). Over one-third (36.1 percent) of the women sentenced to transportation at the Newcastle quarter sessions were married, as were over one-fourth (28.1 percent) of those sentenced at the Northumberland quarter sessions.[34] Some of the husbands of these women may have been involved in criminal activities, but many were just artisans, tradesmen, or other skilled workers—people who, it might be assumed, could provide adequately for their families. The occupations of the convict women's husbands—which were sometimes noted in their trial records—included barbers, blacksmiths, block makers, butchers, carpenters, cordwainers, dyers, flax dressers, hatters, hoopers, husbandmen, malt grinders, mariners, miners, pedlars, sailors, shovel makers, soldiers, tailors, weavers, wheelwrights, wig makers, wool combers, and yeomen.[35]

The presence on this list of sailors and soldiers may be an indication that women were stealing to support families affected by the decline in their husbands' war-based employment, which occurred several times throughout the century. The presence on the list of husbandmen and yeomen may be a pointer to the changes taking place in agriculture. In both cases the records are insufficient to be certain about such conclusions. What the trial records may be reflecting, however, is that some male occupations were affected by seasonal factors and that, over the transportation period, there was breakdown in the importance of the rural family as a production unit with interlocking roles and with a "family wage" as the dividend. Rural exodus, commercial employment, and "independent wage" earners were the result.

The new employment environment was also increasingly gender segmented and this created problems for women who were traditionally responsible for the home-based care of children, the sick, and the nonproductive elderly. The changes made it necessary for them to seek the type of employment that would allow them still to fulfill their domestic responsibilities—but such work was usually low status and low paid and was often sheer drudgery. Many women took in washing or became charwomen (*chairwomen* was the contemporary parlance for this general household cleaner) or outworkers in the needle trades (as mantua makers, milliners, seamstresses, trimmers, and so on). These were occupations that allowed women to work with their children close by. However, as women became increasingly marginalized in the labor market, some of them supplemented their income with theft. The occupations of washerwoman and chairwoman are well represented in criminal trial transcripts. Margaret Annis and Mary Harvey were two chairwomen transported on the *Sukey* in April 1725, and so were Rose Robinson and Catherine Herring, who were transported on the *Italian Merchant* in 1745.[36]

Court records show that a very large number of transported women had one or more aliases which, in some cases, may have indicated what might be called today a "de facto" or "common law" marriage. In the first half of the eighteenth century marriages were based on the proposition that what created the married state and constituted the marriage contract were the promises of a couple freely given to bind themselves to each other and live together as man and wife. Even before consummation such a marriage would, in principle, be sustained by the courts against any subsequent marriage. A public ceremony in church or before witnesses was viewed only as a *repetition* and solemnization of the primary promissory and contractual act. It was not until 1753 that the British Parliament passed *An Act for the Better Preventing of Clandestine Marriage* (26 Geo. II, c. 33), which regularized marriage law. From 1754 onward, marriages had to be performed and witnessed in the couple's parish church after the publication of banns or with a valid license. From 1753 a contract that was previously deemed marriage could no longer be considered such, and any woman who contracted to live with a man in the old way without all the precise ceremonial forms required by the act was no longer legally a wife.[37] Clergyman who did not comply with the law could be convicted of "Sexual Offences—Other" and sentenced to transportation for fourteen years. This was the fate of the Reverend John Grierson in 1755 and the Reverend John Wilkinson in 1756.[38] Ann Bowers, who was described at her 1725 trial as "spinster, alias wife of Nicholas Bowers," may or may not have had a common law marriage of the type that predated the Marriage Act. Women indicted of receiving goods stolen by their husbands were sometimes described as "[name], alias wife of." This may have been an indication of court skepticism—that a woman was claiming to be married to avoid being charged as accessory after the fact. It was not valid in law for wives to be charged as accessories to crimes committed by their husbands. One woman had a very complicated marital identity, being described at her trial as "Mary Walker, widow, alias Hitchman, spinster, alias Smith, widow, alias Bouch, wife of Bouch of Stepney."[39] Some other women used multiple surnames (and different forenames), suggesting more devious motives. Such a one was the aforementioned Catherine Davis, alias Mary Shirley, who used the given names Catherine, Mary, and Elizabeth.

Having a family did not automatically guarantee that a woman would have its support. Some families were quite glad to see an errant member transported. In April 1759 twenty-two-year-old Elizabeth Ricketts was actually prosecuted by her stepfather, James Walker, for stealing three gowns worth 45 shillings from his wife (Elizabeth's mother). The mother, who took the stand at Ricketts's trial, reasoned that Elizabeth was an out-of-control delinquent and that if she were not punished for this lesser offense she would end up being hanged on the gallows at Tyburn because she had become mixed up with "a gang of wicked persons, pickpockets, and the like."[40] In 1754 Sarah Merchant, otherwise Sarah, wife of Jebus Merchant, otherwise Sarah Saunders, was indicted for stealing three sheets, a bed quilt, a brass fender, silver spoons, and china from her landlord, John Price. In her petition to the king she stated that she was "married to a man of fortune who had deserted her" and that her prosecution was a "scheme of her husband's friends to get rid of her." Despite the stolen goods having a combined value of 78 shillings, the king (or his officers) seems to have been persuaded by her story because Merchant's sentence was respited and no punishment at all was recorded.[41]

Despite the desperate desire of many (probably most) women to remain at home, transportation may have held out the hope of relief to those whose lives in Britain had become intolerable for reasons of poverty, social dislocation, or community hostility. It offered obvious advantages to the significant number of capital felons reprieved from the gallows (about 62 percent of those originally sentenced to death). However, in 1744, when the aforementioned Catherine Davis, who had been reprieved for transportation in 1741, was sentenced to a third term of transportation for shoplifting, she begged the court "to give her what punishment they pleased, and not transport her; for she would rather be hanged than transported again."[42]

Others were not only apprehensive about transportation but believed it to be less humanitarian and more severe than the physical corrections of whipping, branding, or burning on the hand.[43] Mary Stanford (the London thief who so ruefully confessed to the ordinary of Newgate the details of her progression from a pious Christian country home to complete drunken abandon in London) said that she "preferred hanging at home to transportation abroad," and was of the opinion that "living in foreign parts was worse than a disgraceful and shameful death at home."[44] Elderly and infirm women feared they would not survive either the rugged voyage across the Atlantic or the hard life they would encounter in America. Some women, like a Scottish prisoner named Helen Mortimer, were just as terrified of remaining in jail because "no merchant nor Shipmaster" would risk having them aboard. Mortimer suffered from "Hysterick fits and several other dangerous diseases" and was "much too weak and destitute to transport herself."[45]

If adult women were apprehensive about transportation, what must have been the feelings of little girls? How could they possibly have imagined what lay in store for them? While there is only scant documentary evidence for female transportees who were under the age of sixteen when they were banished to Maryland, there were probably a considerable number because the age of criminal responsibility in Britain was then only seven years. A census taken in Maryland in 1755 showed that 5 percent of the female convicts then serving were under sixteen.[46] One such convict was ten-year-old Mary Johnson.

In the most deprived, dilapidated, and dreary areas of the London parishes, dank, gloomy, rat-infested cellars were rented out to tenants whose poverty was dire in the extreme. In fact, "to have a cellar in St. Giles" was a common catchphrase for squalor and misery.[47] In 1730 Mary Johnson and her mother were living in such a cellar in the Westminster parish of St. Martin's-in-the-Fields. In December of that year Mary was tried at the Old Bailey for stealing goods from their landlady while she (the landlady) was out. Mary was convicted of grand larceny, sentenced to transportation for seven years, and carried to Maryland on the *Patapsco Merchant* in March 1731. Also on board were thirty-six adult women, including several who had been sentenced to death for serious crimes but pardoned on condition of transportation for fourteen years. Of these women, Constance Buckle had been involved in a violent assault and robbery, Mary Smith was a prostitute and pickpocket, and Honour Davis had pressured a servant girl called Mary Parsons to steal goods from her master and pawn them so she would have money to pay Davis for fortune telling. When Davis predicted "great things" in Parsons's future, it is unlikely that the naïve servant and dupe imagined these might include seven years of servitude in America.[48] As Parsons and Davis were transported on the same vessel, it is not likely that their onboard interactions were particularly cordial. If the experienced master of the *Patapsco Merchant*, Captain Darby Lux, took any steps to keep little Mary Johnson away from the baleful influence of Buckle, Smith, and Davis, there is no record of it.

A few of the convicts awaiting exile fought determinedly to evade their destiny and did their very best to abscond. In June 1758 and again in October 1771 the *Gentleman's Magazine* reported foiled escape attempts by Newgate prisoners.[49] The entries describe the prisoners only as "transports," but as men and women were not housed separately in the prisons, it is very likely that women were involved in these attempts.

The *Worcester*, which departed London in February 1719 under the command of Captain Edwyn Tomkins, was one of the first vessels to carry a sizeable number of convicts to Maryland after the Transportation Act was passed. On board were fifty-nine men and thirty-eight women, all from London or Middlesex. All of the women except one (who had been involved in a serious robbery with violence) had been convicted of various types of relatively minor theft or pocket picking. More than thirty years later, in December 1752, the *Greyhound* left London for Maryland under the command of Captain William Gracie. On board were seventy-seven men and thirty-six women. The profile of the *Greyhound*'s female convicts was remarkably similar to that of the women on the *Worcester*. Thirty-five were from London or Middlesex and all but two (who were receivers of stolen goods) had been convicted for theft. The profile of the convicts on the two ships gives a clear indication of how quickly the provisions of the Transportation Act were implemented in the area of Britain with the highest crime rate and how consistently they were applied over a long period.[50]

Contemporary periodicals regularly reported on how the war on crime was being waged, and citizens could track the workings of the Transportation Act through the "Historical Chronicle" for the month in the *Gentleman's Magazine* or a similar section in another publication. Several times each year a paragraph similar to the one transcribed below (though generally less lurid) would appear in the *London Magazine*, the *Historical Register*, or the *Gentleman's Magazine*:[51]

> Thus ended the sessions at the Old Bailey when seven malefactors received sentence of death, viz Thomas Beck and Peter Robinson for the High-way; Dorothy Fosset for stealing two guineas from a person in drink, Richard Wentland for a street robbery, Anne Wentland, his wife for forcibly taking from Henry Park ten pounds, James Phelps and William Hurst for stealing goods out of a house at Hendon. Hurst was held up at the Bar to receive sentence and died on the back of one who was carrying him to the cells.

The two women pleaded their bellies; Wentland only was found pregnant; twenty-five were ordered for transportation; three to be burnt on the hand and four to be whipt.[52]

Like all women who "pleaded their bellies," Dorothy Fosset and Anne Wentland had to be examined by a specially empanelled "Jury of Matrons" to assess whether they "were with quick child." In the eighteenth century just over half of the women who made this plea were successful. Although neither Fosset nor Wentland turned out to be pregnant, they were subsequently conditionally pardoned and transported to Maryland for fourteen years.[53]

Unless their petitions to remain in Britain were successful, women "cast for transportation" faced an exile that, from the point of view of those in authority, would effectively and simultaneously help to solve problems of orderly civil governance, remove a pervasive threat to social stability, and eliminate a menace to the rights of property holders. By being dispatched to America, the convict women who (together with their male colleagues) compositely represented all these dangers would leave behind (or so the governing class hoped) a cleansed and relieved community. Employers and mistresses would no longer have to fear their depredations and sinister presence. They would be well out of sight and mind. For the women themselves the prospect of transportation was severance—from family, from familiar environs, and from a society within which they had spent their whole lives and of which they had knowledge and some understanding.

3
Bound for Maryland

Before the implementation of the Transportation Act in 1718, the arrangements for conveying convicts to the American colonies were somewhat haphazard. While some merchants were conscious of the profits to be made by selling convicts as indentured servants, many captains were reluctant to carry them because of the dangers they posed to the safety of both vessel and crew. Some of those pardoned on condition of transportation had been expected to make their own travel arrangements but, being loath to leave their homes and families, never did so. They remained in Britain, only to revert to "their former wickedness." This sort of problem continued to be experienced in Scotland even after the English law was applied there in 1766. Women had often been refused passage because their disposal as servants in the colonies had proved too difficult.[1]

In drafting the new act, the solicitor general (Sir William Thomson) and his committee explicitly acknowledged the deficiencies of prior transportation arrangements and sought to correct them with the new statute. Thus the Transportation Act created a new legal foundation for those whom the courts had "cast for transportation" to be conveyed to shipping contractors who would be legally bound to transport convicts regardless of their age, sex, or physical condition and to assume responsibility for their safekeeping on board. The contractors would no longer have the option of picking and choosing which convicts they would ship to the colonies and which they would leave behind (see appendix 4). They were obligated to take everyone—even those with little economic value. In order to ensure that removal took place, these contractors were adequately paid and, in addition, were granted a property right in the convicts' labor for the term of their sentence—a right they could sell upon arrival in America. Hefty penalties applied if a contractor failed to comply with the terms of the contract.

The implications of these statutory requirements were that the convict women bound for Maryland were first a cargo for shipment and profit and then little more than chattels for sale—human commodities whose circumstances were not unlike those of slaves, albeit not in perpetuity. It was no coincidence that many of the contractors for the convict business were "Guinea men"—those who had experience in the slave trade—and were well positioned to exploit the opportunities that the convict trade provided. They had on hand vessels fitted out with holds that could securely carry large numbers of people and had crews that had been drilled in dealing with potentially mutinous passengers.[2] Jonathan Forward, James Gildart, Lyonel Lyde, and Samuel Sedgley were all slave traders who became involved with convict transportation.

The business was undoubtedly very profitable. In the later years of the transportation period, general merchants such as the half brothers William Stevenson and James Cheston recognized the attractive returns and decided to include convicts among the other goods they shipped regularly to Maryland. Stevenson told his brother that "the trade would not be worth carrying on without the convicts" and predicted later on, rather gleefully, that "the trade will make us genteel fortunes and sales of convicts run up amazingly."[3] Merchants who dealt in the dry goods needed by the colonists would sometimes leave such goods unshipped if they were able instead to load a cargo of convicts.[4] The convict trade meshed together very nicely with the trade in tobacco and other commodities such as wheat, flour, lumber, and pig iron—convicts were sent out to the colonies and commodities were brought back from the colonies in the same vessels.[5]

There were other attractive features to the business as well. It required only modest capitalization—Stevenson & Cheston began in 1767 with 1,500 pounds and one vessel. With the addition of William Randolph in 1768, the firm's capitalization rose to 9,000 pounds and several vessels; it then became the largest trader of convicts in Bristol, shipping 93 percent of all the convicts sent to Maryland between 1768 and 1775.[6] There was a ready retail market which, if it were overdependent on credit, offered few distribution problems. Moreover, if they were careful to schedule their voyages around court calendars, shippers could match convict supply to periods of peak market demand—the late spring and early summer months for tobacco planting or the late summer and early fall for harvesting.[7] Costs could be underwritten by the per capita subsidies paid by the Treasury for each convict shipped from London and its surrounds or by those paid by county justices, who raised special county levies for the purpose. These payments compensated the merchants for convict mortality and the fact that some convicts—such as old women—had no value in the colonies. They smoothed the variability of year-on-year trading returns and they often cross-subsidized poor results from the trade in other products such as tobacco.[8]

On the downside, the trade was highly competitive and transportation arrangements were often "left to the most corruptible class of Public Officers."[9] Connivance and bribery were also necessary to secure the favor of jailers who provided convicts to the contractors at the ports of departure. In 1769 James Cheston was advised by his partners that he need not have any worries about "our scheming neighbors" (that is, competitors) because "we have secur'd all the Goals [*sic*] round about."[10] Getting paid, however, was also a constant problem. The problem of "the punctuality of remittances" was a constant refrain in nearly every letter between William Stevenson and James Cheston.[11]

Many merchants from ports all over Britain and Ireland were involved in the convict trade at one time or another during the transportation period. Their commercial interests and the nature of the trade itself meant they neither invited any scrutiny of their activities nor left much evidence of these behind. Perhaps this was deliberate; some of the principal shippers were neither savory nor reliable and their affairs would not have stood much scrutiny.

Jonathan Forward who, after ingratiating himself with the solicitor general William Thomson, was appointed by the Treasury in 1718 as "Contractor for the Transports" for London, Middlesex, and the home circuit counties, was, beside being a merchant and slave trader, a highly litigious man with underworld connections (including the notorious thief taker Jonathan Wild).[12] Forward was succeeded by Andrew Reid, who was said to be "a person against whom almost every species of complaint was made."[13] Reid held the post as government contractor until 1763, when he was succeeded by his associate John Stewart. Horatio Sharpe, who was governor of Maryland from 1753 to 1768, regarded Stewart as "unreasonable and greedy."[14] After Stewart died in 1772 his partner, Duncan Campbell, maintained the business until the outbreak of the War of Independence, from which time Campbell became superintendent of the infamous convict hulks on the Thames River in England.[15] Of the Bristol contractors (sometimes regarded as among the most humane of the shippers), Samuel Sedgley was a bankrupt and William Stevenson misappropriated the firm's funds to cover losses resulting from his incompetent management of his family finances.[16]

Despite the requirement of the act that all those sentenced to transportation had to be carried to the American colonies, some provincial contractors still refused to take women or were slack about doing so. This was because women were neither as marketable as male convicts nor did they offer such satisfactory returns. In August 1723 the Common Council of Bristol voted a sum of 10 guineas to obtain pardons for seven prisoners (mostly women) "who have laine long in Newgate under sentence of transportation and no person would take them." After Martha Williams was sentenced in September 1740, she was faced with the possibility of an additional six months in jail after the Bristol Court adjourned before authorization had arrived for her transportation. In 1725 two young women in County Durham were found guilty of a highway robbery between Gateshead and Sunderland and sentenced to death. They apparently received a reprieve but were still in jail five years later awaiting transportation.[17] If convicts were deemed insufficiently fit to be transported, judges might order that they remain in prison. Such was the fate of an Exeter woman, Mary Middleton, who was convicted of stealing in 1719. Whether she served her entire sentence of seven years in prison or whether she died is not on record.[18]

In order to maximize their returns, the contractors had to calibrate their business so that their expenditure on the convicts' care and safety was neither so high that it would reduce potential profits nor so low that it would increase the likelihood of losses. The economics of transportation meant a certain amount of "cargo wastage" was not necessarily detrimental to overall business performance. Its governing principles showed it to be just a branch of the slave trade. Horatio Sharpe believed the contractors made exorbitant profits on the backs of inhuman cruelty and that they obliged the masters of ships to take on board twice the number of convicts they should safely be carrying with little concern for the consequences.[19]

In a matter-of-fact description of the transportation business, the central characteristic experience of the convict women between their departure from jail and their sale in Maryland—the Atlantic crossing—might be missed. The lapsed time between their sentencing and their embarkation was sometimes only a few days, but it could also be several months, even when there were no shipment problems. The *Historical Register* in 1719 noted that on July 10, 1719, Susanna[h] Cook, Elizabeth Curry, Elizabeth Dawson, and Mary Wood had been "ordered for transportation" at the Old Bailey along with twenty-two men.[20] These same women can be found among the list of passengers on the *Susannah and Sarah*, which sailed for Maryland in October 1719. Also aboard were women who had been sentenced at the Old Bailey in May, September, and October 1719.

The removal of those sentenced at the Old Bailey or in the courts of Surrey and the home counties was usually quite prompt but not always. If a trial had resulted in a death sentence but a reprieve was sought, the delay could be years. Alice Impey, who was sentenced to death for several felonies in February 1746 but later reprieved, was not transported until 1752.[21] As they waited for their appeals to be determined and then, if reprieved, for a transportation date, women continued to endure appalling prison conditions.

The convict women's journey to Maryland began when they were taken from their prisons and marched to a quayside, where they would board flat-bottomed lighters used to load vessels riding at anchor instead of tied up at wharves. In London, convicts boarded the lighters at docking points along the Thames River—those from Newgate went down the hill to Blackfriars within sight of St. Paul's Cathedral. Convicts from Southwark boarded further down the river beyond the East End at Blackwall. All vessels leaving London underwent a customs search or "second clearing" at Gravesend in Kent, and additional convicts were sometimes loaded there.[22] Convicts from the provinces were boarded in other trading ports such as Barnstaple, Bideford, Bristol, Liverpool, Lyme Regis, Newcastle,

Plymouth, Portsmouth, or Whitehaven. In Bristol the convict vessels were intentionally moored at some distance from one another for security reasons. Irish convicts, who mostly came from the county of Leinster, were loaded in Dublin.[23]

The *Gentleman's Magazine* of May 1736 provides a glimpse of one convict transfer in London. It highlights how privileged transports did not mingle with the common herd and that class distinctions prevailed even among criminals (the men mentioned were "distinguished" lawyers turned highwaymen):

Monday 17
One hundred felons convict walk'd from Newgate to Black-Fryars and thence went in a close lighter on board a ship at Blackwall. But Wreathcocke the Attorney, Messrs. Ruffhead, Vaughan and Bird went to Blackwall in two Hackney coaches and Henry Justice Esq., Barrister at Law, in another two hours after the walking felons attended by Jonathan Forward. These five gentlemen of distinction were accommodated in the Captain's cabin which they stored with provisions for their voyage.[24]

On this same ship (the *Patapsco Merchant*), Ann Brewer, Ann Brown, Ann Hopkins—all convicted of theft at the May sessions of the Old Bailey—and thirty-seven other women traveled belowdecks as close-packed cargo in the hold. Only the possession of means allowed convicts the privilege of traveling as passengers in cabins. Before she was executed at Tyburn in March 1741, Mary Young, alias Murphew, alias Mary Webb, alias Jane Webb, alias Jenny Diver, a notorious gangster and pickpocket, gave an account of her life to the ordinary of Newgate. She claimed that before she was transported to Virginia she accumulated "as many goods of one sort or other, as would almost have loaded a wagon." When she boarded the transport vessel she thus had the funds to ensure she "was treated in a quite different manner from the rest of the transports."[25] Funds put in the hands of captain and crew generally secured accommodation privileges not available to convicts without such means.

The transfer procedure did not change much during the transportation period. Thirty years later, the *London Magazine* of June 2, 1764, provides another glimpse: "69 transports (56 men and 13 women) were taken from Newgate and put on board a lighter at Blackfriars which carried them to the transport ship [the *Dolphin*] at Blackwall. Thirteen of them who were indisposed, were carried in two carts to the waterside. None were allowed to travel in coaches."[26]

These transfers were often grim processions. As mentioned in chapter 1, eighteenth-century punishments were designed in large part to act as deterrents to would-be wrongdoers. Deterrence involved a public ritual of shame including the pillory, the stocks, the whipping post, and the gallows. The procession of shack-

Representation of the Transports Going from Newgate to Take Water at Blackfriars, undated (possibly 1735). (Rayner and Crook, *The Complete Newgate Calendar,* 593.)

led convicts to transport ships in a chained coffle was part of the deterrent ceremonial. As they shuffled along they were jeered by mobs of often drunken and violent onlookers (including children) who shouted obscenities and often pelted them with mud and stones.

One night in May 1773 the *Hanover Planter,* which was anchored in the Thames near Blackfriars, was due to be loaded with over a hundred convicts bound for Annapolis. A large rabble gathered near the prison steps at Newgate to observe the transfer, but in the early hours of the next morning, a watchman came out to tell the waiting crowd that there was no point in hanging around because the convicts' departure had been delayed. Among those roaming the city at this witching hour were two virtually feral girls from the parish of St. Giles's—Mary Smith and Sarah Topham, aged twelve and thirteen. Deprived of their anticipated amusement (and a glimpse of their own future fate), they went off to drink ale—or so they said by way of alibi at their trial the following month when they and two co-offenders were convicted of violent theft and highway robbery.[27]

Convicts from provincial jails often suffered prolonged humiliation, as they were sometimes transferred to their point of shipment chained on horseback—two to a horse. They too were jeered and pelted with stones and handfuls of dirt by onlookers. At the appearance of a convict public sentiment felt should have been executed, the crowd would cry out, "Hang the dog!" and so forth. Sometimes the crowds so frightened the horses that the prisoners were thrown off.[28]

A few convicts even had to undergo supplementary formal punishment before they departed. Jean Grey was a Northumberland innkeeper who had aided Thomas Jameson—a well-known Newcastle printer and engraver who was facing bankruptcy—to launder (via her bar trade) counterfeit 5 pound notes forged by Jameson. After their joint indictment in 1766, Grey repudiated her accusation of forgery and, as a consequence, Jameson was acquitted at the assizes. He abruptly left the city soon afterwards. Jean Grey was then charged with perjury and convicted at the summer assizes. She was sentenced to transportation, but prior to embarkation, she was required to stand in the pillory for an hour. "Several thousand spectators" turned out to witness Grey's public disgrace.[29]

Once on board the transport vessel, the women were usually stowed between the hold and the main deck, though sometimes they were accommodated in the hold itself. A partition at the masthead was supposed to separate them from the male convicts. The ships lay too low in the water to allow the portholes to be opened; a hatchway onto the deck provided what little air and light the women could expect.

Although Moll Flanders was a fictional character, novelist Daniel Defoe had firsthand knowledge of the convict trade and how it affected the transported prisoners. So when Moll says, "We were for that night clapped under hatches, and kept so close, that I thought I should have been suffocated for want of air," it can be taken as a realistic reaction of convict women to their shipboard conditions.[30] A visitor to one of John Stewart's ships who had gone to bid farewell to a prisoner declared: "All the states of horror I ever had an idea of are much short of what I saw this poor man in; chained to a board in a hole not above sixteen feet long, more than fifty with him; a collar and padlock about his neck and chained to the most dreadful creatures I ever looked on."[31]

The convict women were usually transported in small, slow vessels, mostly of less than two hundred tons, designated (according to the number of masts and overall size) *ships*, *brigantines*, or *snows*. Sometimes larger vessels, called *frigates*, were used, and these carried greater numbers of convicts as well as cannon. At least two vessels—the *Eagle* and the *Anne*—had formerly transported slaves from Africa. Others, including the *Rodney* and the *Loyal Margaret*, were completely unseaworthy.[32] In 1768 a group of convicts bound for Maryland on the *Rodney* were driven off course and badly battered by storms. The vessel eventually made shore in Antigua in the Caribbean. Eleven convicts had died and the rest were in a deplorable condition, covered in sores and vermin. Many had been forced to eat their shoes to survive.[33]

Once the convicts were loaded, the vessels would leave as soon as possible. Duncan Campbell claimed that he usually carried an average of 200 convicts per voyage.[34] One of his ships, the *Justitia*, carried as many as 238 on one voyage. James

Cheston's letters show that the vessels used by Stevenson, Randolph & Cheston carried smaller loads—between 53 and 97 convicts. The transport vessels might also carry indentured servants or free passengers and immigrants. Because the courts of the northeast of England seldom generated more than 20 convicts in a single year, vessels from the north of England rarely carried more than 30 in total, including voluntary indentured servants and other passengers.[35]

Besides the convicts and other passengers, the ships often carried a cargo of dry goods for the American market, including items such as glass, nails, blankets, sugar, paint, and linen. When the *Thetis* arrived in Annapolis from London on December 3, 1757 (a Saturday), it was carrying 128 convicts, including up to 53 women, and a huge range of goods. The following Thursday a prominent notice headed "Just Imported" appeared in the *Maryland Gazette*. Placed by James Houston, it provided details of an onboard sale of the goods brought in on the *Thetis*. The items available included refined sugar, cheeses, beer (casks and bottles), pickles, mustard, and snuff. There were also buckles, hats, material for breeches, shoes and pumps, sheeting, stockings (worsted and silk), a wide variety of fabrics—chintz, flannel, lawn, linen, and osnabrigs—ruffles and handkerchiefs, rugs and blankets. Household items included books and magazines, chamber pots, chinaware, cups and saucers, decanters, earthenware, frying pans, glassware, knives, medicines of all sorts, plates and dishes, and razors. There were also tools—lancets, cutlasses, surgeons' instruments, hoes, nails, and "several other things too tedious to mention."[36] It was perhaps ironic that the women who occupied the hold—such as the London thieves Mary Allen, Catherine Bourne, Rachel Dimsdale, Hannah Fordham, and Sarah Gascoyne—had been convicted of stealing (variously) handkerchiefs, pieces of linen, plates, ribbons, rugs, stockings, and many other items similar to those on the sale list.[37]

Once on board the transport vessels, the women were slightly better off than male convicts in that their iron fetters were usually removed when the ship reached open waters and they enjoyed more freedom. Male convicts remained chained throughout the voyage owing to the well-justified fear of mutiny.[38] On some vessels women were able to earn a little money by doing laundry for the crew.

In the enclosed world of the vessel and its predominantly male culture, there was plenty of scope for sexual opportunism and exploitation. In December 1757 a free passenger—a Welsh poet and clergyman named Goronwy Owen—boarded the *Trial* with his family to travel to Virginia, where he had accepted a teaching post at the College of William and Mary.[39] Also on board were a large number of convicts. While the *Trial* was waiting for a convoy of ships to gather in Portsmouth harbour (Britain was then at war with France), Owen sent a letter to one of his closest friends in Wales, Richard Morris, describing the conditions on board.

Sailors are exceedingly vile men. As God is my saviour, each one of them has taken to him a mistress from among the female criminals and they do no work but couple like animals in every corner of the ship. Five or six of them have got the pox (forsooth!) from the women. And there is no doctor here at all but me, who have Dr. Shaw's book with me, and following that I am patching them up somewhat with the old drugs that are in the [medicine] chest here. I am sometimes afraid of getting it myself by being among them.[40]

Some convict women prostituted themselves (or tried to) for special favors. The captain of the *Trial* sent a woman to Goronwy Owen whom the Welshman assumed was to assist his wife in looking after their three little boys. He was mistaken. "There is one of them here [in the cabin] but it is to serve this gentleman's penis that she has been brought here, not to attend my wife."[41] Duncan Campbell referred to an (unnamed) woman entering into a relationship with Captain Somervill of the *Justitia*. According to Campbell, the woman "had much ascendancy over him."[42] In August 1749 Catherine Davidson who, having received a conditional pardon, was being transported for life on the *Thames*, became similarly involved with the ship's foremastman, John Greek.[43]

But if some women traded sexual favors for benefit, others were defenseless against attention they did not want. In 1787 Captain Arthur Phillip of the Royal Navy, an experienced naval officer and soon-to-be governor of the new penal colony in New South Wales, was undertaking his detailed planning for the organization of the first fleet of convicts to be sent to Botany Bay. He wrote: "Strict orders to the master of the transport should be given that they [the convict women] are not abused and insulted [raped and harassed] by the ship's company, which is said to have been the case too often when they were sent to America."[44]

One of the first transport ships to leave Britain after the passing of the Transportation Act was the *Eagle* (a "Guinea ship") under the command of Captain Robert Staples. When it set sail in August 1718 it was carrying thirty-eight women including Mary Cooper (a shoplifter), Mary Hunt (a coin counterfeiter), Mary Jones (a housebreaker), Mary Willoughby, and Mary Adsey. These last two had both been sentenced to death but reprieved on condition of transportation.[45] It is probably fairly safe to assume that none of these women had much comprehension of the place to which they were going. Nevertheless, they might at least have expected their destination to be "Maryland or Virginia" in accordance with the agreement upon which the contractor, Jonathan Forward, was being paid by the Treasury.[46] In fact, all the convicts on the *Eagle* were landed in South Carolina, having first been intercepted by a pirate vessel in the Atlantic.[47]

Pirates, mutiny, enemy interception, and shipwreck were just some of the dangers the women might encounter during their voyage, if indeed they survived it at all.[48] Even when voyages were relatively uneventful, the shipboard mortality was appalling. In the early years a rate of 15 percent or greater was common. In 1720, of sixty-one convicts on board the *Honor*, twenty [33 percent] died before reaching Maryland. Two years later, thirty-eight of the ninety-five convicts who left Britain on the *Gilbert* died on the voyage (40 percent).[49] On the previously mentioned voyage of the *Thetis* in 1757, twenty-eight convicts and the captain all died before reaching Annapolis (a death rate of 19 percent). By the 1770s there had been some improvement, but the rate over the whole transportation period was probably about 10 percent. In April 1779, Duncan Campbell told a special committee of the British House of Commons that he had been carrying convicts for at least twenty years and that "rather more than a seventh part of the felons died, some of Gaol Fever but rather more of smallpox." He observed that the number of women who died during the voyage was only half that of the men, which he attributed to "their constitutions being less impaired and to their sobriety."[50]

The mortality was not entirely the fault of the contractors or captains who, after all, were keen to maximize their profits by landing as many living convicts as possible. As John Howard was to report in the 1770s, the English jails were filthy and the prisoners undernourished, with many suffering from typhoid, "jail fever" (the term usually given to a type of typhus fever spread by the ticks and fleas on rodents), and other serious illnesses. Elizabeth Ling and Mary Pitt, who were listed for passage to Maryland on the *Tryal* in May 1751, died in Newgate before they could depart.[51]

Some transportees were described as having "black feet" that prevented them from walking. This was almost certainly an indication of scurvy, the vitamin deficiency disease so prevalent among sailors or anyone whose diet was vitamin deficient because it did not include fresh food and vegetables. When someone has been afflicted with scurvy for a prolonged period, watery fluids collect in the lower extremities of the body, causing bruising, a loss of weight-bearing capacity, and sometimes gangrene.[52] Contractor Andrew Reid asked the justices of Coventry to deliver the felons directly to his ships after their conviction, as "carrying them to any of the Gaols about town is of great detriment to their health." He also asked that the convicts and their clothes be washed thoroughly before boarding, as he felt nothing contributed more to making a ship sickly than "nastiness" which, he said, had a "very bad effect when one hundred unclean persons are cooped up between a ship's deck."[53]

In the stale atmosphere and close confinement of the belowdecks accommodation, contagion was inevitable and infectious diseases spread rapidly—aided by the lice and vermin that infested dirty vessels. After the *Elizabeth* arrived in Maryland in October 1773, James Cheston advised his partners (by way of justifying medical expenditures) that he had "never seen the Disorder [probably typhus] anything like so inveterate before, those who have survived having had three or four relapses. Indeed the Mate, Second mate, Doctor and some of the hands are more like ghosts than living men."[54]

In 1750 Gottlieb Mittelberger, who was an organist and music master in the duchy of Wurttemberg, was commissioned to take out a specially built organ to a German congregation in New Providence, Pennsylvania. Mittelberger traveled across the Atlantic on the *Osgood*. The ship was carrying hundreds of passengers, including German and Swiss "redemptioners" or "palatinates"—men who made a pledge to pay off the full or partial cost of their passage by working as servants. Mittelberger wrote a grim and vivid description of his crossing and although his account seems highly overwrought, the convict women, who had never been to sea and thus did not know what to expect, may have shared a common experience with similar anxieties and fears:

> When the ships have for the last time weighed their anchors . . . the real misery begins. . . . During the voyage there is on board these ships terrible misery, stench, fumes, horror, vomiting, many kinds of sea-sickness, fever, dysentery, headache, heat, constipation, boils, scurvy, cancer, mouth-rot and the like, all of which come from old and very sharply salted food and meat, also from the very bad, foul water, so many die miserably. Add to this the want of provisions, hunger, the thirst, frost, dampness, anxiety, want, afflictions and lamentations together with other trouble . . . and the lice abound so frightfully especially on sick people that they can be scraped off the body. The misery reaches the climax when the gales rage for 2 or 3 nights and days so that everyone believes the ship will go to the bottom with all human beings on board. In such a visitation, the people cry and pray most piteously.[55]

As cargo, the women were not provided with any human comforts. Some slept in berths that were only eighteen inches wide and others on the hard boards of the deck floor. When vessels leaked, those in the hold might actually lie in water.[56] Though some women came aboard pregnant, no special arrangements were made for their accouchement. During childbirth women were attended by the ship's surgeon, often a very young man with little obstetric experience. Many did not survive the experience. Gottlieb Mittelberger claimed that on the *Osgood* the bodies of the women who died in childbirth and their babies were tossed overboard without ceremony—in one case a woman's corpse was just pushed through a porthole because taking it up to the deck was too difficult. Catherine Davis and Hannah White were both convict women who gave birth en route to Maryland; Davis's baby died.[57]

Although their voyage could take from seven weeks to three months, there is no evidence that any masters of transport vessels made special arrangements to keep the convict women occupied or exercised. Men played games of chance with dice and drank when they could bribe the crew to give them liquor; women may have shared these activities.[58] The better-off planters of the Chesapeake (such as William Byrd of Virginia) imported alcohol from Europe in bottles, kegs, and barrels and these were sometimes carried as cargo on convict ships. The planters complained that their wine and beer never arrived safely and intact. Perhaps the convicts and/or the crew were responsible for the "leakages."[59]

The provision of food varied. On some vessels the women received a ration that included bread, salted meat, peas, oatmeal, and molasses, plus gin on Saturdays. On other ships they received a diet composed almost wholly of carbohydrates— "ship's biscuit," potatoes, and beans. If the rations were properly administered, the women would have received about twelve hundred calories each day.[60] The water supplied was often inadequate. Goronwy Owen told Richard Morris: "For a fortnight we have had to drink foetid water or choke (for there is not a drop of small beer in the ship)."[61]

Like the contractors, many captains (and vessels) continued in what was a specialized business year after year. Captain James Dobbins, who made nine voyages to Maryland, was said to be (though not by a convict) "a Gentleman of Honour in whom strict Discipline and Humanity are equally tempered in his behavior towards these unfortunate wretches."[62]

Dobbins needed to be a disciplinarian, as some of his charges, especially the men, were dangerous and there were several convict mutinies during the transportation period. On a voyage of the *Thames* in 1750 a petty thief named Dorothy Gale—who was being transported for having stolen a linen sheet—alleged that one of her fellow female convict passengers had murdered a third woman. Although the allegation was plausible, an inquiry by a magistrate could not find any evidence to sustain the charge.[63]

Discipline was not always tempered by any humanity. In 1764 Captain Thomas Spencer of the *Albion* kept his cargo "subdued" by "bleeding a few." In the same year Captain James Brown of the *Colin* maintained discipline on his ship by "firing among the convicts and crippling some."[64]

In September 1742 Catherine Davis was convicted and sentenced to transportation for stealing nearly seven yards of thread lace in the Whitechapel milliner's shop of William Coverley—she said she wanted it for baby clothes. Before she left London on the *Forward*, her husband, Lewis Davis, approached the master of the vessel, Captain John Sargent, and made provision for his very pregnant wife to receive special consideration during the voyage.[65] Davis, who was described as a periwig maker from the parish of St. Bartholomew the Less, was very concerned for Catherine, who had already spent two months in Newgate. He gave Sargent between 2 and 3 guineas and some silver buttons to ensure that for the remainder of her pregnancy his wife would be lodged comparatively comfortably in steerage rather than being confined with the other felons in the hold.[66]

Despite the monies he had received from Lewis Davis, as soon as the vessel was off the coast of Kent, Captain Sargent sent Catherine belowdecks to join the other convicts—supposedly because she might spread infection to the crew if she remained in steerage. The ship was tossed by storms and took on water. After her delivery and the death of her child, Catherine became so ill she was not expected to live either. Anticipating her death, Sargent rifled through her boxes and appropriated her valuables (he disdained the box containing "childhood linen"). Sargent also stole from other convicts on board and sold one woman gin and cheese at such inflated prices that he effectively extorted from her all the money she was taking to Maryland. Sargent was later charged with "Piracy and Robbery." At his pretrial hearing at the Admiralty Court, he claimed the watches and other valuables he stole were "gifts," even complaining: "It was a little enough present from a felon."[67] The charges were eventually dropped and his trial did not proceed.

During a voyage of the *Justitia* in March 1743 under the command of Captain Barnett Bond, those on board were subjected to a regime of terror and sadism that eventually saw Bond charged with murder. For reasons of his own (and despite adequate water supplies), Bond strictly controlled the water ration allowed to the 163 convicts on board. The ration was so stringent that their tongues began to split and some were reduced to drinking their own urine. Bond extorted any money that the convicts had and keelhauled those who would not pay up. Although she had only just given birth, Hannah White was threatened with this treatment but, overcome with terror, somehow managed to obtain half a crown to pay off Bond. She must have rued the crime that landed her in Bond's clutches—the theft of some kitchen hardware and a few books, including one called *Dr. Anderson's Royal Genealogies*.[68]

By the end of the *Justitia*'s voyage, forty-five people had died. Among the dead were four women—Ann Masham, Dorothy Roberts, Margaret Robinson, and Grace Thomas. Roberts had stolen large quantities of ribbons, buttons, linen, and other fabrics from a draper; Robinson had betrayed the trust of a little girl by stealing from around her neck a coral necklace and a gold locket.[69] Both women deserved to be punished in accordance with the law, but this fate? Bond declared himself "Heir to all the Felons that should happen to dye while under his care" and took everything left in the possession of the dead.[70]

In December 1766 Maryland passed the Quarantine Act, imposing a fine of 10 pounds per head for each convict unless the ship's master had taken an oath that they were free from jail fever or smallpox upon landing.[71] In 1772 the fine was increased to 50 pounds per head. The contractors and their factors did every-

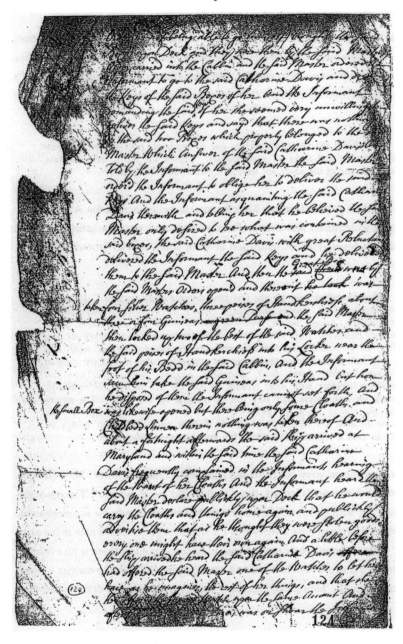

Part of the evidence of John Johnstoun concerning Catherine Davis in the pretrial hearing against Captain John Sargent in March 1744. (High Court of Admiralty: Oyer and Terminer Records, HCA 1/19: Criminal Papers, 1735–1744: Charges against Captain John Sargent. Courtesy of the Public Record Office, Kew, UK.)

thing possible to have the act disallowed by the proprietor, Lord Baltimore, but their objections were overridden and the measure achieved some improvements. John Stewart and Duncan Campbell made their ships "more airy by opening a range of ports on each side between decks."[72] Sedgley and Co. furnished their ships with ventilators, and later Stevenson, Randolph & Cheston installed gratings on one of their ships. The firm did not, however, install a ventilator because William Stevenson thought "pumping in such a torrent of fresh and cold air when perhaps they [the convicts] are in a sweat, must be rather a prejudice and besides, Guinea men do not carry them" (the economics of the slave trade were the standard).[73] In 1768, when Stevenson, Randolph & Cheston bought the brand-new and specially modified *William*, the partners calculated that by bringing in convicts who were healthy, they would avoid the loss of profit usually attributed to deaths on the passage. They even considered the regular engagement of a competent doctor to travel out on their spring and fall ships.[74]

Some captains went to great lengths to assure the Maryland public that they were not landing diseased convicts. A Baltimore merchant named Jonathan Plowman placed an advertisement in the *Maryland Gazette* of July 9, 1767, notifying the importation and sale of *healthy* seven-year servants. He mentioned specifically that a malicious rumor was circulating suggesting the servants had "jail fever," but this was quite untrue. In support of his assertion he included in his advertisement a copy of the quarantine oath made by Captain James Morrison of the *Blessing's Success*.[75] Morrison's sworn oath stated he had sailed from London on April 11, 1767, with sixty-five convicts, one passenger, and twelve sailors. Smallpox had broken out among the convicts and eight had died. The ship's doctor then inoculated all those who had not previously had the disease. For the previous six weeks no one on board had had jail fever, smallpox, flux, or any other infectious disorder.

Duncan Campbell seems to have made some effort to ensure his female charges were adequately dressed for their voyage. On December 8, 1773, he wrote to Mr. James Bare ordering a quantity of clothing to be sent to Captain Finlay Gray of the *Justitia*, which was to sail the following month with forty-six convict women on board. The list included eighteen women's gowns, twenty-four dozen petticoats (he noted "these two items were dear last year"), twelve linen handkerchiefs, twenty-four shifts, and eighteen pairs of women's yarn hose. In the margin of his shopping list, Campbell wrote the direction, "I trust you will take care that these are as good as can be had at the prices."[76] Not all women were so cared for. Some wore coarse dowlas shifts and petticoats or clumsy canvas gowns issued by the merchants at Gravesend. Some just had patched or ragged bodices, hats, and cloaks.[77]

Despite the passage mortality rate and the rigor of the ocean crossing, the majority of the women convicted in Britain and Ireland survived their journey to be sold into servitude. Captains who delivered their cargoes successfully after coping not only with the hazards of a long voyage but with the ever-present threat of convict uprisings, disease, and piracy, might earn a commission from the sale proceeds.[78]

～

For a business so heavily subsidized by the Treasury and by county levies, the trade in convicts remained throughout the whole transportation period largely unaudited and unsupervised by any statutory or independent authority except those concerned to ensure that removal was timely and delivery was made. Various governments of the Hanoverian period were so anxious to see the back of their criminals that they seemed to have no interest in either the often-dubious profiteers to whom they assigned the convicts or the ways in which these merchants conducted their business. The interaction between government policy, its administration, and the men and women under sentence ended with the assignment of the convicts to the contractors. Unlike the slave trade, this ongoing traffic in white humankind attracted no liberal attention and little public awareness. There was no one of the ilk of William Wilberforce, who was later to be so effective in rousing political and societal opinion against the slave trade. The consequence was a regime of what was often officially sanctioned mistreatment and callous cruelty. If this went unnoticed it was because, from the British government's viewpoint, the convicts had forfeited their rights as citizens, the contractors were providing a useful service, and transportation was (by its measure) "a striking success."[79]

4
Arrival in the New World

For the Puritans who emigrated to Massachusetts and other parts of New England in the seventeenth century, the trial of the Atlantic crossing was a test of their faith and fortitude. It was a pilgrim's progress on the way to both a promised land and a primordial garden in which they hoped to establish a new and upright society. Similarly, the arrival in 1634 of the *Ark* and the *Dove* at St. Clement's Island in Maryland with about 140 settlers was the beginning of another colonial endeavor in which idealism—the ideal of religious toleration—was to be the guiding principle. The colonial proprietor, Cecil Calvert, the second Lord Baltimore (and a Catholic) envisaged Maryland as a sanctuary for his persecuted coreligionists, an environment in which Anglican Protestants might be persuaded to return to the (true) Catholic faith and a sort of beachhead for the conversion of the Native Americans to Catholic Christianity.[1] This principle of toleration was subject to enormous stresses because of the religious turmoil of the seventeenth century in both the mother country and the colony. It did not survive the Glorious Revolution of 1688, after which the government of the Calverts was overthrown by a faction of Calvinists, Puritans, and Presbyterians.[2] Not everyone in Maryland was content with Lord Baltimore's vision for his colony as a religiously tolerant society that had one foot in the traditional world—with a feudal land-tenure system and autocratic proprietary powers—and another in the modern world—with its reliance on science, capital investments, innovation, and risk taking as a means of accumulating wealth.[3]

Even though King George I restored the Calvert family's proprietary rights in 1715, Maryland's Catholics continued to suffer discrimination from the Protestant majority and were disenfranchised in 1718. Nevertheless, the founding sentiment and moral value of toleration was not completely extinguished. By 1776 notions about liberty and freedom of conscience and the separation of church and state were fundamental to the Declaration of Independence and the rhetorical language of the new republic.

In the Chesapeake society of the eighteenth century, ideas of freedom and liberty were still tied very firmly to privilege and a cadre of white adult males. Thomas Jefferson wanted as few restrictions on his own liberty and natural rights as possible, but he did not favor such rights for those unfit to use them (such as slaves and servants).[4] Even so, the presence of British convicts in the Chesapeake colonies offered a glaring reproof to notions of liberty, no matter how circumscribed these might have been. This was not only because of the convicts' criminal status (which implied moral corruption) but because they were white and freeborn women and men reduced effectively (if not at law) to a chattel-like condition—at least for the period of their sentence. Also, as the population of Maryland became more dominated by those who were native born, the convicts were prone to be regarded less as erring fellow countrymen and women and more as menacing foreigners. They were thus always likely to be treated either as something less than human or with contempt, and this is exactly what happened not long after they started arriving in large numbers after 1718.

Despite being needed as a source of labor in Maryland, the convicts were depicted almost immediately as if they were invasive serpents who would instigate the fall of an innocent people.[5] In the earliest years of convict transportation to Australia—which began just five years after the trade to Maryland finally ceased—women convicts were described by their overseers as "damned whores," "depraved," "dissolute," "lazy," "mischievous," "poor mothers," and "full of vice and villainy." It is probable that all these epithets—which showed both a disdain for their nonconformance to gendered norms of female respectability and a fearfulness of their sexuality—would also have been thought appropriate to the women sent to Maryland. When these absconded, some of them were described in similarly derogatory terms.[6] Cecilius Calvert, principal secretary to the lord proprietor's court in England, remarked to the governor of Maryland, Horatio Sharpe, that "it was truly hard upon the Province that the Scum and Dregs of the People sent should be the Cause of Ruin to Honest men there."[7]

In the summer of 1719, Maryland's elected Assembly met to discuss the sudden influx of felons and decided to draft legislation aimed at impeding and regulating the trade. A bill was prepared, but the upper house secured its postponement—apparently on the grounds that hasty action would be unfair to the shipping contractor Jonathan Forward. Needless to say, Forward strongly resented any attempts at regulation, but in any case, the governor refused to accede to the Assembly's draft bill.[8]

In 1723 the Maryland House of Assembly succeeded in passing *An Act to Prevent the Great Evils Arising by the Importation of Convicts into This Province and for the Better Discovery of Such When Imported.*[9] The preamble to the act suggests that the reappearance of what the colonists called "Newgate birds" was causing grave disquiet—though this was really due to the large number of male ruffians arriving rather than the smaller number of women—by 1755 one in every twelve white males in Baltimore, Anne Arundel, Charles, and Queen Anne counties would be a British convict.[10] The act stipulated that those buying convicts would have to enter into a renewable annual good-behavior bond of 30 pounds on behalf of each convict purchased. This sum would be forfeited if the convict committed any offenses within the bond period. The act also provided for fines to be levied on owners, factors, and the masters of vessels for noncompliance with several regulatory measures, all of which were designed to connect names with purchasers—and hence establish responsibility in the event of further criminality.

Though sympathetic to the colonists' fears, Lord Baltimore (the fifth Lord Baltimore, Charles Calvert, 1699–1751), was not pleased with what he saw as an attempt to undermine the authority of the British Parliament, which had implemented the Transportation Act. He dissented to the Maryland act the following year (1724).[11] In conveying his dissent to the Assembly, the lieutenant governor, Charles Calvert (the proprietor's uncle) commented, "I could heartily wish they [the convicts] were sent to any other of His Majesty's plantations but while we purchase, they will send them and we bring the evil upon ourselves."[12] When the Maryland Assembly heard of the proprietor's decision, it considered a remonstrance to the king.

Meanwhile, in August 1723 the Baltimore County Court issued a warrant directed to the sheriff commanding him to take into custody all convicts until they or their masters could provide a good-behavior surety. Jonathan Forward's factors claimed that the imposition of this bond denied them their property rights in the convicts. The dispute caused quite a kerfuffle, with charge and countercharge being made by Forward's factors and local officials. The matter was resolved in Forward's favor.[13]

The next attempt by the Assembly to regulate the trade came in 1728 with *An Act to Prevent the Abuses of Concealing Convicted Felons and Other Offenders Imported into This Province and for the Better Discovery of Them.*[14] This act was designed to ensure that the crimes for which felons had been convicted and the terms of their sentences were known to both purchasers and colonial officials alike. It required every ship's master to bring an authentic testimonial of each felon's conviction and the number of years she or he was to serve. This act was not disallowed because it was to regulate, not prohibit, the importation of convicts.[15]

In 1751 the Assembly passed *An Act to Make the Testimony of Convicted Persons Legal against Convicted Persons.* This act was intended to prevent the criminal collusion that was alleged to occur because convicts were "disabled from being witnesses against each other."[16] In the same year, after a period of heavy importations, the magistrates of Baltimore and Anne Arundel counties took it upon themselves to renew the requirement for a good-behavior bond for each convict purchased.

This time the Provincial Court overruled the justices, saying they had "exceeded their jurisdiction."[17]

In 1754, when Maryland was attempting to raise revenue to fight the French and Indian War (the American theater of the Seven Years' War), the Assembly imposed a duty on each servant imported "to serve for the term of seven years or more"—that is, convicts.[18] The contractor John Stewart filed an objection to this duty as being "directed against his business," though other contractors paid it without protest. This act was allowed to stand, but Stewart's factors refused to pay the duty, and the requirement was abandoned two years later. In 1766 the Assembly passed *An Act to Oblige Ships Coming into This Province to Perform Quarantine* because diseases were being spread by incoming convicts. In 1767 the whole quarantine issue was thoroughly aired in letters to the *Maryland Gazette* because a Mrs. Blake of Queen Anne's County and twenty of her slaves had died of "jail fever" (probably typhus) the previous year.[19] From this highly emotional correspondence it is evident that the fear of convicts that had prompted the 1723 act was still very much alive among colonists more than forty years later.

A final regulatory act was passed in 1769 in a period when incoming British convicts comprised more than one-third of all immigrants received by Maryland.[20] This was a supplementary act to that passed in 1728 and was aimed at further tightening the obligations on the masters of ships to provide a full transcript of each imported felon's conviction so they might not pass as "persons of character or be received as witnesses to the great vexation and prejudice of this province."[21]

It was into this suspicious and hostile community that every year the despised female felons were delivered for sale.[22] Yet despite the suspicion and hostility, many of Maryland's citizens were willing to buy and to keep on buying convicts for a period of more than sixty years.

After weeks at sea, how welcome it must have been for the women to know that they were nearing their destination as they passed through the Virginia Capes to the Chesapeake Bay beyond. Like all new arrivals, they were probably awed by what they could see of the bay's vast size, its thousands of miles of shoreline, its maze of inlets, and the many large rivers that emptied into it. William Eddis, an Englishman who arrived in 1769 to become surveyor of customs in Annapolis, wrote home, "A few weeks since, the Thames was the most considerable river I had ever beheld; it is now, comparatively, reduced to a diminutive stream."[23]

Annapolis was usually the first port of entry for convict vessels. Here they cleared customs and, providing they did not have to be quarantined (as was often the case when the convicts or crew were afflicted with smallpox), landing certificates were issued to their masters. When quarantine was required, a vessel might wait at anchor for up to three weeks before being allowed to land its cargo. Captains feared not being able to "take the [quarantine] oath" because this hindered the benefits of

Shipping notice in the *Maryland Gazette,* October 26, 1748, announcing the arrival of a snow with a cargo of convicts. (Collection of the Maryland Historical Society, Baltimore.)

Annapolis merchant David Ross advertised his convict servant sale in the *Maryland Gazette,* October 26, 1748—the same day his cargo of felons arrived from Britain. (Collection of the Maryland Historical Society, Baltimore.)

getting the convicts to market early and quickly reloading with export commodities for the homeward journey.[24]

Once the necessary clearances were received, the agents (usually called "factors") for the British firms took charge of the sale transactions, which they tried to conclude as quickly as they possibly could. In the early years Jonathan Forward's factors were John Moale and Daniel Russel.[25] Others who were involved in a major way were an Eastern Shore merchant and major slave dealer called Thomas Ringgold (1715–72), who was a prominent member of Maryland's society and operated out of Chestertown in Kent County.[26] In the 1760s and 1770s, other factors included Matthew Ridley of Baltimore and also James Cheston, the Baltimore-based partner of Stevenson, Randolph & Cheston in Bristol. James Braddock, who was based on the Eastern Shore in Talbot County, represented the merchants James Gildart and John Gawith of Liverpool, Lancashire. He was receiving convicts from them as late as June 1775.[27]

On the Eastern Shore, when transport vessels put into port at Oxford near the mouth of the Tred Avon River in Talbot County, it was apparently the practice of at least one captain to fire a gun as a signal to alert nearby planters that a new supply of convicts had just arrived.[28] Another means by which buyers were made aware of the availability of convict servants was via an advertisement in the *Maryland Gazette.*

Factors often used descriptions in their sale notices that displayed a type of ironic euphemism. These included "King's Passengers," "His Majesty's Seven-year Passengers," "Passengers of Note who are destined to tarry for seven years," "King's Passengers of the *old sort.*" Also occurring, of course, was the more prosaic "Seven Year Servants."[29] These descriptions were probably not intended to fool anyone, but perhaps the plain word *convicts* was too direct. Baltimore's Matthew Ridley commonly referred to both indentured servants and convicts as "servants" as if, to him at least, the differences between them were trifling.

If the convicts available did not interest buyers at one port, they would be tried elsewhere. In June 1770, having sold almost half a shipment at Annapolis, James Cheston wrote to his partners that he had "no doubt but the remainder will go off well at Baltimore."[30] Similarly, on the Eastern Shore, if the convicts did not sell at Oxford, they would be tried at Chestertown. The women might be shopped from place to place until they had all found purchasers. Because convicts (unlike slaves) represented a comparatively small investment, they did not usually attract retail buyers over long distances; purchasers were generally from areas close to local ports.[31] In 1755 a census of Maryland's population showed that in the lower Eastern Shore counties of Worcester, Dorchester, and Somerset, the total number of convicts was only ten.[32]

Convict sales were held on the transport vessels and strongly resembled slave auctions.[33] This was deeply shocking to anyone witnessing them for the first time, but to residents of port towns the sales were a familiar part of life. Indentured and convict servants, often mingled together, were brought up on deck, where the men and women were separated. One historian has described them as "a woebegone, weary, largely silent group of men, women and children faced with a strange procedure they could not control but would determine their fate."[34] An eyewitness to a 1758 sale of one hundred male and female convicts in Virginia stated, "I never see such pasels of pore Raches in my Life, some all most naked and what had Cloths was as Black [as] Chimney Swipers, and all most Starved by the Ill [usage] in their Pasedge By the Capn, for they are no bater than many negro Slaves."[35]

Once the convicts were lined up on the deck, interested customers then came aboard to inspect the merchandise. In deciding whether to make a purchase they would carefully question the ship's captain and the factors about the health, origins, skills, and cost of those who were of interest. They considered each convict's demeanor and tried to assess trustworthiness—would the convict be likely to run away before contract completion? In accordance with the law of 1728, prospective buyers were shown each convict's criminal record, which stated for how long and in which jail he or she had been incarcerated. This had a bearing on assessing a convict's state of health—a critical consideration if purchasers were not to waste their investment. In a sense the men and women were perishable goods whose "expiration date" had to be carefully calculated. However, the health assessment only went so far. There is no evidence that women were ever stripped naked at these sales.[36]

As with any product, the convict women were prepared for sale so as to maximize their appeal, though this was no easy task when the women had been at sea for about three months and some had been devastated by smallpox and other illnesses. The masters of ships (some of whom received a commission on sale proceeds) ensured that the convicts washed, had their hair trimmed, and put on clean clothes. This was necessary to minimize the "peculiar smell incident to all servants just coming from ships."[37] The odor may have been especially pungent in the heat and humidity of Maryland's summer months.

Occasionally, women were encouraged to wear wigs or their "best Head Dresses."[38] Sometimes the presentation of the convicts involved fraud. In 1737 a vessel arrived in Annapolis with no fewer than sixty-one indentures (to serve as testimonials) signed by the mayor of Dublin in Ireland, and twenty-two wigs. Both indentures and wigs were denounced as "an arrant cheat detected, being evidently brought for no other purpose than to give a respectable appearance to the convicts when they should go ashore." It was believed that the convicts were to be passed off as indentured servants, for whom a better price could be achieved from those buyers who thought them superior.[39] Despite the efforts put in to make them respectable, it seems that newly arrived convicts were instantly recognizable. In 1757 an advertiser for a male runaway convict named James Griffiths noted, "He appears like a servant just come off a ship and has a bundle of old clothes with him."[40]

A long verse narrative about the (supposedly) firsthand experiences of James Revel, a convict who was allegedly sent to the Chesapeake, provides a glimpse of convict women in the sale process:

Against the planters did come down to view,
How well they lik'd this fresh transported crew.
The Women separated from us stand
As well as we by them for to be view'd.

And in short time some men up to us came,
Some ask'd our trades, and others ask'd our names.
Some view'd our limbs, and others turn'd us round
Examining like Horses if we're sound.

Some felt our hands and view'd our legs and feet,
And made us walk to see were compleat.

Some view'd our teeth, to see if they were good,
Or fit to chew our hard and homely food.[41]

As the convict women waited for their sale transactions to be concluded, they might have looked ashore with some curiosity. Having survived the crossing and reached their destination after months at sea, their anguish at exile may have sharpened but they were probably relieved to find themselves in a bustling port rather than a barren wilderness—though some would shortly relocate to plantations that were miles from anywhere. At this juncture, like all immigrants, these outcasts were probably experiencing a mix of fear, trepidation, and hope.

In the first thirty or forty years of the transportation period, the women who arrived in Annapolis would have viewed a place of "very irregular appearance, and in size and form but a very poor town."[42] They may have noticed unpaved streets and many taverns, inns, and small businesses. The women who arrived after about the 1760s would have gained quite a different impression. Although the port still looked to be "more of an agreeable village than the metropolis of an opulent province," and the town's total population was only just over a thousand, there had been a building boom and several streets were lined with elegant and architecturally refined town houses.[43] In the 1740s the women who arrived at Chestertown in Kent County may have passed through a handsome three-storied brick building erected in 1746 by the Ringgold family and used as the customshouse.[44] Those who arrived at Oxford in Talbot County would have been processed in that town's tiny clapboard customshouse, which had been built in the seventeenth century. While passing through the town, they may have glimpsed the Robert Morris Inn, built around 1710–1715—probably of more interest to them. Those who arrived in Baltimore would have seen only a rural village with scattered small houses set among fields—in 1760 the town's population was still only twelve hundred (see the illustration of Baltimore in 1752 in chapter 7). The women's impressions of all the new sights and sounds would begin the process by which they would develop a sense of a place and location. This would be critical to their overcoming loneliness and feelings of alienation. Without such a sense they might succumb to depression and despair during the many years that stretched ahead.

William Eddis—the observant Englishman who had been so struck by the size of the Chesapeake Bay—noted that if convicts had sufficient financial means they could pay the colonial factor for the shipper's property right in their labor. They were then "free to pursue their inclinations or abilities."[45] Eddis's comment highlights the fact that transportation was banishment for the sentence term, but it was not in itself a commitment to labor—although most convicts, being destitute, were sold so the shippers could recoup their transportation costs and make a tidy profit as well. The price that these better-off convicts paid for themselves was based on

The Oxford Customs House. This building is an exact replica (constructed in 1976) of the original customshouse erected in the seventeenth century. (Courtesy of Leon Reed.)

that which they might have fetched as servants. Those with insufficient means to satisfy the factor in total could make part payments and then be sold for a lesser term of servitude than the usual seven or fourteen years.

Such transactions were common knowledge. When Daniel Defoe's Moll Flanders visits her husband in Newgate to urge him to seek transportation rather than suffer the infamy of a public execution, she tells him that money would ease his passage, as captains "were generally speaking, Men of good humour and some Gallantry and a small amount of Conduct, especially if there was any Money to be had, [and] would make way for him to buy himself off, when he came to Virginia."[46]

It is not known how many women were able to buy out their sentences, but when the *Elizabeth* arrived in Maryland from Bristol in June 1775, two women "paid cash" to James Cheston.[47] These were Judith Rendall [Randall] from Dorset, who had received a death sentence but had been pardoned on condition of transportation for fourteen years, and a Warwickshire woman named Mary Hobson, who had been convicted at the Lent quarter sessions of that county.[48] A different sort of "self-purchase" occurred in 1745 when Elizabeth Cane, who had been convicted for receiving stolen goods, arrived from London to begin a sentence. She was sold to a planter, from whom she was then bought by her brother who lived in Massachusetts. Elizabeth left Maryland to join her brother in New England but,

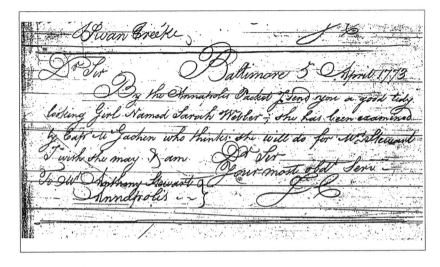

Letter to Anthony Stewart from James Cheston regarding his order for a female servant, April 5, 1773. (James Cheston Letterbook, 1772–June 1776, Cheston-Galloway Papers, box 8, Maryland Historical Society, Baltimore.)

upon reaching Boston, she found he had died and she, as the beneficiary of his will, became the owner of herself. Cane traveled back to Britain, where she was arrested for returning early from transportation. Although this was a capital offense, she was reprieved and sentenced again to be transported.[49]

The factors who handled convict sales often had preexisting customer orders that they met when convicts with the desired appropriate skills became available. Women were rarely specified, but James Cheston's correspondence does provide some examples. On April 5, 1773, Cheston wrote to Anthony Stewart (a person of significance in Annapolis) and advised him that he was sending a "tidy looking girl named Sarah Webber," who had "been examined by Captain McGacken who thinks she will do for Mrs Stewart." On the same date he sent John Chapman a woman who "has been used to all kinds of household work and can sew."[50]

In November 1774 Thomas Smyth, a sometime factor and merchant, wrote to James Cheston asking him to choose from among his shipment from Bristol a woman to be "a cook and manager for my shipyard . . . one from the country would be most probable to suit me best." When the *William* arrived in December, Cheston sold Smyth a married woman from Worcestershire, Elizabeth Smith, who had been convicted for stealing at Old Swinford.[51]

Most convicts were bought singly or in lots of two. In the years between 1767 and 1775, 739 incoming convicts were distributed among 405 buyers.[52] There were, however, some wholesale purchasers, called "soul-drivers," who bought "lumps" of multiple convicts. An indentured servant named John Harrower noted in his diary that the soul-drivers made it their business "to go onb[d] all ships who have in either Servants or Convicts and buy sometimes the whole and sometimes a parcell of them as they can agree, and then they drive them throughout the Country like a parcel of Sheep untill they can sell them to advantage."[53] Rosannah Edwards, who arrived on the *Elizabeth* in June 1775, and Ann Bolton and Judith Williams, who arrived on the *Isabella* a month later, were sold to soul-drivers named William Walters (or Waters) and Richard Gattrell (or Gartrall). These men bought a total of twenty-two convicts from the two ships.[54]

In Maryland, soul-drivers led their convicts out from Baltimore on foot—sometimes shackled—or by wagon, riverboat, or raft. They traveled along networks of rough roads or walking trails as well as rivers and streams. Their destination was the sparsely settled "backcountry"—an imprecise geographic term for those lands close to a frontier that was, year by year, expanding west. In 1730 the area that became Frederick County eighteen years later was still heavily forested; by 1755 it was the second-most populous part of the province. In the backcountry the pioneer settlers had "to struggle with nature for a livelihood. Mountain tracts separated them from their kind and kindred and to the west of them lay the vast and unknown wilds."[55] But gradually small market centers developed, and over time these might acquire a store, a warehouse, a mill, and possibly a simple church. At such centers the soul-drivers offered their human commodities for sale.[56] The realities of the frontier sometimes intruded upon the trade. In 1774 James Cheston advised his partners that his usual arrangements for backcountry sales had to be suspended because there was a war being conducted there against the Shawnee and Ottawa peoples.[57]

Sale prices are an indication of why convicts were an attractive option to those seeking additional labor without a substantial outlay. Prices for healthy convicts were only about one-third those for slaves and, at the end of the service term, buyers probably had no obligations with regard to the provision of tools and clothes as they might have with indentured servants.[58] The usual convict service term was seven years—two or three years more than that for indentured servants—but it could be for fourteen. When capital prisoners were reprieved they were sometimes ordered transported for life, but their servitude terms never seem to have been longer than fourteen years. The price for a convict with a fourteen-year sentence was about 4.9 percent higher than for a convict with a seven-year sentence. However, in the years toward the end of the transportation period, servitude may not have exceeded seven years even when sentences were for longer periods.[59]

As in all human capital transactions—then as (is often the case) now—the same variables applied. Men were more valuable than women, the skilled were more valuable than the unskilled, adults were more valuable than adolescents or children. Female convict prices were generally about 23 percent lower than prices for male convicts. By comparison, prices for American-born female slaves were between 10 and 20 percent lower than those for males slaves.[60] The firm Stevenson, Randolph & Cheston appears to have thought 10 pounds for women was "a very low price." In 1779 the shipper Duncan Campbell stated he sold "common male convicts, not artificers, for £10 per piece, females for about £8 or £9 and those who were of useful trades from £15 to £25." He disposed of the old and infirm "to those humane people who chose to take them," but with some he "was obliged to give premiums."[61]

When the *Isabella* arrived in Maryland in July 1775, one of the convicts on board was Jane Aston, a married woman from Shropshire who had been "cast for transportation" for fourteen years at the Lent quarter sessions held in Shrewsbury. Aston was described as "an unfortunate, poor woman to be found a kind master," and James Cheston sought out Richard Moale to purchase her. Moale, who operated a store in Baltimore that supplied imported goods to those living in the surrounding county, was apparently one of the "humane people," and he responded favorably to Cheston's approach.[62] This arrangement was unusual—Stevenson, Randolph & Cheston mostly disposed of old, unhealthy, or unskilled "residues" in a wholesale batch or "lump." This was because these convicts were too expensive to clothe, feed, and accommodate while waiting for a better price at retail, and delays also threatened the merchants' sailing schedules.[63]

Convicts who were demonstrably unfit or disabled in some capacity posed a major disposal problem for the merchants, who sometimes just gave them away. Matthew Ridley wondered what to do with a woman afflicted with "a very bad leg," and George Woolsey faced the same dilemma over another woman with "a sore breast" (possibly breast cancer). He also had to dispose of "a fool" and "a verry old convict woman that says she can spin." His comment suggests he was skeptical that she could.[64]

Sometimes merchants made sales that later proved so unsatisfactory purchasers demanded their money back. Nicholas Hobbs, one of James Cheston's customers, complained that a young woman for whom he had paid 15 pounds was a bad bargain because she was given to having fits and doctors were unable to provide a cure. Hobbs accused Cheston of having known of her condition. Matthew Ridley was berated by a customer who had bought a woman who soon showed signs of a serious mental illness. Sometimes merchants gave partial refunds to buyers who had reasonable complaints in order to maintain a reputation for business probity.[65]

The gender gap in sale prices referred to above may have been partly due to a lack of recognition of female capabilities as "skills" deserving a premium. Yet a check of trial and other records shows the convict women included breeches makers, cooks, dairy workers, dancing mistresses, farm servants, glove makers, housekeepers, house servants, laundresses, leather dressers, mantua makers, milliners, quilters, seamstresses, spinners, spoon casters, stay makers, storekeepers, and weavers.[66] It may be thought that skills for teaching dancing were at a low premium in a colony focused on tobacco production, but actually the opposite was the case. Dancing was a very popular pastime, and there were resident teachers in Chestertown, Annapolis, and other places. Moreover, itinerant dancing masters "rode from manor to manor, from plantation to plantation . . . to rehearse growings-up in the steps of the minuet, the Sir Roger de Coverley, the gavotte de Vestris, the Allemands, the Russian waltz or the lively reels."[67]

But specialized skills were not often those most required by the general run of purchasers, who wanted servants or laborers for field work on tobacco plantations. Although women could usually cope with most aspects of this work, heavier tasks might be beyond them—and there was always the risk that they might become pregnant. After one convict sale, James Cheston told his partners that "he had received a good price, *notwithstanding* the women amongst them."[68]

In disposing of convicts, factors pushed for quick sales but were willing to extend credit because they did not want to be left with unsold convicts, particularly "late in the season." For payment they accepted bills of exchange, cash, produce (such as tobacco), or part cash and part produce.[69] Market conditions affected sales and a glut of convicts and servants could drive down prices. In June 1775 James Cheston lamented, "I am taking every step in my power to dispose of the convicts tho . . . with 160 that is just arrived and two or three more parcels that is expected, leave but an indifferent prospect,—at any rate, prices must be lower and longer credit given."[70]

The types of people who purchased convict women at either shipboard sales or via agents ranged from the richest men in Maryland (of whom many were also major slave owners) to those much less well off economically, with personal estates whose worth was between (approximately) 100 pounds and 500 pounds and who often could not afford the large investment needed to buy slaves. Yet slavery and indentured servitude went hand in hand, and the same Maryland counties that were the best markets for slave labor were also the best customers for imported servants, including convicts. Although it is not fully understood why those who could well afford slaves also bought convicts (and white indentured servants), it has been postulated that this probably had something to do with the growing diversification of Maryland's economy. Another view is that bound service had not yet been racialized and that the availability of skills—white or black—determined purchasing decisions. Other considerations may have been youth and the characteristics associated with gender—for example, a white middle-aged woman may have been thought a more appropriate child's nursemaid than an adolescent slave.[71] As in any other transaction, buyers revealed their own perceptions and prejudices regarding suitability. Certainly, convicts and other bound servants were in demand for skilled and semiskilled tasks right up to the War of Independence, but they were wanted for unskilled work as well. Some masters may simply have wanted servants who could speak English—particularly in women bought for domestic service, who would be interacting significantly with the women of the household.[72]

Actual sales records survive for only three of the vessels that transported convicts to the American colonies—the *Margaret*, which departed London in May 1719, and the *Elizabeth* and the *Isabella*, which departed Bristol in April and May 1775 respectively. The *Isabella* also carried indentured servants. Some of the buyers of convict women can be identified in land records, estate inventories, the pages of the *Maryland Gazette*, or because they were of some colonial significance.[73] Providing a profile and some background information on these buyers allows a partial understanding of the sorts of environments in which some of the convict women were destined to serve out their sentences.

When the *Margaret* arrived in Annapolis in August 1719 under the command of Captain William Greenwood, twenty-seven convict women were available for sale. Thomazin Elby from Surrey was sold to Dr. Charles Carroll (1691–1755), who was on his way to becoming a member of the colony's rich elite. Dr. Carroll had emigrated from Ireland in about 1715 and had set up practice as a physician and surgeon (or chirurgeon) in Annapolis. Within a decade his interests as a planter, merchant (trading with the West Indies, Spain, Portugal, Britain, and other American colonies), land speculator, importer and, later on, iron producer would completely overshadow his medical practice, though he did not give this up entirely until the last decade of his life. Upon his death, Carroll left to his son and namesake, Charles Carroll (called "the Barrister" to distinguish him from several other bearers of that name), a "handsome fortune" of 15,000 pounds, including his Annapolis home—part of which is now located on the campus of St. John's College in that city.[74] Dr. Carroll appears to have bought convicts over many years, as evidenced by the advertisements for convict runaways he placed in the *Maryland Gazette* from time to time. For example, he advertised for Mary Rider in the issue of April 19, 1749.[75]

Seven of the convict women on the *Margaret* were bought by Patrick Sympson (sometimes styled "Captain") and William Black of London Town—a small town on the South River not far from Annapolis and a popular port for the entry, sale, and distribution of slaves. Sympson and Black were partners, planter/merchants, expediters of the Chesapeake tobacco consignment system, credit providers, and intermediary agents for British and colonial interests. Sympson was the son-in-law of an English merchant named Gilbert Higgonson whose firm was engaged in importing slaves on behalf of Maryland investors; Sympson acted as Higgonson's local agent in this and other commercial activities. Sympson also operated a store in London Town from which he sold a huge variety of imported consumer goods including luxury items for members of elite families—especially James Carroll, a kinsman of Charles.[76] The convict women may have been intended for roles in Sympson and Black's diversified business empire, but it is more likely that their purchase was a wholesale transaction and that they were bought to be sold individually to planters not living within reach of Annapolis. Sympson and Black jointly bought a total of eighteen male and female convicts from the *Margaret*, and each separately bought four convict men as well.

John Welch, the buyer of Winifred Haynes, was a landholder and planter in Anne Arundel County, and Daniel Carter, the buyer of Martha Barker, was also a planter. Haynes and Barker were both from inner London parishes and neither seems to have been particularly sharp. Haynes had been a weekly servant to Isabella Sutherland for three or four years when she uncharacteristically stole and pawned some items of clothing. She said at her trial, "I did not design to steal them, but intended to redeem them and bring them again." Martha Barker had stolen and pawned various items of pewter and hardware and household equipment which, being marked with the owner's name, aroused the pawnbroker's suspicion immediately.[77]

Joseph Pettibone, who bought London woman Elizabeth Dobbs, was a twenty-one-year-old tobacco grower who owned a small plantation called Pyney Plain on the northern side of the Magothy River in Anne Arundel County. When Pettibone died in March 1728, his total estate was valued at just over 142 pounds.[78]

At the *Margaret* sale, a Mrs. Bransome bought a Surrey woman named Abigail Green, alias Harvey—probably to be a domestic servant. Green would have been a somewhat awkward inclusion in any colonial household. She had been indicted at the Surrey quarter sessions in October 1718 for picking the pocket of one Jero Hockney, whom she had accosted in a street near the church of St. George the Martyr in Southwark. She had subsequently stolen from him a linen bag containing gold and silver with a total value of 16 pounds. The details in the indictment suggest Green was a street prostitute as well as a thief.[79]

Nearly every county had counterparts to the wealthy Dr. Carroll—several even more affluent. Peter Galloway, who bought Surrey woman Sarah Naggs from the *Margaret*, was part of a Quaker family that dominated the mercantile community of Maryland's Western Shore. His son, Samuel Galloway (who was James Cheston's father-in-law), had business connections with many other prominent citizens, including Thomas Ringgold and Dr. Carroll. Galloway was involved in trade with Jamaica, Barbados, Madeira, and Ireland—usually dealing in mixed cargoes. The Carrolls (and there were two major branches of the Irish Carroll family in colonial Maryland—the Anglican and the Catholic), the Tilghmans, the Galloways, the Ringgolds, and a relatively small number of other families formed a sort of county elite whose members were leaders in social, governmental, and economic affairs. These men served variously as vestrymen, justices of the peace, grand jurors, assembly delegates and, of course, bankers to those of lesser means. Their wives and womenfolk were leaders of society and fashion and lent refinement to colonial activities.[80]

The names of most of the other purchasers of the convict women who arrived on the *Margaret* are not easily traceable. The "Gustavus Hesseltine" to whom Elizabeth Symonds was sold may or may not have been Gustavus Hesselius, a well-known artist and portrait painter then practicing in Maryland.[81] On the other hand, Hesseltine may have just been a clerk.

Further information on individual purchasers of convicts over the transportation period expands an understanding of the future destiny of the women convicts. In October 1731, twelve years after the arrival of the *Margaret*, Dr. Carroll, his kinsmen "Charles Carroll of Annapolis" (1702–82) and *his* brother, "Daniel Carroll of Duddington" (1707–34), plus two other members of Maryland's elite— the wealthy and powerful Benjamin Tasker Sr. (1690–1768) and Daniel Dulany Sr. (1685–1753)—provided the capital to develop an ironworks on eighteen hundred acres beside the Patapsco River. This was the Baltimore Company, which smelted ore to produce pig iron for export to Britain. The company prospered and expanded to two furnaces and a number of forges. The original investors, plus Charles Carroll of Annapolis's son, "Charles Carroll of Carrollton" (1737–1832), would continue to be involved in this business for many years to come. Convicts were purchased regularly for the Baltimore Company's workforce.[82] They also absconded regularly and thus featured frequently in runaway advertisements placed in the *Maryland Gazette*. Anna Maria Norman was a German woman living in England when she was sentenced at the Lent Assizes in Kent in 1745. She was transported on the *Italian Merchant* and arrived in Maryland around October 1745. She escaped from the Baltimore Company almost exactly twelve months later, in October 1746. The operators of other ironworks also advertised for runaway convict women, such as Frances Barret, who ran away from the Northampton ironworks in 1780.[83]

Charles Carroll of Annapolis had an extensive estate (12,500 acres by the 1770s) at Elk Ridge in the fertile piedmont of western Anne Arundel County. This was Doohoragen Manor, and it was partly managed by white overseers. The principal overseer was Captain John Ireland, a Yorkshireman who had misspent his youth and run through a family fortune before serving in both the French and Austrian armies. He arrived in America in the late 1750s. He soon encountered the Carrolls, for whom he worked tirelessly for the rest of his active life. The Carrolls provided John Ireland with eight slaves of his own and, it seems, with convicts as well, because he advertised for runaway convict servants in both 1759 and 1761, including "John Burrows and his wife."[84] Whether John Ireland's early life made him more or less sympathetic to the circumstances of the convicts can only be a matter for conjecture.

In 1774 (or thereabouts) in the last decade of the transportation period, James Braddock arrived in Maryland from Britain. He settled near the Miles River in Talbot County on the Eastern Shore and started buying and developing land especially around Church Creek and an inlet known as Church Cove. In 1775 and 1776 Braddock advertised on several occasions for convict runaways in both the *Maryland Gazette* and the *Pennsylvania Gazette*, always noting that they spoke in a Lancashire dialect. It is a reasonable assumption that these convicts had all been shipped by Gildart & Gawith—the Liverpool merchants and slave traders whom Braddock represented—but no records exist to show whether they were shipped so they could be offered for sale to planters or other settlers or whether it was always intended that they be deployed in Braddock's land-development projects. Two of his male runaways were described as "sawyers and labourers," so these may have been involved in forest clearance. A female convict runaway, Ann Wilson, was probably a domestic servant to Braddock because he knew enough about her skills at housework to make specific mention of them in his runaway advertisement.[85]

Not long before the time Braddock was active in Talbot County, Lord Baltimore (Frederick Calvert) was opening for settlement his proprietary landholdings in western Maryland. Speculators and developers hurried there to secure the most desirable tracts. A surveyor named Francis Deakins (1738–1804) and his brother William obtained warrants for hundreds of acres of this land—sometimes in partnership with others. As the War of Independence loomed, "committees of observation" were formed to provide county governance. Such a committee was formed in Frederick County on January 24, 1775, and "leading citizens" Francis and William Deakins were appointed members. In addition Francis was appointed a member of two district committees (for Georgetown and for Sugar Loaf Hundred) that were to raise funds to purchase arms and ammunition. After the Revolution and the establishment of the United States, Francis Deakins must still have been highly regarded because, in April 1787, the government of Maryland chose him to survey the lands west of Fort Cumberland and lay these out into fifty-acre lots for veterans of the Continental army. At some point in his career, Francis Deakins also operated a "mercantile house" in Georgetown.[86]

In June 1775 (five months after Francis Deakins was appointed to the Frederick Committee of Observation and to the district committees), one of Stevenson, Randolph & Cheston's vessels—the *Elizabeth*—arrived in Maryland from Bristol. On board were 104 convicts, including 13 women. Despite being busy in so many activities to do with the impending war, Deakins seems to have found time for his business interests; he purchased seven of the *Elizabeth*'s convict women—

one each from Dorset, Somerset, and Wiltshire, two from Warwickshire, and two from other unidentified jurisdictions—as well as twenty men.[87] Although it is not possible to state with any certainty why Deakins needed quite so many convicts or how they were deployed, the population growth and economic expansion of the western backcountry was creating a continuing demand from settlers for both white servants and slaves. It seems highly probable that Deakins was acting as a servant wholesaler for the settlers. Deakins was himself a slaveholder and may have sold slaves as well as convicts.

Another purchaser of women from the *Elizabeth* was Captain Charles Ridgely, who owned a fleet of merchant ships, mills, quarries, orchards, and a general merchandising business in Baltimore. In 1762, just as the Carrolls had done, Charles and John Ridgely established an ironworks in Baltimore County to produce pig iron for export. In 1770, from just one vessel, Charles Ridgely bought fifty-five convicts for his Northampton ironworks.[88] From the *Elizabeth* Ridgely bought Mary Garrett from Oxfordshire and Ann Greenaway from Warwickshire.[89] These women may have been destined for the ironworks or for another part of his highly diversified empire, where they would join other convicts, slaves, white indentured servants, and hirelings.

In addition to the information cited above, other sources reveal that convict women were bought (probably to work as domestic servants) by small businessmen (a butcher, a land agent, a fulling mill operator, a miller, a surveyor, a tailor, a tavern keeper, and a wigmaker were just some of those who advertised for runaway women in the *Maryland Gazette*). They were also bought by widows, by "gentlemen," and even by a magistrate.[90] In the years after their arrival some convict women were prosecuted in the county courts, and the names of their masters appear in court records. Samuel Owings and William Hamilton, who were respectively the owners of Jane Ellis and Frances Humphreys, both held land tracts of several hundred acres, suggesting they were medium-scale planters.[91]

The sales records are insufficient to show the distribution of the convict women among well-to-do, middling, and poor settlers. However, while buyers represented a variety of occupational and income groups, it is probable that the largest single number of purchasers were not wealthy but included some of the poorer planters whose estates were worth between (approximately) 100 and 500 pounds. These comprised about one-third of Maryland's planter households near the end of the colonial period.[92] An Englishman who visited Maryland in 1745, Edward Kimber, noted that some planters "have been originally of the convict class." In the doggerel poem by "James Revel," he states that his master "was a man but of ill-fame, who first of all a Transport thither came."[93] These sorts of people could not afford to buy laborers for purposes other than the production of cash crops. The women they purchased would, in all likelihood, be involved in sowing, weeding, worming, and harvesting tobacco or grain, or perhaps controlling a team of oxen while guiding a plow.[94]

Arriving convict women may or may not have been oblivious—or indifferent—to the fact that they were disdained by Maryland's governing class, feared by many of its citizens, and regarded with suspicion as moral contaminants. Although they may have deduced that they were valued by the shipping contractors and the factors only for the profits they might yield, they may not have appreciated that they were regarded by their purchasers initially as cut-price servants and, as time went on, in much the same category as slaves.[95] They would possibly have feared their purchasers would try to wring the most out of them during their term of servitude. They were not entirely bereft of all rights at law but were almost certainly unaware that a Maryland statute of 1715 stipulated: "Masters, &c. not providing Lodging and Cloathing, for their Servants, or burdening them beyond their Strength, debarring them of necessary Rest, excessively beating and abusing them, or giving them above Ten Lashes for any one offense, may, on Conviction in the County Court, be fined a sum, not exceeding 1,000 lbs of tobacco."[96]

∼

Whether the convict women were actually resourceful individuals who were ready to adapt to their new circumstances and justify their purchasers' investment is not something that can be established through evidence, but the multiple adjustments they had already made as they experienced incarceration, family separation, banishment, the Atlantic crossing, arrival in an unknown world, and the commercial sale of their own selves (or, technically, their labor) suggests that many would find their feet and deal successfully with whatever their future held. Yet any type of indentured servitude was something of a gamble. The women might be reasonably treated or cruelly abused outside the purview of authorities. Their masters might be pleased they had acquired additional hands for which they had not had to make a significant outlay or they might be burdened with servants who were disinclined for anything except escape. The outcomes for both the convict women and their purchasers depended to a large extent on luck.

5
Servants and Masters

After the sale process was completed, the factors handed over the convict women to the strangers who were to be their masters—effectively their owners—and with whom they were likely to spend the next seven, or possibly fourteen, years of their lives. Despite the interval since their sentencing in Britain, legally their punishment was only just beginning. Their sentence and servitude ran in tandem and started when they arrived in Maryland.[1] During this term, unless they died, committed another offense, ran away, or were advertised for sale, the women essentially disappeared from view as they undertook employment that was virtually unregulated, frequently harsh, and occasionally cruel or callous. The reasons for this were both deliberate and/or situational but can be understood within the framework of Maryland's contemporary circumstances—the new economic, social, and cultural world of the convict women.

Dominated geographically by the vast bisector of the Chesapeake Bay, Maryland was a region of great demographic and growing economic variation. It stretched from the wetlands of the lower Eastern Shore to the Great Appalachian Valley in the "backcountry" or western part of the colony from which Frederick County was formed in 1748. Regular accounts by colonial governors to the Board of Trade and Plantations in London provide a progressive picture of Maryland's economy, which, for most of the eighteenth century, was heavily dependent on a single commercial crop, *Nicotiana tabacum*—tobacco. The type most commonly grown in Maryland was "Orinoco" (or Oronoco) a light-colored, air-cured variety that possesses good burning qualities. It was favored in Europe, whereas the other principal type of tobacco—"Sweetscented"—was the preferred choice of British consumers. In the 1720s, spurred by the development of an efficient marketing system in Europe, demand for tobacco expanded there, and a growing taste for snuff created a whole new set of consumers. In every part of Maryland growers responded to rising tobacco prices with an increase in output. The numbers of planters raising the crop also increased. However, the five counties on the peninsula bounded by the Chesapeake Bay and the Potomac River—Anne Arundel, Calvert, Charles, Prince George's, and St. Mary's—dominated production. In the middle of the century the

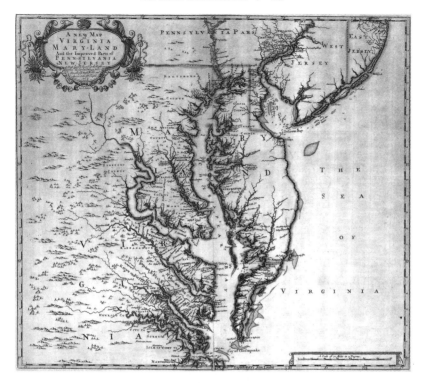

A New Map of Virginia, Maryland and the Improved Parts of Pennsylvania and New Jersey,
taken from a 1685 map by Christopher Browne that was revised by John Senex and published
in 1719. (Courtesy of the Maryland State Archives.)

high price of tobacco inhibited agricultural diversification and restrained the development of marketing networks and urban centers of the type that developed
only a short distance away in Pennsylvania.[2]

Yet from about the 1730s—particularly on the Eastern Shore but in other areas
as well—planters (particularly German and Scotch-Irish settlers) began to move
away from monoculture and started to raise wheat, corn, and oats. This diversification was probably a response to different soils as well as the prohibitive distance
from markets and shipping.[3] Maryland's other exports included meat, lumber,
staves, furs, and pig iron which, as stated in the last chapter, was being produced
by a number of different ironworks on the Patuxent and Patapsco rivers.[4]

Yet tobacco remained the dominant export commodity. In 1771 Maryland's tobacco exports constituted approximately one-third of all that produced in North
America. As a crop it was twice as valuable as coffee and rice, the next most important commodities exported from mainland America to Britain and elsewhere.[5]

The dependence on tobacco meant that Maryland's economy was susceptible to downturns whenever tobacco prices were low. At such times the colonists had no means to buy imported manufactured goods and were obliged to produce their own "country-made" cloth or, as one official reported, "go naked." By 1776 there was quite an extensive network of local industries that, if they did not supplant them, at least supplemented the supplies of manufactured goods that had previously been exclusively imported.[6]

In 1720 the population of Maryland was approximately 62,000, of which around 18 percent was black. By that date the majority of the white population was native born and, as one early eighteenth-century governor noted, "by the name of Country borne distinguish themselves from the rest of her Majesty's subjects."[7] By 1755 the population had reached 153,564 (107,208 white, 42,764 black, and 3,592 "mulatto"). In 1770 it was approximately 220,000, of which about 31 percent was black.[8] In the early part of the century Annapolis was the largest town, but even by 1760 it had a population of only 1,000 people occupying fewer than two hundred houses. By 1760 Baltimore (at 1,200 people) had overtaken Annapolis in size. This was because Baltimore was a deep-water port and had better access to the backcountry. Nevertheless, Annapolis remained the center of influence and the seat of government.[9]

The rapidly expanding population in this predominantly nonurban, agricultural, and plantation society and a limited supply of land meant that, for most of the eighteenth century, only about 40 percent of the free male population actually owned land. Where new opportunities might have been sought on the far western frontier, 21 percent of the land was owned by just thirteen men and the lord proprietor controlled further vast holdings that he did not really start opening for settlement until the 1770s. All these economic factors meant that a majority of the ordinary inhabitants of Maryland fared worse economically than those living elsewhere in colonial North America.[10]

In 1759 Father John Mosley, a Jesuit priest and missionary, was based at White Marsh in Prince George's County on the Western Shore. He traveled widely on his pastoral duties throughout the province and found the people to be "very poor and not to be compared in riches to the rest of our colonies." Eleven years later, when stationed at Tuckahoe in Talbot County on the Eastern Shore, he wrote touchingly of "miserable, abandoned families in poverty, want and misery."[11] Poverty was closely intertwined with the indebtedness of the typical colonist—a symptom of the economics of the tobacco trade.

Maryland's planters included those who were involved on a large scale and who, like Dr. Carroll and his kinsmen, frequently had other business interests, those who had their own smaller plantations, and those who leased modest holdings from a landlord as tenants. All planters involved in the production of tobacco had significant labor needs, and many of the convict women were purchased specifically for work in the fields. At the beginning of the eighteenth century a single laborer was expected to tend about ten thousand tobacco plants spaced out over two to three acres. Also, because the soils were being rapidly depleted by tobacco (a single field could be used only for three successive years), growers had to keep clearing land to create new acres for production—some fields had to lie fallow for twenty years before being replanted with tobacco. The continuing need to put new fields under cultivation plus the need of additional land for growing corn, grazing livestock, and accessing timber, led the writer of *American Husbandry* to conclude that "a planter should have fifty acres of land for every working hand; with less than this they would be distressed for want of room."[12]

The convict women who had been purchased by planters in the summer would reach their new plantation homes at that point in the tobacco growing cycle when the crop was either about to be or had just been harvested. The production of tobacco began in February, when seed was sown in small seed-raising beds. From about late April until June, the seedlings would then be planted out in knee-high mounds, or "hills," set some four feet apart in the cleared fields with approximately four thousand or five thousand plants to the acre. The young plants had to have bud tips and leaves removed to promote growth and they also had to be kept moist— which required the beds being cleared of weeds with a hoe. The plants were constantly at risk from insect pests—flies on the plant bed, ground worms that thrived in damp soil and could quickly level the seedlings, and green hornworms (which were an even greater threat) that had to be picked off daily from the pointy leaves that some likened to the ears of foxes, though the convict women were probably indifferent to such fancies.

After continual attention for about four months, the crop was harvested around the end of August or early September. The cut plants were then hung in a ventilated tobacco house that provided a protected shelter to store the tobacco and allowed it to be cured by air circulation. This curing took place over about five or six weeks, after which the plants were taken down, the stalks removed, and the leaves bound into bundles and prized into hogsheads. These were very large wooden barrels that, when fully packed with tobacco, weighed about a thousand pounds (455 kgs). Only after November was there any lull in the relentless cycle, though planters also had to attend to their other crops and their cattle, sheep, and hogs, which aided household self-sufficiency.[13]

On the largest landholdings, planters might have a hundred African slaves or more distributed among several "quarters." On smaller estates there might be twenty to fifty, and on the smallest five or fewer. In 1720 many smaller landholders held no slaves at all, but by 1760 46 percent of all planters held some slaves. As mentioned in the previous chapter, although purchasers of convicts were rep-

Tobacco field. (Copyright © Dimitar Bosakov/123rf.com.)

resented in all wealth groups, it was the people with estates worth between (approximately) 100 and 500 pounds who, if they could afford any additional labor, were most likely to have bought convicts because these were more affordable than slaves; cheap labor enabled small planters to maintain a toehold in the colonial economy.[14]

A planter who purchased a female convict would rarely expect from her seven (or possibly fourteen) years of fully productive labor. Convict servants were initially inexperienced—those from Britain's urban areas may never have used a hoe, a plow, a sickle, or other farming implements before, all of which were necessary for the cultivation of tobacco. They had a high mortality rate, and they tended to run away—particularly in the early years of their sentence when their adjustment was at its most difficult.

Although producing tobacco involved fairly constant labor for about ten or eleven months each year, the work itself, even if tiring, was not particularly heavy—though hoeing did need a strong back. Thus the convict women would have been quite acceptable as field hands. In fact, despite the constant risk that pregnancy posed to the economic interests of their masters, white female servants had one very special advantage in Maryland during the transportation years. Unlike all men (free or slave), free black women, slave women, and female "mulattoes," the convict women (like other white women) were not "taxable," so that by employing them, a planter could maximize his production of tobacco without paying excise.[15] This was allegedly one reason for the overproduction of substandard leaf that led to poor returns in the early years of the century. In the 1720s, after a long slump in tobacco prices, there were two attempts to improve leaf quality (and prices) by limiting the amount of tobacco each planter could produce for every taxable worker he owned. There was much hostility to this approach. On both occasions the question of whether women servants would continue to be exempted was considered. The first act did not pass, and the colony's proprietor disallowed the second. Eventually, after the passing of the Maryland Inspection Act of 1747, tobacco quality was raised by means of a preshipment inspection rather than by limiting cultivation, and women continued to be bought as field hands. Despite the tax advantages of women laborers, field work never became an exclusively female occupation, and the experiences of male and female convicts who worked as field laborers were not dissimilar.[16] Some convict women may have felt aggrieved at having to do field work on a regular basis, as it was more common for women in rural England to work in the fields only at harvest time when extra hands were needed.[17]

The records do not show whether the convict women were good workers, but it can be inferred that they were certainly good enough from the advertisements placed by their masters when they ran away and by the rewards offered to retrieve them. Of course, masters were concerned about the loss of their investment and a financial asset, but it is doubtful that they would have been willing to pay much of a reward to recover completely useless or nonproductive women who might have been more trouble than they were worth and for whom, if a planter decided to cut his losses, there would still be disposal costs.

Because the convict women were required solely for their labor, the planters are unlikely to have either cared or given any thought to whether they might have needs of their own—for example, compatible fellow workers of the same age and/or gender who might offer mutual support and companionship and perhaps thereby increase their productivity. On plantations where the workforce was racially mixed, some convicts regarded it as degrading that they should have to work as field hands alongside slaves. Their sharing of a common lot with people they tended to look down on was a source of resentment to them.[18] Some were even given to complaining that slaves were better treated, though the unfortunate slaves were likely to be newly imported and thus recovering from their own capture and transportation ordeal and suffering an even greater sense of dislocation. Many slaves did not even share a common language. One convict, after returning to London, cautioned potential wrongdoers lest they should end up going "among the Negroes to work at the hoe / in distant countries void of all relief / sold for a slave because you prov'd a thief."[19]

In eighteenth-century Britain "blackness" and the physical attributes of black people were easily grasped symbols of their supposed laziness and inferiority in culture and status.[20] These were attitudes that were further developed in the slaveholding Chesapeake, with elite white women equating the level of a slave or servant's skin pigmentation with her capacity for efficient domestic service and obedience—the lighter her skin, the better she was supposed to be as a house servant. Being British, the convict women may have brought contemporary racial prejudice with them to Maryland, but the fostering of racial prejudice might have suited some masters as a useful means of social and sexual control. It would be interesting to know the fate of a black London woman named Elizabeth Jones, who was indicted in 1735 for stealing a few items of clothing with an assessed total value of 10 pence. She was convicted and sentenced in April and transported to Maryland on the *John* in December of that year. Being black, a convict, and a servant, Jones would have had a triple "status handicap" in the colony.[21]

Over time the sheer propinquity of white servants and black slaves meant that the convict women inevitably crossed the racial divide and struck up friendships or alliances with slaves and, as will be described below, engaged in intimate pairings with black men as well. When Elizabeth Willoughby stole a horse to run away from John Drummond of Cecil County in October 1750, she put her trust in two of Drummond's slaves, Jack and Pobb. Drummond described these men respectively as "a cunning, sensible fellow" and "an old, stupid fellow," though his chagrin may have influenced his opinions. In October 1757 when Anne Sayer ran away from James Bleake and Anne Milton, she did so with a "pretty tall" twenty-year-old slave named Tom and a tall twenty-five-year-old English convict—coincidentally also named Tom—Thomas Rogers. The advertisers, James Bleake and Ann Milton, alleged that Sayer had stolen her indenture papers and that Rogers had probably forged a pass for himself as well as a bill of sale for Tom.[22] The information in the advertisement suggests that all three young people were in close cahoots as they conspired to escape. Implicitly, their scheming had to be based on a high degree of mutual trust.

Even when convicts did have other white coworkers, they could not always communicate with them. Many indentured servants (and at least one German convict woman—Anna Maria Norman) were from continental Europe, and those from Britain and Ireland frequently had heavy accents or spoke in regional dialects.[23] In the 1720s Daniel Defoe claimed that "there is as much difference between the English Tongue, as spoken in the North of England, and the same Tongue, as spoken in the West, as between the French spoken in Normandy, and that of Gascogne and Poictou."[24] Regional dialects were still deeply rooted in many rural districts at the end of the eighteenth century, and occasionally major distinctions in language were to be found even in the same county.[25] Servants from regional areas of Britain were even said to have "different habits and different modes of thinking."[26] Advertisements for runaways often noted their language status: "a Highlander who speaks broken English" or "born in the west of England and speaks bad English." A woman from Wales named Grace Jones was, rather puzzlingly, said to speak in "broken Dutch."[27]

In 1758, when twenty-two-year-old Sarah Davis from Essex ran away from Paul Rankin of Prince George's County, he placed an advertisement in the *Maryland Gazette* to locate her. In this notice Rankin said he lived eight miles away from Queen Anne Town, situated on the Patuxent River. If Sarah Davis were heading for this village, she probably walked all the way as there was no reference to her stealing a horse. As a consequence of the Maryland Inspection Act of 1747, Queen Anne Town had been designated an inspection station for tobacco being exported to Europe and it had a warehouse, a racetrack, a few houses, and some civic buildings. Sarah Davis would not have passed unnoticed, particularly as she may have gone there specifically to seek out company. Rankin said she had a "palavering tongue," implying she was, in his opinion, much too talkative—often an indication of someone who is naturally gregarious but whose circumstances are isolating.[28]

It does not require much imagination to appreciate how lonely many convict women may have felt on the plantations and how alien an environment these must have seemed to women from the city parishes of busy eighteenth-century London or the smaller cities of Bristol, Dublin, or Newcastle-upon-Tyne. Even today some of the places where tobacco was grown in Maryland nearly three hundred years ago—for example, along the Sassafras River near Earleville in Cecil County—are sparsely populated areas of farmland and forest.[29] Those women who were from rural areas are likely to have found the large land tracts utterly different from the closely cultivated fields of Britain and Ireland and the more intimate contact with friends and neighbors that was so characteristic of rural living in Britain at that time.

It was not unknown for convicts who were family members to be transported on the same ship; what is not known is how frequently they were bought by the same purchaser and stayed together during their servitude (which would have alleviated their isolation and loneliness). There are, however, some documented instances of this happening. When the *Isabella* arrived in Maryland in July 1775, surviving sale records show that Charity Jones and her (likely) husband Timothy Jones were both sold to John Welch (also Welsh) Jr., a planter. In 1750 an advertisement appeared in the *Pennsylvania Gazette* seeking information on a forty-seven-year-old Irish woman named Mary McCreary and her twenty-four-year-old son (both convicts) who had run away together from Bohemia Manner in Cecil County. In 1758 William Clayton of Queen Anne's County advertised in the *Maryland Gazette* for forty-year-old "lusty" Mary Jackson (a convict) and her fifty-year-old "well-set" husband, John Jackson, an indentured servant but not a convict.[30]

Before the women could become fully effective agents of plantation production, they had to become "seasoned"—or immune to their new disease environment. To the colonists, becoming seasoned usually meant suffering and recovering from a bout of malaria or "ague and fever." Malaria was still endemic on both shores of the Chesapeake Bay, particularly in August and September, because of "the vast multitudes of mosquitoes" that had not yet been eliminated from the region's tidewater swamps. In the first half of the century it was the likely cause of an exceptionally high death rate among pregnant women.[31] In 1720 in one of his regular reports to the Board of Trade and Plantations in London, Governor John Hart wrote: "The climate is unhealthy, especially to strangers occasioned by the excessive heat in summer and extreme cold in winter; the vernal and autumnal quarters are attended with fevers, pleurisies, etc."[32] In 1771 William Eddis also described how debilitating he found "the intense heat which prevails during the summer and the extremity of cold in winter."[33] There were other risks too. The shallow wells dug by Tidewater colonists became easily contaminated and bred typhoid fever and other diseases.[34]

Some women died soon after arrival. Elizabeth Field was convicted at the Old Bailey on October 12, 1726, for receiving several bundles of clothing she knew to be stolen. Field seems to have been an "old lag"—a regular crook who spoke an underworld argot. She had told the thieves she would "lock anything that they could speak with, though it was the King's Crown"—that is, she would buy anything they could steal. Sentenced to transportation for fourteen years, Field arrived in Maryland on the *Rappahannock Merchant* in June 1727. She was dead four months later.[35]

Women who survived seasoning were sometimes weakened and less well able to withstand other diseases such as dysentery and influenza, or "distempers," which were year-round phenomena. From time to time there were epidemics—"winter fever" in 1750, smallpox in 1752, and (in Queen Anne's County) "jail fever" (typhus) in 1767.[36] An official report asserted that "white servants lose much of their time by sickness, which still increases the expense."[37]

The scarcity of experienced medical practitioners and the distance from towns meant that some Chesapeake planters assumed the role of doctor to their families and servants, confident in their ability to make diagnoses and apply remedies—and also to demonstrate their authority and control over the bodies of their servants and slaves.[38] Local suppliers such as James MacGill could provide the planters with "an assortment of good fresh MEDICINES, Chymical and Galenical imported from London . . . and a compleat new Set of Surgeon's Instruments, a small collection of new Books on Surgery, Physic, &c."[39]

Some of the remedies administered by the planters may have been in accordance with contemporary practice, but they cannot have helped the patient very much. For influenza, where the risk of dehydration must be carefully managed, they gave ipecacuanha or tartar water as an emetic to "induce the vomits," as one planter put it. Similarly, for malaria they purged and bled the patient—not the best thing to do considering one of the symptoms of malaria is anemia.[40] Most medical treatments, whether they were delivered by amateurs, lay practitioners, or professionals, were based on Galenic humoral theories and relied greatly on purges and stimulants. At least one Annapolis physician, Dr. Alexander Hamilton, found that "Jesuit's Bark" was useful in treating malaria—a shrewd observation because the bark contained a substance similar to quinine. Convicts may have been treated with this product because it was readily available for 12 shillings currency per pound in Hamilton's own apothecary's shop. Women afflicted with syphilis (French distemper), such as the convicts encountered by Goronwy Owen on the *Trial* in 1757 and those returned to merchants by dissatisfied purchasers, would have been treated with mercury.[41]

Although it is likely that most convict women were assigned to field work, which was, in the main, ungendered, convict servants also took on domestic service roles that were more gender specific—cooks, general servants, kitchen maids, housemaids, laundresses, quilters, and seamstresses. This was particularly the case in the urban households for which many convicts were purchased. About a quarter of the advertisements for runaway convict women were placed by townspeople who resided in or near Annapolis.

As the eighteenth century wore on, Annapolis became the place where more than a few prosperous mercantile families based themselves and built fine houses to reflect their status. The elite women who headed such households were, unlike their rural counterparts, freed from a repertoire of tasks to do with production and domestic manufacturing and processing. With the ready availability of consumer goods, they were able increasingly to focus their energies and attention on the genteel upbringing of their daughters and the refinement and beautification of their homes. Cleanliness became a mark of urban sophistication, but the work needed to achieve the high standards required—the washing, scouring, scrubbing, dusting, and polishing—was done by slaves and servants.[42] Winifred Jones may have fulfilled such a domestic role, as she was a convict servant to Captain (later Major, then Colonel) Thomas Sheredine (1699–1752). Sheredine was a Baltimore County landholder and a man of civic prominence who between 1732 and 1749 was an elected delegate for that county in Maryland's Assembly. He was also a member of the Episcopalian church, a presiding justice, and on two occasions (in 1729 and 1751) Baltimore County's elected high sheriff. Sheredine resided in Annapolis when the Assembly was in session.[43]

The urban households of the nonelite were sometimes a multifunctional combination of familial and economic activities. The household might occupy a building of several stories, with a business (such as a tavern) at ground level and a residence upstairs.[44] Hannah Boyer was bought by an Annapolis tavern keeper named Catherine Jenings, and may have worked as a general servant as well as assisting in the tavern.[45]

The roles of convict women assigned to domestic service in the households of the more prosperous farmers or plantation owners were probably much broader than those of their urban equivalents. While "James Revel" claimed that on the plantation where he served there were "four servant women in the house / to wait upon the master and his spouse," this would not have been a common situation.[46] Rural servants were more likely to assist their mistresses with a huge range of tasks integral to the self-sufficiency of planter households, such as collecting and chopping kindling for the fire, preparing food, laundering, spinning yarn, sewing, making cloth and clothes, quilting, and knitting stockings. Other tasks might include milking, churning butter, and making cheese. Some may also have assisted with making cider, as this was a woman's task until the end of the eighteenth century. Inventory information reveals that cidering equipment was located in "women's spaces," such as the kitchen, the dairy, or in the area where women made textiles, so they could check frequently on the brew.[47]

Rural domestic servants also worked outdoors tending orchards and kitchen gardens where, according to season, were grown fresh vegetables such as beans and peas, cabbages, carrots, corn, onions, potatoes, and squash. Any surplus was dried for winter consumption. They sometimes looked after small barnyard animals and poultry and assisted in raising grain crops that contributed the cereal component of the planter family's diet (bread, hominy, and mush).[48]

The role of their mistresses in the lives of the women convicts is elusive. While most mistresses would have been the wives or daughters of the convict women's masters, some—perhaps widows—would have headed households themselves and bought convicts on their own account. The few surviving sale records for arriving convicts list just a couple of names of female purchasers. In August 1719 when the *Margaret* arrived in Annapolis, a Mrs. Bransome purchased Abigail Green from Surrey, and a Rosanna Lees purchased Ann Spurgeon. In July 1775, when the *Isabella* arrived, an Elizabeth Harrison of Charles County purchased Bridget McCarty.[49] It is highly likely there were many other female purchasers because a number advertised for convict women when they ran away. The advertisers included Alice Davis, Ann Milton, Sarah Monro, Rachel Pottenger, and Catharine

Jenings. Their notices do not provide any details that were much different from those in advertisements placed by men. A possible exception may be the advertisement that was placed for Elizabeth Crowder by Sarah Monro. In this Monro acknowledged Crowder's quilting skills, and being a quilter herself, Monro was in a good position to judge. The shared work of sewing and quilting does not seem to have made friends of Monro and Crowder, who ran away only a year into her sentence.[50]

If it did not lead to female friendship, the proximity of white servants and mistresses in circumstances of potentially great intimacy did at least create opportunities for cooperative collaboration. But the enforced closeness may also have produced abuse. Despite their proximity, mistresses—especially mistresses of the households of Maryland's elite families such as the Carrolls, Dulanys, Galloways, and Tilghmans—probably sought to preserve a class-based distance between themselves and their servants. They are likely also to have been uneasy about their convict servants' criminal backgrounds and wanted to keep the women at arm's length.

In writing about the relationships between servants and mistresses in Virginia's plantation houses, historian Kathleen M. Brown relates how the mistresses of those houses used tone of voice, body language, clothing, the division of labor, and the creation of special off-limits ("sacred") places within the home as means by which they could establish social boundaries and confirm differences in status in spite of their closeness to their slaves and servants.[51] Unfortunately, there is simply no adequate source material that might throw light on or could sustain any assumptions about typical relationships that Maryland's convict servants had with their mistresses—or other female family members of the households in which they worked.

The convicts may have made friendships with slave women and/or with other white servants. When Margaret Tasker ran away from the Baltimore Company in 1764, she did so with a white indentured maidservant called Sarah Skinner. Tasker took with her a great many items of clothing that her master surmised were for Sarah, who was "meanly clad" and had with her only a pair of shoes and some stockings. The content of the advertisement provides the outlines of a friendship based on a common goal—escaping—and the very human consideration of another's basic needs.[52]

Despite there not being any diaries, letters, or much other documentary evidence for the lives of the convict women, the material circumstances of their day-to-day lives can still be established somewhat convincingly by examining the estate inventories and accounts in Maryland's eighteenth-century probate records. These inventories (supported with archaeological evidence) provide enough information to furnish a sort of economic biography of every person of property, whether a member of the elite or the poorest planter. When appraising an estate, assessors overlooked nothing, not even a cracked cup without a handle—they certainly did not miss the human property of servants and slaves.[53]

Kitchen equipment might include peels and piggins, churns and querns, crocks and cranes, Dutch ovens and roasting kitchens, skillets, trivets, spiders, and spits.[54] Although the names of some of these items are no longer familiar, most were associated with cooking over an open fire, which burned all year round. Actually, a kitchen with these utensils would have been very well equipped; most inventories do not include such a great range of equipment. In one inventory in which two servants comprised 21 percent of the entire estate of 58 pounds, 13 shillings, and 6 pence, they were listed along with four pots, two pewter dishes, three pans, a small looking glass, and two spinning wheels. Ironically, one of the servants in the inventory was a London convict, Barbara Black, who had been transported for stealing household items including a sheet.[55] Some of the poorer households boasted nothing more than a single pot or pan for braising meat (principally pork) or making stews. Even essentials—bowls, cups, plates, and spoons—are missing from the inventories of these lower-value estates, suggesting substitutes were improvised, such as wooden trenchers made with an adze, bowls carved from dried gourds, or spoons whittled from bits of a tree branch. Gourds were also used as drinking vessels.[56]

Inventory and archaeological evidence confirms that these poorer planters built simple houses of traditional earth-fast post construction that were little changed from those of a century before—probably because tobacco cultivation was labor intensive and any available funds were spent on labor rather than comfortable accommodation.[57] Containing as few as two or three rooms, the houses of these poorer planters often had dirt floors, unglazed windows, and log furniture. Having no lamps, after nightfall their inhabitants were dependent on firelight.

As estate values ascend (particularly into the brackets representing the planters most likely to purchase convicts), inventories indicate lives that, though they may have had a higher level of material comfort (beds and bedheads appear, for example), were nevertheless frugal and indebted.[58] When he died at thirty, Joseph Pettibone, who purchased Elizabeth Dobbs from the *Margaret* in 1719, left a small estate valued at 142 pounds, 6 shillings—of which about half was owed to creditors.[59] Not much suggests that the convict women in these meagerly equipped households were provided for separately in any meaningful way. Indeed, in some households they may have been fully integrated into their master's family life, sharing meals and sleeping within the house.[60]

In 1656 John Hammond in his promotional tract *Leah and Rachel; or, The Two Fruitfull Sisters, Virginia and Mary-land* wrote: "Whereas it is rumoured that Servants have no lodging other then on boards, or by the Fire side, it is contrary to reason to believe it: First, as we are Christians; next as people living under a law, which compels as well the Master as the Servant to perform his duty; nor can true labour be either expected or exacted without sufficient cloathing, diet, and lodging; all which both their Indentures (which must inviolably be observed) and the Justice of the Country requires.[61]

If this were really true in the seventeenth century, it was not so a century later when women actually did doss down beside the hearth or on straw in the loft or stables—at least in marginal households where accommodation was at its most meager. Even in the houses of the well to do, accommodation for servants was often segregated from the master's view—in the basement of the plantation or town house, where the kitchen, cellars, and other service areas were located. If they had ever possessed habits of cleanliness and order, these would have soon faded, as there were no special provisions for servants to wash themselves.[62]

The only known letter from a female servant, who may have been a convict but was definitely indentured, was written by a young woman called Elizabeth Sprigs. Sprigs was a servant in the household of Richard Cross, who was a member of a planter family with landholdings near Baltimore called Cross's Park and Cross's Lot.[63] The letter which, considering the flourishes of the penman, was almost certainly written on Sprigs's behalf by a professional letter writer, was sent to her father in London. It came to light only because the ship on which it was carried to England met with some sort of misadventure on the voyage and everything on board was impounded, to be held forevermore by the High Court of Admiralty. The letter starts with an apology to her father for her "undutifulness" and acknowledges that she had "offended in the highest degree." She then refers to her "former bad Conduct." All these phrases suggest criminality or perhaps just delinquency. The letter proceeds:

> O dear father, belive what I am going to relate the words of truth and
> sincerity, and Ballance my former bad Conduct to my sufferings here, and
> then I am sure you'll pitty your Destress Daughter. What we Unfortunat
> English People suffer here is beyond the probility of you in England
> to Conceive, let it suffice that I one of the unhappy Number, am toiling
> almost Day and Night, and very often in the Horses druggery, with only
> this comfort that you Bitch you do not halfe enough, and then tied up
> and whipp'd to that Degree that you'd not serve an Annimal, scarce
> anything but Indian Corn and Salt to eat and even that begrudged nay
> many Neagroes are better used, almost naked no shoes nor stockings to
> wear, and the comfort after slaving Dureing Master's pleasure, what rest we
> can get is to rap ourselves up in a Blanket and ly upon the Ground, this is
> the deplorable Condition your poor Betty endures, and now I beg if you

have any Bowels of Compassion left show it by sending me some Relief, Clothing is the principal thing wanting, which if you should condiscend to, may easily send them to me by any of the ships bound to Baltimore Town Patapsco River Maryland, and give me leave to conclude in Duty to you & Uncles and Aunts, and Respect to all Friends.

> Honored Father
> Your Undutifull & Disobedient Child
> Elizabeth Sprigs[64]

By itself, Elizabeth Sprigs's letter is evidence only of the unhappy circumstances of one abused young woman on a marginal plantation. Yet the observations of several contemporaries suggest that her experience was actually commonplace, if not standard. Father Mosley wrote that "servants had no choice of masters but the highest bidder at publick sale carrys them off to be used at his mercy, without any redress at law." He went on to describe these men as being "in general cruel, barbarous and unmerciful."[65] The fictional Polly Haycock described her plantation master as "cruel, haughty and mercenary, without any soft sentiment of humanity in his breast. Like most of the tribe of planters he had no appetite but for money; nor pleasure in any pastime but torturing the unhappy wretches in his power."[66] William Eddis, the observant Englishmen who had come to Annapolis in 1769, commented in one of his letters home about the different forms of bound labor in Maryland. "Negroes, being a property for life, are almost in every instance under more comfortable circumstances than the miserable European over whom the rigid planter exercises an inflexible severity."[67]

The reasons for this severity are not hard to gauge. Many small planters had a difficult life themselves and were unlikely to have much sympathy left over for the hardship of others. These masters also had "a prepossession in many cases" that the convicts were "supposed to be receiving their just reward due to repeated offenses."[68] On plantations where all the labor was bound and some was bound in perpetuity, the likelihood that a master's treatment would vary greatly between indentured servants, convicts, and slaves was slight. If anything, slaves came off best because they had a permanent asset value and regular indentured servants worst because, as William Eddis said, "their owners too generally conceive the opinion that the difference is merely nominal between the indented servant and the convicted felon."[69] If Eddis was right, being a convict did not add a great deal more to the burdens of being a female servant with a binding indentured labor agreement. There again, in marginal households, often the only difference between the circumstances of the convict women and their master and his family was the formers' unfree status because their work, tasks, and accommodation were not dissimilar.

If the convict women had, like Elizabeth Sprigs, "scarce anything but Indian

Honred Father   Maryland Sept:. 22. 1756

My being for ever banished from your sight, will I hope pardon the Boldness I now take of troubling you with these, my long silence has been purely owing to my undutifullness to you, and well knowing I had offended in the highest Degree, put a tie to my tongue and pen, for fear I should be extinct from your good Graces and add a further Trouble to you, but too well knowing your care and tenderness for me so long as I retaind my Duty to you, induced me once again to endeavour if possible, to kindle up that flame again, O Dear Father, belive what I am going to relate the words of truth and sincerity, and Ballance my former bad Conduct to my sufferings here, and then I am sure you'll pitty your Distressed Daughter, What we unfortunat English People suffer here is beyond the probability of you in England to Conceive, let it suffice that I one of the unhappy Number, am toiling almost Day and Night, and very often in the Horses druggery, with only this comfort that you Bitch you do not halfe enough, and then tied up and whipp'd to that Degree that you'd not serve an Annimal, scarce any thing but Indian Corn and Salt to eat and that even begrudged nay many Negroes are better used, almost naked no shoes nor stockings to wear, and the comfort after slaving during Masters pleasure, what rest we can get is to rap ourselves up in a Blanket and ly upon the Ground, this is the deplorable Condition your poor Betty endures, & now I beg if you have any Bowels of Compassion left show it by sending me some Relief, Cloathing is the principle thing wanting, which if you should condiscend to, may easily send them to me by any of the Ships bound to Baltimore Town Patapsco River Maryland, & give me leave to conclude in Duty to you & Unkles & Aunts, and Respect to all Friends

Please to direct for me at Mr. Rich'd Crosss to be left at Mr. Luxes Merch't in Baltimore Town Patapsco River Maryland

Honred Father
Your undutifull & Disobedient Child
Elizabeth Sprigs

Elizabeth Sprigs to her father, September 22, 1756. (High Court of Admiralty: Oyer and Terminer Records, HCA/30/258. Courtesy of the Public Record Office, Kew, UK.)

Corn and Salt to eat," they may have been at risk of developing a skin condition called pellagra which had unpleasant symptoms often confused with scurvy. Long before Sprigs wrote her letter, the Maryland courts had decided that servants needed to have an appropriate diet and that this should include meat as well as beans and corn.[70] Richard Cross seems to have been ignoring this requirement.

In an extensive examination of the private punishment of servants and slaves in eighteenth-century Maryland, C. Ashley Ellefson has found that it was not just the struggling small planters who took out their frustrations on their servants and that the rigid class structure of the period was also to blame. Those who belonged to "the more fortunate classes"—the planters, merchants, and the free population—generally believed they were superior to their servants and slaves and thus could do with them whatever they liked. Servants and slaves were often the helpless victims of a colonial tolerance for the exploitation and pain of others. Even the law, which stipulated a master's minimum responsibilities for his servants, entitled him to whip a servant with up to ten lashes without reference to a magistrate—and up to thirty-nine lashes if the magistrate so ordered.[71]

On plantations and in businesses that were not marginal—those owned and controlled by well-to-do or elite and wealthy families—the treatment of servants was not always noticeably better. Peter Galloway, Dr. Charles Carroll, Charles Carroll of Annapolis, Benjamin Tasker, Daniel Dulany, and Charles Ridgely are all on record as having treated severely their convict servants.[72]

Servants had a right at law to petition the courts for relief from excessively harsh treatment from their masters, and very occasionally they did so. Elizabeth Whitney, alias Dribray, was one convict woman who took such action. She had been transported from London in May 1740, and two years later was a servant to William Mattingly of Baltimore County who, she alleged, was cruelly abusive. Now Whitney had employed violence herself—she had nearly strangled a man while robbing him of his wallet—and it might be thought she could look after herself. Yet the charge was proved, and in March 1742 Mattingly was duly fined. Similarly, in 1728 Martha Anderson brought to court some type of complaint against her mistress, Sarah James, though this may not have proceeded to a hearing. There was, however, a strong disincentive for any servant to bring an action for abuse because the justices (who owned servants themselves) were likely to side with the master and impose a penalty on the petitioner for lying. Moreover, only masters, not servants, could serve on juries.[73]

As in Britain, the law governing servants was administered within the context of a society concerned with the primacy of property rights and a scant regard for any competing interest. Judges were mindful that the owners of servants were entitled to benefit from their investment; harsh and exploitative practices were part of the day-to-day reality of servitude. In 1747, however, the *Maryland Gazette* reported on the suicide of a male convict called Elisha Williams who was a servant in the Annapolis home of Hannah and John Senhouse, the latter a shoemaker and currier (leather tanner). In his charge to the jury the coroner stated: "Too often [the] rigorous Usage and Ill-treatment of Masters . . . is the Cause of many Servants making an End of themselves one Way or other."[74]

~

Maryland's laws strongly protected the interests of masters whose female servants became pregnant during their servitude, and women paid heavily for having an illegitimate child. Theoretically, servitude imposed a condition of celibacy. Pregnancy was punished because it meant lost time and thus threatened a planter's livelihood. If a woman died in childbirth, it could mean the loss of the planter's entire investment.

During the transportation period the Maryland law governing sexual relations was *An Act for the Punishing of the Offences of Adultery and Fornication*—which was passed in 1715 by the Assembly. In 1749, in a move that reflected a shift toward less public shaming of those who transgressed moral boundaries (at least in white pairings), the Assembly passed an *Act for Taking off Corporal Punishment Inflicted on Females Having Base-born Children; and Other Purposes therein Mentioned.* This somewhat modified the 1715 law in regard to corporal punishment and updated the level of applicable fines.[75]

In spite of the penalties, unmarried servant women became pregnant anyway, and indictments and trials for "bastardy" were frequently listed in Maryland's court proceedings. In the twenty years between 1728 and 1748, there were more than four hundred indictments for bastardy in Queen Anne County alone. How many of these indictments involved convict servants is not completely clear. Indicted servants (convict and indentured) and free women frequently shared the same or similar names, and the court records only occasionally mentioned that a defendant was a "seven-year servant." In Baltimore County however, sixty-nine women who appear to have been convicts were indicted for bastardy between 1673 and 1783 (four for mulatto bastardy after 1718).[76]

Court records that *do* allow the certain identification of defendants as convicts show that some women were indicted on multiple occasions, including seven of the sixty-nine Baltimore County women mentioned above. Such a one was Hannah Howard, a London thief, who was transported in 1733. She was charged with bastardy at the Baltimore County Court in August 1742 and again in 1744. Ann Ambrose may have been indicted and convicted on three separate occasions within a ten-year period.[77]

Laws on sexual relations were based on the idea that moral wrongdoing such as fornication or adultery should be punished. A woman's indictment usually stated that, on a certain date, she had permitted "an unknown person then and there to have carnal knowledge of her body and to beget then and there a bastard child to the high displeasure of Almighty God and to the evil example of all others." Moreover, bastardy was an offense that was "contrary to the peace of the said Lord Proprietary that now is his good rule and government and against the form of the Act of Assembly in that case made & provided." Laws also recognized a master's entitlement to compensatory extra service from a female servant in order to recoup any costs he might incur as a consequence of lost productivity during her pregnancy, confinement, and during the early years of her child's life. Court judgments put it thus: "for trouble, loss of time, disgrace and charges in her lying in."[78] County courts were principally concerned to ensure that illegitimate children did not become a charge on the county and thus sought to establish paternity in order to obtain payments for maintenance and upkeep.[79] If a woman "did refuse to discover the Father, or begetter" of her illegitimate child, she could be heavily fined and, if no one would pay her fine, could be "whipped on her bare body 'till the blood do appear."[80]

A 1727 law—*An Act Directing the Payment of Fees Arising Due on the Prosecution of White Servants Which Shall Hereafter Be Imported into This Province*—required that "Bastard Children of Women Servants shall be maintained by the Master or Owner of such Servants, during the Mother's servitude."[81] The mother had the length of her servitude extended for an extra twelve to twenty-four months to repay her master for the "trouble of his house" and labor lost—an overgenerous reparation for what was probably only a few weeks of downtime.[82] If neither the woman's master nor the "discovered" father was prepared to meet the costs of an illegitimate child, then after it was weaned, the justices of the county court might bind it out to a suitable home with some compensatory inducement and directions for its future education and training.[83]

On the larger tobacco plantations, where, as the century wore on, slaves comprised a larger and larger proportion of a planter's workforce, the men with whom convict women were most likely to come into contact were slaves. If they engaged in sexual relations—what the law termed "inordinate copulations"—with these fellow workers, they combined illicit activity with social and legal taboos on interracial sex and miscegenation. If the women bore children, they were prosecuted for the crime of "Mulatto Bastardy."[84]

In June 1755 Maria Newman was indicted and convicted for mulatto bastardy at the Charles County Court. Newman was perhaps inclined to be a risk taker— she had been a prostitute in London and was transported for robbing one of her clients of a valuable ring and 10 guineas in gold.[85] In June 1739 Ann Farthing, who arrived in Maryland on the *Falcon* in March 1733, was similarly indicted for mulatto bastardy at the Kent County Criminal Court in Chestertown. Farthing was described as being a spinster of St. Paul's Parish, Kent County, who had, on May

1, 1738, committed fornication with an unknown Negro man. Farthing declared she was "in no sort guilty of the premises upon her imposed by the indictment." The court did not believe her—the child was ipso facto evidence. The clerk, James Smith, recorded her sentence thus: "That the aforesaid Ann serve the term of seven years according to Act of Assembly for committing the fornication aforesaid. And also pay the sum of five hundred and sixty-nine pounds of tobacco. Costs accruing on the premises aforesaid to the several officers of this court &c."[86]

Jane Ellis was a convict servant to planter Samuel Owings when she was indicted for mulatto bastardy at Baltimore County Court in August 1755. Perhaps surprisingly, the court found her not guilty of the charge. She was sentenced instead to serve an extra nine months to compensate her master for time lost during a period when she had run away and for charges to a doctor for curing her of "French distemper"—a contemporary term for syphilis.[87]

In March 1745 Frances Humphreys was living in Baltimore County when a jury found her guilty of mulatto bastardy.[88] She had had a previous conviction for (white) bastardy two years earlier, when she was sentenced to receive fifteen lashes. Upon her second conviction the Baltimore County Court ruled that Abigail, her daughter, be sold to Humphreys's master, William Hamilton. The girl would have been bound to Hamilton until she reached the age of thirty-one. This was the usual arrangement for a servant's mulatto child. If a master was unwilling to accept such responsibility, the child would be bound out—that is, sold—to another master (proceeds to the county) to serve until the age of thirty-one.[89]

Despite the punitive consequences for mulatto bastardy, some women seem to have been unable or unwilling to forego the behavior their sentences were intended strongly to discourage. During her servitude with William Brawner, a Charles County planter, Ann Nelson was twice indicted for mulatto bastardy in a period of just over two years.[90] Winifred Jones, the aforementioned house servant to assemblyman Major Thomas Sheredine, was successfully prosecuted three times for having a child by a "Negro," but Sheredine's estate inventory indicates that at the time of Sheredine's death from smallpox in May 1752, Jones actually had five mixed-race children, each bound to Sheredine until the age of thirty-one.[91]

As with white bastardy, a conviction for mulatto bastardy could entail a woman being heavily fined or, if unable to pay, whipped. Additionally, however, a conviction (such as Ann Farthing's) required that a servant "shall finish her Servitude, together with Satisfaction for Damage, and shall again become a Servant for Seven years."[92] Margaret Lewis, a London thief who was transported on the *Patapsco* in 1731, was a servant to Thomas Hands in Anne Arundel County when charged with "bastardy and miscegenation" in 1741. She was ordered to serve Hands for an additional twelve months and then to serve a further seven years to satisfy the County Court.[93]

Only masters could give permission for women to marry during their service (successful labor arrangements could not allow the competing authorities of master and husband), and servants who contracted an unsanctioned marriage could be required to serve an extra year of service. A law passed in 1664 proscribed marriages between white and black people.

Although illegitimate births were not at all uncommon, the stigma of bearing an illegitimate child, whether white or of mixed race, connected the convict women to other marginalized members of Maryland's colonial society. These included slaves, free black people, and other white women prosecuted for illegitimacy or other sexual offences, and helped to confirm further their social status as pariahs. If their illegitimate children were of mixed race, these would occupy a place in the social order only nominally different from the place occupied by their enslaved kin.[94]

Some of the convict women may have offered sexual favors to their masters hoping for lighter work or other special privileges. Others may have had to endure unsought sexual attention from their masters and male members of their master's family as well as from fellow servants.[95] William Byrd was a Virginian planter and the member of an elite colonial family whose diaries survive for the years 1709–12 and 1739–41. In these he frequently recorded how he and his companions took advantage of female servants and other women they regarded as being socially or racially distant from themselves.[96] Byrd is likely to have had counterparts in Maryland—if perhaps not quite so boastful about their machismo. In any case, domestic workers in Britain were all too often expected to service sexually the men of the household, and it may not have been a novel experience for those women who had been servants before transportation. In the years between 1767 and 1775, James Cheston sold forty-eight convict women, but he subsequently refunded a portion of the purchase price to the buyers of four of them. This was because, post-purchase, the women had been "discovered" by their buyers to have a venereal disease.[97]

In the medical thinking of the period, having a venereal disease made the women unsuitable for child care, food preparation, and other female household chores. Eighteenth-century literature on venereal diseases alleged there was risk to children of contagion should they be nursed by an infected female servant or come into contact with the servant's sweat or skin.[98] A venereal disease also carried the implication that a woman may have been a prostitute in Britain or Ireland, and therefore a more "professional" criminal than her papers suggested. Obviously, venereal diseases made women less appealing for sexual contact—something their masters may have learned too late and lived to regret. However, despite the sexual opportunity offered by the proximity of the convict women, they were valued primarily as workers, and masters did not really want all the complications of pregnancy and the obligations stemming from bastardy charges.[99]

It is more than likely that the convict women's sexual activities did not involve only heterosexual encounters, and some women may have been homosexual themselves. In 1751 the *Gentleman's Magazine* reported the transportation to Virginia of "an impostress dressed in man's apparel who had married seven wives. The first six being virgins were deceived by artifice, but the seventh, a widow, soon discovered her bedfellow."[100] Some of the convict women were also cross-dressers, though their motives seem more to do with the opportunities offered by such disguise rather than a means of expressing sexual identity. Women occasionally dressed as men in order to break out of the custodial confinement of parents, husbands, and masters and to gain access to opportunities (such as military service) otherwise denied to them. It allowed them to travel at liberty without male guardianship and to receive higher wages.[101] In 1753 a Yorkshire woman named Sarah Knox ran away from David Currie, who placed an advertisement for her in the *Maryland Gazette*. He thought Knox might be dressing in men's clothes and pretending to be a male doctor.[102] Another runaway woman—merely called "Elizabeth" in the advertisement placed to locate her—was said to be passing herself off as a soldier. John Ducker of Annapolis surmised that his runaway convict servant, Frances Burrowes, would change her name and "appear in man's apparel"—a not infrequent runaway stratagem.[103] Cross-dressing was subversive because it blurred lines of gender and sexuality and thus, for these women, actually altered the conventional experience of being female. If the adjectives used in the advertisements are any guide, it was also deeply unsettling to men.

The punishment of female sexuality was an aspect of servitude that was significantly different for male and female convict servants. Unless male convicts were explicitly named as the putative fathers in bastardy cases or were charged with some sexual offense such as adultery, fornication, or rape, they did not have to worry about being fined or whipped merely for engaging in sexual contact, nor were they legally required to undertake extended service periods as punishment or for any lost time.

~

The labor performed by convict servants meant economic survival for some planters—their time was money. It was also essential for those who provided planters with domestic and household labor. Yet some women were apparently able to find ways of taking time off from work to enjoy themselves. In 1764 Margaret Cane was a convict servant to Benjamin Philpott of Port Tobacco in Charles County. At that time Port Tobacco was a very busy place. It was the county seat, a naval port of entry and, like Queen Anne Town, an inspection station for export tobacco. It had a popular racetrack and it was also where Benjamin Philpott operated a tavern or public house. When Cane ran away, he advertised for her in the *Maryland Gazette*, forewarning the masters of ships that if they carried her off they would do so "at their peril." Besides providing a list of the clothing that Cane was likely to be wearing or had taken with her, Philpott's notice stated that "she is fond of a drink and likes sailors' company very much." He also said, to aid identification, that Cane had been so severely burned as a child that "her little finger and that next to it lay in the palm of her left hand." It is tempting to judge Philpott as a kindly master who valued Cane as a worker and tolerated her roistering out of sympathy for the awful injury of her fused hand. It is more likely he found her refractory and licentious but was concerned at losing his investment. He offered 6 dollars as a reward for her return.[104]

Each October or November a huge fleet of vessels arrived in the Chesapeake Bay from England in order to collect the tobacco harvest. Their captains remained in the bay area probing its many estuaries and anchoring at plantation wharves until their vessels were fully laden.[105] Not infrequently tobacco collection held the vessels over until the following summer, and when sailors found they had time on their hands they made their way to any settlement that had a race course or taverns and public houses ("ordinaries") that served good beer, rum, and cider—made not only from apples but other fruits as well.[106] As a timeless social lubricant, drink brought people together and aided joviality and amiability. In such a setting it is easy to imagine Shropshire woman Mary Owens—a fresh-complexioned "hussy" who spoke in dialect—taking snuff and dimpling as she threw back her head with laughter, displaying a gap-toothed smile. When she ran away in 1767 her master, William Simpson, cited the dimple on her left cheek and missing teeth as distinguishing characteristics.[107]

Where there was social activity there was also often music—the most important recreational element for laboring people who, even without instruments, could enjoy singing and dancing. In fact, just as it was for elite families in the colonial Chesapeake, dancing was a favorite recreation of working people—jigs, reels, and other hearty country dances.[108] Some convicts did have musical instruments— Mary Jackson's husband possessed a set of bagpipes, and a male convict named Elisha Bond was a fiddler. When he ran away from a Kent County plantation in October 1747 his owner, Michael Hackett, placed an advertisement in the *Maryland Gazette*. This asserted that the lusty, bushy-haired, forty-five-year-old from Devon "understands fiddling having one with him."[109]

Alcohol was essential to colonial life—water was often brackish or too contaminated for drinking, milk was not widely available, and tea and coffee were luxuries for the very wealthy. Colonists also used alcohol in cooking, as a cleaning agent, and as medicine, but consuming alcohol was something that usually took place in gendered settings with men drinking in male groups—often outdoors—at public festivities, militia musters, elections, and so on. Women drank indoors with their families or at gatherings for events such as childbirth.[110] At a time when the home was regarded as the usual arena for women, those who ventured out into predominantly male spaces such as taverns confirmed the marginality of their status and the deviance of their behavior from seemly and respectable female norms. For their pleasure the convict women would be judged more harshly than male convicts, for whom such activities were not a transgression of gender roles. Without respectability, the women were likely to be deemed sexually available (whether they were or not), fair game for those with a lecherous intent.[111]

In 1975 Carville Earle, a Maryland geographer and historian, conducted a multi-layered and detailed study of All Hallows Parish in Anne Arundel County from 1650 to 1783. Earle showed how the rhythms of tobacco production conveniently matched the traditional Christian calendar—periods of sacred observance coinciding neatly with slack times for planters. Thus Whitsun, Easter, and Christmas were all celebrated both as holy days and, in the modern sense, as holidays. Quakers, who were of sober habits, actually complained that when they held meetings at these times, they had to endure "a great concourse of idle and profligate white people and great crowds of Negroes that assemble together . . . drinking to excess and behaving in a riotous and turbulent manner."[112]

Although Sunday was (by law) supposed to be strictly observed as a day of rest, and "grinding corn on the Sabbath" could be cause for indictment by a grand jury, some convicts apparently spent their Sundays looking after their own gardens. White parish residents were expected to attend church, though there is no evidence that convict women did so.[113] Those who were Irish were probably Catholic and, although the captains of incoming vessels had to swear they were not bringing "papists" into Maryland on penalty of paying a fine, it is clear from Father Mosley's accounts of his life in Maryland that he spent much of his time ministering to the needs of a large Catholic population.[114] This certainly included regular indentured servants and probably convict servants also. Some of the convict women bore names that suggest they were Jewish (for example, Ann Abraham, Rachael Isaacs, alias Jacobs, Susan Moses, and Sarah Jacobs, alias Sikes), but it is not known whether they were interested in observing their faith in any way—there were certainly no synagogues in Maryland until the nineteenth century.[115]

∾

Convict women were purchased right up until the War of Independence because they were inexpensive, there was a dependable and regular supply, and there continued to be a need for their labor. The value of many of them lay in what they could produce—not, for example, whether they might make good future settlers or suitable wives for colonists (as was sometimes a consideration in deciding which women would be transported to Australia). Unlike slaves, they were not a self-perpetuating labor force—many of them merely allowed small planters to survive economically from season to season. The frequently harsh treatment of women on plantations and in other workplaces such as ironworks was governed by the need of their masters to maintain their productive capacity for the greater period of their sentence term and be compensated for any time out from this purpose. Should the owner of a convict woman die, his investment was not necessarily lost but merely passed to the owner's estate; their labor was disposable property. Their treatment and conditions might be in accordance with Maryland's laws and compliant with the terms and inherent nature of compulsory servitude, but they were, nevertheless, inherently exploitative and debased further the women's already fragile and marginal status.

6
Escape

The lives of servants and rural laborers were routinely burdensome on both sides of the Atlantic during the eighteenth century, but the hardships of Maryland's convict women were heightened by their severance from family, friends, and—for those from rural areas—familiarity with a deeply rooted culture that was rich in folk tradition. Their hardship was also heightened by their dehumanized and (in some instances) degendered status. They were stigmatized as malefactors, thieves, and ne'er-do-wells who were either at or nearly at the bottom of the social pile. All these factors are likely to have exacerbated their difficulties and at times made their lot seem unbearable. As a consequence, many were motivated to escape their situation by fleeing from their masters and setting out for the Carolinas, Delaware, Pennsylvania, or the Rappahannock River in Virginia—any place far enough afield for them to pass unrecognized and where they might find a vessel that would take them home.

Running away was inherently risky. If servants were found more than ten miles from where they lived and had neither a note from their master nor a pass issued under the county seal and they were unable to give a good account of themselves before a magistrate, then they could be deemed runaways and suffer accordingly.[1] Yet in the years between 1728 and 1780, the *Maryland Gazette*, the *Pennsylvania Gazette*, the *Maryland Journal and Baltimore Advertiser*, and other journals or newspapers carried eighty-four advertisements (some duplicates) for sixty convict women who had run away from Maryland masters. The notices—invariably introduced by the phrase "Run [or ran] away from the subscriber last [date]"— appeared among other classified advertisements for runaway slaves and indentured servants—and often adjacent to those for lost horses and strayed cows. These advertisements show that some women ran away within just a few months of their arrival—although the median time for running away was around fourteen months. A few women appear in these advertisements on more than one occasion, indicating that they were not deterred from trying to escape even after an unsuccessful attempt.[2] About half the advertisements gave ages for the runaways—the youngest was eighteen, the oldest forty-seven; the median age was twenty-nine and a half. Convict women ran away at about double the rate of other indentured servant women despite the much greater number of unconvicted indentured servants. Between 1750 and 1759 the *Maryland Gazette* published advertisements for nine convict women and five female indentured servants.

The descriptions in these advertisements were necessarily extremely rich in detail, as each functioned as a type of pre-photographic-era "Wanted" poster. They show the ways in which masters attentively surveyed their servants—even making inventories of their characteristics—perhaps displaying the prudence of a careful property owner but also as an aid to control. The owners may actually have anticipated that their servants were likely to abscond and kept precise descriptive notes by way of a contingency plan. Charles Ridgely was one master who is known to have maintained detailed records of the white workforce at his Hampton farm and Northampton ironworks in the early 1770s, listing physical and personal idiosyncrasies.[3]

The detail in the advertisements is not only a guide as to how masters regarded the servants over whom they had authority and power, but it usefully invests names with unique personal characteristics and assists the process by which various aspects of the convict women's lives can be discovered. As with some of the evidence given at their trials, the accumulated catalog of details in the advertisements helps to make the convict women come alive as individuals (sometimes vividly) and to show how they asserted their personalities and, to some extent, subverted their status. As well, the information given over many years is consistent enough to allow the reasonable inference to be drawn that these women were a representative sample of Maryland's female convict servants—if perhaps less risk averse or more daring than those who never attempted to escape. This is despite the fact that the total number of advertisements represent approximately 1 percent of the number of women estimated to have been transported to the province. However, it should be noted that in the 1720s runaway advertisements did not always mention whether a servant was a convict. Also the *Maryland Gazette* was not published at all between December 1734 and January 1745 (and in other years the proprietor sometimes suspended publication for months at a time), and information for the *Maryland Journal and Baltimore Advertiser* is available only between 1773 and December 1775. It is probable that not all runaways were advertised (it may not have been worth offering a reward for women, who were of less value than male convicts), and owners may not have wanted to advertise in newspapers published a great distance from where they lived. Some women may have wanted to run away but were not bold enough to do so—particularly without a male protector. About one-fifth of the runaways escaped with a fellow servant or servants. There was a noteworthy gender difference in the likelihood of running away—men were far more likely to attempt escape than women.[4]

RAN away from the Subscriber, living in *Annapolis*, on the 23d of ~~this follow~~ *May*, a Convict Servant Woman, named *Hannah Boyer*, about 23 or 24 Years of Age, pitted much with the Small Pox, has a Scar in one of her Eye Brows, not very tall, but a very strong, fresh coloured, robust, masculine Wench. She had on and took with her, a blue Jacket, an old whitish Cloak, a brown Petticoat, a double Mobb, an Ofnabrigs Shift, a small striped check'd Apron, a Plaid Petticoat, and Night Gown, no Shoes nor Stockings; but without doubt will change her Cloathing; she had a Horfe Lock and Chain on one of her Legs. Whoever takes up the said Servant, and brings her home, shall have Twenty Shillings Reward, if taken in *Annapolis*; if taken 10 Miles from home, Twenty Shillings Reward, besides what the Law allows, paid by

* *Daniel Wells.*

Daniel Wells placed this notice when Hannah Boyer ran away from him wearing a "horse lock and chain" on her leg. (*Maryland Gazette*, May 28, 1752, *Maryland Gazette* Collection, January 2, 1752–October 19, 1758, M 1279, Maryland Historical Society, Baltimore.)

At a time when petticoats grazed the ankles and gowns usually had half-length sleeves with cuffs or, from about the 1740s, deep ruffles that covered the elbows, the physical details cited in these advertisements suggest that the women had been closely, perhaps intimately, observed by their owners before they ran off—assessed and appraised as the property the women had virtually become.[5] Masters knew that although clothes and hairstyles could be changed, deformities or scars could not, and the advertisements contain many examples of such identifiers. Thus Paul Rankin, who was Sarah Davis's master, noted she had many scars on her back— welts from being whipped during a previous period of service. Thomas Lewis, Isabella Pierce's master, said that "if examined" she would be found to have large scars on her ankles—an indication that, either during or prior to her service with Lewis, Pierce had worn metal shackles and these had cut into her skin.[6]

Metal restraints on convicts were not unusual; three advertisers shamelessly noted their female escapees were wearing iron fetters or "horse collars" and chains. One of these was an eighteen-year-old girl named Margaret Tasker from Cheshire. In November 1763 Tasker was transported from Whitehaven on the *Betsy* and purchased in Maryland on behalf of Thomas Harrison and Company to work in the Patapsco Iron Furnace—though in what capacity is uncertain. Two months later (in January 1764), she ran away with another woman. Joseph Watkins, the manager of the furnace, advertised for her return. He described her as wearing an iron collar. It seems Watkins fitted all his convict servants with such collars, or "pothooks," because most of his runaway advertisements refer to them. Even if Tasker had not been assigned to do the heaviest tasks in the furnace, any work in such a place was likely to have been dismal, hot, and physically exhausting for anyone so young—let alone someone who was also half blind—the advertisement mentioned that Margaret Tasker had only one eye.[7]

Not surprisingly, the appearance of the runaways, who were often from a background of socioeconomic deprivation and had endured filthy prisons and a nonnutritive diet for months on end, does not sound very prepossessing. Descriptions such as "round-shouldered," "pot-bellied," "bloated under the eyes," "stooped," "stooped in the shoulders," "limping," "scarred," "pitted with smallpox" (or "pockfretten") were all used. Nothing went unrecorded—Mary Owens's pigeon-toed walk and her missing front teeth, the scar running through Hannah Boyer's eyebrow, the "blemish" in Sarah Wilson's right eye, and the "small blemish" in one of Frances Burrowes's eyes. Also noted was the "remarkable mole" on the left cheek of Mary Brady and the fact that the index finger on Anne Pervis's right hand was much smaller than all her other fingers.[8] Height was often noted: Mary Osbourn (or Osborn) was only four feet tall (1.22 m), Elizabeth Lloyd was four feet, eight inches (1.42 m), and Mary Jackson was "lofty"—well over five and a half feet (1.73 m).[9]

Even when the women were unimpaired, their masters' descriptions (even if factual) conveyed a distaste for their lack of pulchritude. A "flat, freckled face," "a very homely face," "large white eyes," "little black eyes," "a long, sharp nose," "small and spare," "a swarthy complexion," "a thin visage," or "very fleshy" were the sorts of details they included. The Annapolis surgeon and businessman Dr. Charles Carroll must have passed a careful diagnostic eye over his servant Mary Rider. He declared that Rider had "a mulatto complexion, much browner than common for persons of *English* birth."[10] The frequent references in advertisements to "swarthiness" and "brown complexions" may have led readers of the *Maryland Gazette* and other papers to infer that the convicts possessed the attributes that masters often associated with a darker skin—disobedience, inefficiency, and a lack of intelligence. It is just as well that the runaways were unlikely to be able to read these hurtful and disparaging assessments of their physical appearance.

Only a few advertisers noted hairstyles—perhaps because changing a hairstyle was relatively easy, and thus not a particularly helpful aid to identification. William Duvall (misprinted in his advertisement as Devall) described Sarah Wilson as having her hair "rolled," John Collar and Henry Weeden noted that their Irish convict servant, Margaret Vyans, had her black hair curled, John Lansdale stated that Mary Osbourn's very black hair was "tied behind," and Sarah Monro advised that her servant Elizabeth Crowder (or Crowther) had cut off her gray hair and would be found to be wearing a "tower," or wig.[11] As runaway advertisements rarely mentioned wigs, this one example suggests that Crowder may have been aping the fashionable residents of Annapolis, where she lived—and from whom she would later seek custom as a quilter. Similarly, because the coiffures of women of style in the eighteenth century required puffs, rolls, and sometimes added hair, Sarah Wilson may also have been attempting to emulate contemporary fashion to aid her adventures in fraud (as will be described below).

In many advertisements the owners saw fit to go beyond physical descriptions to attribute moral or behavioral deficiencies to their escapees—Anne Bailey was said to be "a likely hussy," Elizabeth Hawkins was "bold and talkative," Sarah Robbins had a "bold staring" countenance, Sarah Davis had a "palavering tongue," Sarah Knox was "deceitful, bold and insinuating," Mary Owens was a "sly, artful, hussy," Sarah Plint was "very artful," and Catherine Pardon was "artful and deceiving" (in this period, describing someone as "artful" meant they were cleverly cunning or crafty).[12]

In April 1749, Dr. Carroll's advertisement for the brown-skinned Mary Rider stated she was "much given to drunkenness and taking snuff." William Simpson also drew attention to Mary Owens's snuff taking. As related in the last chapter, Benjamin Philpott stressed Margaret Cane's overfondness for drink and sailors, and Constantine Bull's advertisement for the pregnant Catherine Pardon asserted she was "subject to all manner of vice."[13]

All the comments in the above paragraphs display both the values of an elite class (even when the advertisers themselves were not really part of the elite) and a repugnance for female behavior deemed unseemly and unwomanly by men—being manipulative and self-assertive rather than submissive and modest, talking loudly, drinking alcohol in public places, taking snuff, and engaging in extramarital sex.

The advertisers who made judgmental and negative comments about behavior that was abhorrent to them were part of a society that had very definite views about desirable female qualities and expected women to recognize male authority. For his 1986 book *Tobacco and Slaves*, Allan Kulikoff reviewed marriage and death notices in the *Maryland Gazette* between 1745 and 1767 to determine how these notices depicted the ideal characteristics of men and women. Sixty notices listed the following valued and admired female characteristics: affable, agreeable, amenable, amiable, benevolent, charitable, Christian, esteemed, pious, sensible, virtuous, well accomplished, and having "every quality to make a man happy."[14] Although of course runaway advertisements for female convicts had an entirely different purpose, no such complimentary adjectives ever appeared in them; the only favourable characteristics cited were physical attributes ("strong and healthy") or domestic skills such as the ability to quilt, sew, weave, wash, and iron.

It is not difficult to infer that, because the women did not display those qualities and behaviors deemed desirable in women, the advertisers felt no compunctions about describing them in ways that were inherently degrading. Daniel Wells's views about women who did not comply with his gendered expectations were explicit in his advertisement for Hannah Boyer, who ran away in May 1752. He stated, "She is a robust, *masculine* wench"—which was a bit much coming from a man who had fitted a "horse lock and chain" to one of the young woman's legs. Hannah Boyer had actually run away six months previously—from a well-to-do Annapolis widow, tavern keeper, and property owner named Catharine Jenings. The advertisement placed by Jenings in November 1751 provided a much milder description; it merely stated that Hannah Boyer was of "middle stature and a little pock-fretten."[15] Perhaps she looked less masculine without the iron pothook.

In his 2007 book *The Dress of the People*, clothing historian John Styles writes that "ordinary people of the eighteenth century often chalked out their lives in clothes. Garments appear again and again in their life stories as markers of maturity and achievement, or of struggle and failure." He comments that criminal trials and runaway advertisements can capture only one moment in the personal "clothing biography" of any individual and that, in any case, these sources provide an unrepresentative sample.[16] While this may be largely true, the runaway advertisements provide one of the few sources of information on how the convict women were clothed during their servitude because, when they fled, owners were able to specify carefully how they were dressed and what other apparel they were likely to have bundled up and taken with them—information gained from their nearness to their servants and to their daily scrutiny. Clothing was important because most servants had few garments. These were replaced infrequently, and it was assumed they would be retained because runaways would find it difficult to buy or otherwise obtain new attire. Describing a runaway's clothes was thus almost as good as describing the runaway herself. If her garments had been brought from Britain or Ireland, then these might by themselves provide clues to her origin—for example, her gown might be of a fabric that was recognizably not "country-made."

The three items of clothing almost always itemized in runaway advertisements were a shift (a loose undershirt similar to a chemise with a drawstring neck that varied in length), a gown (which consisted of a bodice—often loosely closed with lacing—joined to a front-opening skirt revealing a separate petticoat), and a petticoat (which was an essential part of the dress, not an undergarment) (see the illustration *A St. Giles's Beauty* in chapter 1, which shows a quilted petticoat). Also listed were aprons, bedgowns (an informal wrap gown worn as ordinary daily clothing—particularly in pregnancy), caps, cloaks (red "cardinals"), handkerchiefs, hats or bonnets (usually of black silk), jackets, shoes, stays, and stockings (woven or knitted). Stays—a shaping undergarment usually stiffened with fine whalebones—were only mentioned in four advertisements, suggesting that convict women mostly did without this support.

In order to maximize the likelihood of recapturing their servants, advertisers often gave explicit details of the actual fabrics from which clothing was made and the patterns woven or printed onto cotton gowns, the color of petticoats, and stockings and shoe materials. Shifts were usually made of oznabrig or osnaburg (a coarse, unbleached, and undyed linen or hempen fabric) or holland (a generic name for linen). Occasionally they were made of fine Irish linen (though these may have been hand-me-downs). Gowns were of calamanco (a fine, glazed wool), camblet (a silk and wool mix), chintz (a polished cotton cloth fast printed with designs in a number of colors), kersey (a coarse woolen cloth), linsey-woolsey (a coarse cloth made with a linen warp and woolen weft), shalloon (a closely woven woolen cloth), or stuff (a broad category of worsted textiles). Most of these fabrics were of a plain weave and, being hard wearing, were suitable as work clothing. The advertisements often refer to linen clothing and, as linen was washable (unlike wool), this is likely to have allowed the convict women greater comfort than sturdier "stuff." The advertisement for Catherine Miller explicitly stated that her petticoat was of "country cloth."[17]

The descriptions in advertisements suggest some clothing was plain and quite dull—Anne Griffith's gown was "partridge colored," Hannah Boyer's jacket was "of drab colour," and others were old or patched. One advertiser stated his servant was in a "tolerable good dress" and another that his was in a "good" linsey-woolsey gown and petticoat and a "fine" linen shift and apron. Dr. Charles Carroll described Mary Rider as having "a good Irish linen shift and apron" and a "new brown and white birds-eye stuff gown." In December 1768, when Isabella Watson escaped for the second time in four years, her owner, John Augustus Frederick Priggs, claimed she was dressed in "a new purple sprig stamped cotton gown and a new blue shalloon petticoat." Priggs was the deputy surveyor for Prince George's County, a landowning "gentleman" of German or Danish origins and a Protestant.

He may have felt a duty to clothe his servants properly.[18] Some masters may have not wanted to admit in a public notice that their servants were attired in rags, and "faded" might thus be read as "worn out."

In 1773, Edward Lloyd, a prosperous Talbot County planter on the Eastern Shore, issued an annual allotment of clothing to each of his female field hands: a petticoat, stockings, a jacket, two smocks, and several yards of cloth.[19] These women were probably all slaves, but it is likely that Lloyd and other better-off planters made similar provisions for their white servants. It was not unknown for masters to hand down to servants garments for which their wives or other female household members no longer had any use.[20] How much choice the women had in clothing issued to them is unknown. If the letter from Elizabeth Sprigs is any guide, some women may have found a way to get word home to their families in Britain asking for new clothing.

The textiles purchased for clothing slaves were in a restricted range of colors— usually white, blue, or green but some of the convict servants' clothes were checked, plaid, striped, or had stamped or woven patterns (sprigs were popular), and some outfits seem brightly appealing, at least on the page. (The St. Giles's Beauty illustration in chapter 1 shows a sprigged gown.)[21] The child-sized Mary Osbourn had a checkered woolen gown with a striped petticoat and blue and white ringed stockings. Catherine "O'Bryan" (who passed as the wife of an Irish convict named James O'Bryan), who ran away from John Ashford in October 1750, had a red, white, and blue striped gown, a blue and white spotted handkerchief around her shoulders, a fine white apron, and a ruffled mobcap. In May 1761 an Irish woman named Mary Barrington ran away from Thomas Miles of Frederick County. Barrington had red hair and was wearing a gown printed with blue and red flowers, a red mantle or cloak, and red stockings—it is unlikely she avoided attention.[22]

Shoes mentioned in runaway advertisements were usually said to be made of leather—specifically calfskin or goatskin—with heels of leather or cork. Elizabeth Edwards's shoes were of red morocco with white heels and were thus unlikely to have been for everyday use. From the advertisement it seems she lived near Snowden's Patuxent ironworks and may have worked either there or on one of the nearby tobacco plantations. Elizabeth Crowder, who was an inside worker (a quilter), had black shoes with new soles. One advertiser said his servant had taken "pumps"—plain shoes with a slightly high heel—but two others specifically mentioned heels that were low or flat. Some shoes were imported (English) and others (like some gowns and petticoats) were "country-made" of cloth such as serge or denim—a reminder that, in the first half of the eighteenth century, making cloth—"homespun"—was an important domestic activity in the Chesapeake; it would become even more so in the years immediately before the Revolution. When Elizabeth Bryan and Margaret Tasker—the furnace worker—ran away, they were both wearing men's shoes, but the fettered Hannah Boyer had no shoes at all.[23]

When Rachel Pottenger (or Pottinger) advertised her missing servant Elizabeth Hawkins, she said she had "thread stockings with silk clocks." While the convict women's stockings were mostly hand knitted (frequently from blue wool), Hawkins's would have been frame knitted with a triangular gore (a wedge insert at the instep) running under the heel from one side of the calf to the other. The tops of these gores were often decorated with silk patterns, interwoven into the knit, known as "gore clocks." The rose and crown motif was very popular. Margaret Tasker's stockings were green with red clocks, and Mary Rider's were blue with whitish clocks. After the invention of the Derby Rib stocking frame in 1758, hosiers experimented with different fibers, designs, and decorations for stockings, moving from the silk gore clock to silk and cotton lace clocks, and later incorporating stripes and zigzags into the knit. It is somewhat surprising that servants were equipped with frame-knitted stockings, which were finer and less durable than hand-knitted thread stockings. Ready-made stockings were, however, certainly available in the 1750s. John Copithorn, an Alexandria storekeeper, advertised in the *Maryland Gazette* in 1757 that he had "women's silk, cotton and thread hose" available for sale. Copithorn's advertisement was only one among a great many that appeared in the *Maryland Gazette* and other papers advising the availability of all kinds of goods. They serve as an indication of the extent to which Maryland was becoming a fully fledged consumer society whose inhabitants—at least its prosperous inhabitants—had access to a vast range of all sorts of household items as well as fine clothes and fabrics and imported footwear.[24]

The hats that were taken or worn by the runaways were usually black—probably high crowned, though this was not stated—and made of silk, felt, or horsehair. This was the same type of hat as was commonly worn by country women in England throughout much of the eighteenth century. Mary Owens had a white straw leghorn hat, and Nell Fitzgerald had a check bonnet that would have had a soft crown, or caul, and a stiffened brim. It is interesting that there were not more references to straw or "chip" hats, which were also widely worn by country women in England—a point of colonial difference perhaps? In the engraving entitled *Representation of the Transports Going from Newgate to Take Water at Blackfriars* (see illustration in chapter 3), all six of the convict women depicted are wearing straw hats over ruffled mobcaps that were probably made of linen.[25] Most runaway women took such ruffled white linen caps with them. Accessories—apart from shawl-like handkerchiefs—were rarely listed. The valuable objects of desire whose theft had led to the transportation of some women—the silver buckles and buttons, gold rings, and jewelry set with precious or gemstones—were entirely absent from runaway advertisements. However, when she first fled from John Priggs in

1764, Isabella Watson, who had formerly been a London prostitute, was said to be wearing "a necklace of large French beads"—she also took "a small looking-glass."[26]

Throughout the transportation period, clothes and the textiles from which they were made were an indication of status and occupation, gentility or servility. The finely woven linen shift of a rich planter's wife would never be mistaken for the coarse osnaburg that was usually worn by servants, even when the two were cut and constructed in much the same way. In fact, these distinctions in clothing were a means of preserving boundaries between mistress and servant. Thus convicts wearing clothes other than those described in the advertisements would be suspected of theft—unless these were faded, worn, and patched and thus obviously hand-me-downs. But even their simple garments could be a vehicle for the fugitives—women who were at the bottom of society—to express themselves.

Slave women were creative in mending their petticoats, skirts, and shifts with materials of clashing colors and patterns, and they made headdresses to assert their cultural identity.[27] Convict servants may have copied their slave colleagues for similar reasons. Their poverty did not create many opportunities for adornment, and they may have seen potential in their simple garments for some sort of self-definition. The advertisement for Anne Griffith (or Griffin) stated she was wearing a dress that was "patched in the body with lighter stuff." Elizabeth Hawkins had a black silk hat that she had trimmed all around with gauze instead of lace. Hawkins had a plaid petticoat covered with blue stuff damask that she had sewn together with "saddle binding" (possibly saddle stitch). Nancy Partinton wore "a bonnet set round with sticks," and—possibly with a nod to African influence—also wrapped her handkerchief around her head and tied it firmly under her chin. Sarah Wilson made "a common practice of marking her clothes with a crown and a B," and Catherine O'Bryan had a cap that "was very much ruffled." Elizabeth Lloyd—the woman from Wiltshire who had stolen bread and bacon when that county was recovering from famine—wore a shift that had detachable or false sleeves "made out of old shirts."[28]

Advertisers sometimes suggested that a motive for running away was to see friends, companions, or maybe even fondly remembered employers. Elizabeth Bryan, who ran away in 1764 from John Thompson of Annapolis, was assumed to have gone to Bladensburg in Prince George's County, where she "had served part of her time with Mrs Cook." She may have just wanted to visit one of Bladensburg's several inns or drinking places, such as the Indian Queen Tavern, or perhaps its popular racetrack. Bryan seems to have made a habit of such unauthorized absences; four years later she was taken up by Daniel Chamier, the sheriff of Baltimore County, who advertised in the *Maryland Gazette* that she had been committed to his custody.[29] Some women fled to find their former sexual partners or to escape the legal reprisals for pregnancy or fornication. Anne Griffith took off

Sketch of Bladensburg, Maryland, Looking Northward, undated, watercolor on paper by Benjamin Henry Latrobe. (Courtesy of the Maryland Historical Society, Baltimore, item ID # 1960.108.1.9.7.)

with her baby in August 1767 to join her husband—"though she has none," the aggrieved advertiser commented rather snidely.[30] Anne Sayer and Nell Fitzgerald were "great with child" when they left their plantations, and several ran away with their actual husbands, sexual partners, or other male acquaintances—"induced to do so" sniffed one master, a doctor named George Buchanan. He seemed peevish not only to have lost his servant, Catherine Davidson, but to have seen his rightful authority subverted.[31]

When women escaped with their fellow servants (and sometimes a group of three servants or slaves went off together), they usually did so under cover of darkness—often stealing horses to get away as rapidly as they could. Once it was daylight they would "lurk in the woods"—staying hidden in the foliage until it was once again nightfall.[32] The advertisements describing these departures are surprisingly vivid, and although no more than vignettes, encapsulate all the dramatic qualities of romantic fiction—more like illicit elopements than illegal breaches of bound labor contracts—where the agency for the action is all with the principals. This cannot have been the intention or the view of the angry owners. In March 1767 Sarah Plint, alias Powell, alias Merchant fled from John McDonall, who lived near Annapolis. She was accompanied by a fellow convict named William Newcomb, alias Dodson—who, before he was transported, had been a butcher in Gloucestershire. Plint was dressed in a striped yellow silk gown with a white cloak and a white hat and rode off on a bay horse with a white star blaze and a blue fringed saddle (cloth). When Elizabeth Willoughby (a "tall and slender Englishwoman") escaped from John Drummond on the Sassafras Neck in Cecil County, she wore a white gown and was mounted on a brown mare with a blue sidesaddle. She was accompanied by a two of Drummond's slaves (Jack and Pobb), who were also on stolen horses.[33] Running away with a slave (let alone two) added risk to the enterprise because a black person would be more easily spotted in a region where most people of color were unfree.

In October 1775 Ann Wilson and William Manly made their dash for freedom from James Braddock of Talbot County. Wilson was a married woman from the small town of Ulverston in Lancashire who had been sentenced to transportation at that county's quarter sessions in January 1775. She had been in Maryland only for a few months when she and Manly (also from Lancashire) galloped off into the night. Manly's name apparently suited him—Braddock said he was "a well made fellow," about five feet, eight or nine inches (1.77 m) tall with black hair, aged twenty-five or thirty. Braddock's advertisement also stated that the much older Ann Wilson—described as "handy at doing housework"—was calling herself Manly's wife and it was very likely that they were intending to "make down the [Chesapeake] Bay." They had taken with them "a new canoe, a frying pan, a tea kettle, several linen shirts and provisions." It appears the two were recaptured because just over six months later Manly again ran away from Braddock (who thought him "a most impudent, infamous villain"). On this occasion he was wearing an iron collar, but there was no information about Ann Wilson.[34]

As touched on in the previous chapter, there were instances of women crossdressing, and being attired in "man's apparel" was not an infrequent runaway disguise. When Frances Burrowes and the unnamed wife of Moses Dykes ran away, their advertisers noted that they were both wearing men's clothing.[35] A more common runaway ruse was to assume the identity of free servants or to change names.

If a servant wanted to leave his or her master's property, it was necessary to carry a pass or authorization issued by the master and stamped with the county seal. If servants were without such a document, it would be assumed they were runaways and they might be punished accordingly.[36] Convicts responded to this restriction on their mobility by forging passes and adopting false names.[37] Isabella Pierce's master said "she had taken with her the indenture of Bridget Castile and will pass by that name." Nell Fitzgerald's master said she was likely to go by the name of Mary Collins. Nancy Partinton's master said she had been issued with a pass in the name of Jane McGhee by Captain Richard Ward Key and would be traveling under that name.[38]

Disguises and deceptions, feints and ruses could have been criminal stratagems learned in Britain or Ireland, but a protean capacity for assuming alternative identities and appearing to be someone else was certainly useful to those convict women who wished to transcend the consequences of transportation and abscond successfully. If they needed to engage in a little "self fashioning," then so be it. One master, Dr. Carroll, showed he harbored no illusions about his servant Mary Rider's boasted skills—she "talks plausibly" and *pretends* to be a seamstress," he commented.[39]

In January 1753, when David Currie of Lancaster County in Virginia lodged a runaway advertisement in the *Maryland Gazette* for his cross-dressing servant Sarah Knox, he stated that she used multiple surnames as aliases, that she had been a camp follower in Flanders, and then had passed for a soldier at Culloden (where her husband had died), and that she might *pretend* to be a dancing mistress. Currie said he had read an extract of a letter from Chester County in Pennsylvania that had been published in the *Maryland Gazette* the previous August. This concerned a quack doctor and surgeon called Charles Hamilton who "seemed to be about forty" and had been peddling medicines around the county. The doctor was suspected of being a woman in men's clothes and, when he was "taken up and examined," this was found to be the case. The "doctor" revealed she was actually Charlotte Hamilton and claimed (to some derision) to be twenty-eight years of age. Currie had a hunch that Charlotte Hamilton and Sarah Knox were one and the same and that her broad Yorkshire brogue would prove it. Having made herself too obvious, Knox was recaptured.[40]

Sarah Wilson was another convict woman who was too ambitious in her self-fashioning and recklessly overreached after she ran away in October 1771. Sentenced toward the end of 1767, Wilson probably arrived in Maryland in the next year or so and was purchased by Frederick County landholder William Duvall. In the previous seventeen years Duvall had acquired more than three thousand acres of land in the western backcountry and had his residence at Bush Creek near the lower reaches of the Monocacy River. He had apparently purchased Wilson to be a maid in his household. When she ran away in October 1771, Duvall placed a runaway advertisement in a local newspaper offering a reward of 5 pistoles for her safe capture and return. Unfortunately, it failed to produce a result—probably because Wilson was no longer in Maryland but had made her way south through Virginia until she eventually reached South Carolina. Two years later her outrageous activities attracted attention and were reported in newspapers as far afield as Massachusetts, New York, Pennsylvania, and Virginia.[41] In July 1773 her story had crossed the Atlantic to be picked up by the *London Magazine* and the *Gentleman's Magazine*. These carried an account of a person who had been plausibly passing herself off as "Princess Susanna Carolina Matilda," a sister to "our sovereign lady," Queen Charlotte. Invited to the homes of the gentry, the "princess" had lavishly promised governmental appointments and preferments in return for substantial loans. Some sensible and cautious people suspected Wilson was a fraud, but it was not until the runaway advertisement was reprinted and a Mr. Michael Dalton (Duvall's agent) arrived in Charleston and "raised a hue and cry for her serene highness," that the game was up. Wilson was then "reduced to her former slavery."[42]

The British magazines repeated an assertion made in *Rivington's New-York Gazeteer* that Wilson was a former servant to the queen's maid of honor—a Miss Vernon—and had stolen some valuable jewels in the royal apartments.[43] They claimed further that Wilson had been sentenced to death but reprieved for transportation upon the intercession of her employer, although there is no record of such a potentially sensational crime or intercession in either the Westminster or Old Bailey's court records. It might have been prudent for the *Gentleman's Magazine* to have checked its back issues, because in June 1767 Wilson had actually been indicted in Westminster for a much more prosaic fraud, and in January 1768 the magazine had covered her quarter sessions trial at some length. At this trial Wilson had been found guilty of swindling a kindhearted shopgirl by spinning her "a piteous tale" of being a countess down on her luck. Wilson claimed she would be able to redeem a substantial sum of money (for which she had a banker's draft) if only she had the proper clothes in which to present herself to the banker, a Mr. Child. The girl had been persuaded to provide Wilson with a full outfit of new clothes on the promise of being paid later. Wilson was found guilty of fraud and deception and was sentenced to transportation. The *Gentleman's Magazine* described Wilson as someone who "has long been a notorious imposter." She had at one time passed herself off as the "Marchioness of Waldegrave."[44]

Wilson was not alone in her aristocratic aspirations. Mary Hambleton, who was sentenced to transportation at the Manchester quarter sessions in Lancashire in 1758, called herself the Duchess of Hambleton or Hamilton. Elizabeth Grieve (or Greve), who was sentenced at the Middlesex quarter sessions in 1774, claimed to be a kinswoman of the Duke of Grafton.[45] Their absurd pretensions and the bravura of their self-fashioning lend a bit of color to the usually rather mundane quality of criminal trials.

Few convicts would have had the necessary flair or chutzpah to pass as princesses, marchionesses, or duchesses when they absconded. Far more typical were nineteen-year-old Nancy Partinton (traveling as Jane McGhee) and Mary Price. Richard Cooke, who advertised for Partinton, described her as having a "down look," whereas Robert Reith said Mary Price had a "sour, down look."[46] Both descriptions suggest sullen insolence rather than deference. Having a "down look" was a rubric much resorted to by masters, who seem to have had definite ideas about how working people—especially their own servants—should deport themselves.

Perhaps Partinton and Price had good reason for their gloomy "down" expressions. Rewards were usually a sufficient incentive for members of the public to look for, locate, and capture the runaways, but they might also be pursued by professional catchers, so there was a high chance of their being recovered. In Maryland runaways had to serve an additional day for every hour of absence and an extra ten days for every single day of absence. The penalties outranked those of all the other colonies in their severity.[47]

The law allowed any person "seizing or taking up Runaways travelling without Passes, and not able to give Account of themselves" to be paid two hundred pounds (90.72 kgs) of tobacco from the runaway's master, but advertisements for runaways often stipulated rewards "above what the law allows."[48] The additional rewards offered varied from 20 shillings to 3 pounds or the equivalent, presumably to reflect the residual value of the runaway. There was often a supplement for distance. Thomas Lane, who advertised for Nell Fitzgerald, offered a reward of 20 shillings if she had to be brought over a distance of twenty miles, 40 shillings if the distance was forty miles, and "£3 if outside the province." Paul Rankin stated he would pay 10 shillings for Sarah Davis, stipulating that "no greater reward will be given, it being the full worth of her when taken."[49] Sometimes rewards were expressed in dollars (the reward offered for Catherine Miller was 4 dollars) or in pistoles (the reward for Sarah Wilson). A pistole was a Spanish coin worth approximately 18 shillings at midcentury.

The reference to worth provides a reminder that the women were effectively chattels with an assessable value. Although their value depreciated until it expired with the completion of their term of servitude, their status was not entirely dissimilar to that of slaves. The women were listed in wills and, has been mentioned, in estate inventories. This saleable and tradeable quality added to the uncertainty of the women's already somewhat precarious and marginal existence. In August 1725, three London women who had stolen linen and other household equipment—Mary Wall, Margaret Pew, and Barbara Black—were each sentenced to seven years' transportation. Mary Wall arrived in Maryland in 1725 and upon arrival was sold to Patrick Sympson (see chapter 4); two years later her value was being assessed as part of Saldine Eagle's estate—presumably the person to whom Sympson (a wholesale supplier of servants) had sold her. Margaret Pew arrived on the *Supply* in 1726; in 1729 her value was being assessed as part of Amos Garrett's estate. Barbara Black arrived in 1733; in 1736 her value was being assessed as part of William Wood's estate.[50] These three women thus all faced a second or third master within three years of arrival.

Other women were lent out to neighbors or advertised for sale when their masters wanted to dispose of them. In June 1745 an unnamed person placed the following sale notice in the *Maryland Gazette*: "To Be Sold: A likely servant woman

John Brice's house (Little Brice House), Prince George Street, Annapolis, undated (probably late nineteenth century). (Courtesy of the Maryland State Archives.)

that has 6 years and a half to serve. She is strong and healthy, can do any household work and understands weaving. Enquire of the Printer here. N.B. Her principal failing is drunkenness."[51] (This was probably the likely reason for the sale). Nearly twenty years later John Brice II, a person who was active in civic affairs as well as being a judge of the Provincial Court, a planter/merchant, and the owner of both a retail store and an attractive house in Annapolis, placed a similar advertisement. His notice stated: "To be sold: A convict woman who has near seven years to serve. She can sew, wash and iron very well, is a sober and exceedingly handy woman. Enquire at the Printing House." This unnamed woman was not snapped up; Brice's advertisement appeared at least twelve times over the next three months.[52]

Servants not "disposed of" through advertisements could be "exposed to public vendue." Some women were sold on multiple occasions. Martha Anderson, alias Blacklock, who arrived from England in 1722, was owned by Sarah James in 1728. In August 1729 she was sold to Nicholas Day for seven months. In March 1730, Day sold her to John Higginson, and in November 1733, when she was reported as a runaway, she was owned by Henry Butler.[53]

～

Throughout the years of their servitude, the convict women's lives were chiefly characterized by precariousness and varying levels of oppression. In an increasingly patriarchal society, they were dominated by their (most frequently male) owners and by a legal system that punished women for the inherent nature and consequences of their sexuality. As women their behavior was often regarded as deviating from acceptable gender norms; as servants they were assessed as a property asset—to appear in estate inventories along with other household equipment. Running away allowed the women some agency in the determination of their future (even if this was actually only short term). Although each runaway probably had her own motives for absconding, they were all making a strike against their powerlessness, asserting their individuality, and allowing themselves the enjoyment of autonomy and unrestricted mobility. The tenacity with which so many of them gambled on freedom, despite the harsh penalties for doing so, indicates that although they were powerless, many had not allowed themselves to become completely dispirited.

7
Going Home and Staying On

Eventually the convict women completed their terms of servitude (and concurrent sentences). Those who remained in Maryland then had good reasons for making themselves as inconspicuous as possible because, as William Eddis said, "the stamp of infamy" was upon them.[1] Those who escaped their masters successfully and returned to Britain before the expiry of their sentences had a more compelling reason for seeking obscurity—returning early from transportation was a capital offense.

Not long after the Transportation Act had been implemented, some of the convicts who had been sentenced to remain in America for seven or fourteen years started showing up again in London. Magistrates asserted and complained that street robbers were felons returned from transportation, and Sir John Fielding deplored mercy being shown to those convicted of returning.[2] In the ordinary of Newgate's account of the exploits of the notorious pickpocket Mary Young, alias Murphrew, alias Mary Webb, alias Jane Webb, alias Jenny Diver, he wrote: "Jenny staid no longer there than to see the Country, for Business in her Way could not be transacted there; so after she had diverted herself as long as she thought proper, she agreed with a Gentleman for her Passage who was bound for England, who brought her over. When she came back, she did not chuse immediately to come to Town, but went and took a Progress round the Countries; and after she had sufficiently tired herself, and the Country People with her Exploits, she came to London."[3]

When Young finally went to the gallows in March 1741, it was for the violent theft and highway robbery of a person named Judith Gardner in which the victim had been robbed of 12 shillings in cash and put in fear of her life. At Young's January trial, it was brought to the attention of the court that she had been transported previously, and this is likely to have influenced the judge's sentencing decision. Yet Young's robbery of Judith Gardner had been a joint enterprise with another woman, Catherine Davis (alias Catherine Floyd, alias Elizabeth Davis, wife of Henry Huggins, alias Mary Shirley) and, while Davis also received a death sentence, she was later reprieved on condition of transportation for fourteen years.

Baltimore in 1752, aquatint engraved in 1817 by William Strickland after a sketch by John Moale, Esq. (Hambleton Print Collection, courtesy of the Maryland Historical Society, Baltimore, item ID # H16.)

The court's decision is perplexing because, as described in chapter 3, Catherine Davis was also a serial offender and had been previously sentenced to transportation for shoplifting in September 1739—though there is no evidence she actually left Britain. After her reprieve for the Gardner robbery in April 1741, Davis was transported to Maryland later that month but, mysteriously, was back in London within the year. In July 1742, she was on trial for shoplifting at the Old Bailey (as Mary Shirley). On this occasion she was acquitted, and nothing was said about her returning early from transportation, but only two months later (as Catherine Davis) she was again before the court for stealing lace from a milliner's shop in Whitechapel. She was found guilty and sentenced to transportation for seven years, which led to her maltreatment at the hands of Captain John Sargent on the *Forward* (see chapter 3). After a second premature return to Britain, she soon went back to her old ways and in April 1744 was indicted (as Mary Shirley) for stealing cotton fabric from the shop of Matthew Wealy and John Rush. At her Old Bailey trial on May 10, 1744, the court was only too well aware of Davis's criminal record because it was read into the trial transcript. Yet she once again escaped a death sentence for early return and instead was "cast for transportation" for seven years. On this occasion she was destined to be sent to Virginia.[4] The possibility of being hanged does not seem to have acted as much of a deterrent either to Davis or to others. Margaret Brown, alias Wilson, alias Long Peg was supposedly transported five times.[5]

In 1753 John Poulter, a notorious English gangster, wrote a confessional tract disclosing all his criminal associates and their various practices and wiles.[6] This was probably an attempt (though unsuccessful) to avoid his own date with the hangman. Poulter alleged that criminals colluded in manipulating the transportation system. He stated, "The [convicts] say they do not mind transportation it being but four or five months' pleasure for they can get their freedom and come home again." He included this assertion in a section headed "The Way That Convicts Return from Transportation and the Only Way How to Prevent Their Return." He offered the information that even before some convicts boarded the transport vessels in England, their freedom would be purchased from the captain for 10 pounds by accomplices. In turn, the captain would issue some sort of note to state the service of these convicts had been paid for and they were free to go where they might once they reached America. However, upon arrival, the "free" convicts would buy passage on another ship and be home within a matter of months. Poulter listed members of the "Coventry Gang"—Rosey Brown, Mary Dawson, alias Brown, Margaret Brown, alias Wilson, alias Long Peg, Eleanor Wilson, alias Sparrow, and Eleanor Connor, alias Tobin, alias Woods—as some of the women who returned early.[7]

Poulter was correct about Eleanor Connor returning early (if she even went), and as he asserted, she may have been a member of the notorious Coventry Gang, which comprised a large number of professional thieves. Despite its name, this gang operated from a base near London and roamed the English countryside looking for suitable targets. Connor was prosecuted in Bristol in 1748 for picking the pocket of a farmer named Hewitt. She was convicted and received a death sentence but, after lingering in Bristol's Newgate prison for two years, was conditionally pardoned by the king—the condition being that she be transported for fourteen years. It appears that she was not happy with that outcome and unsuccessfully petitioned the archbishop of Canterbury to allow her to stay in England.[8]

Connor may have been transported to Maryland from Bideford on a vessel under the command of Captain Whitepair. On the other hand, she may (as Poulter claimed) have fled before being transported, having "bribed some of the ship's crew." In any case, five years later her former Bristol jailor, James Perrit, happened to be in London on business and, as chance would have it, ran into Connor in the street. He had her charged before Justice John Fielding and in February 1754 she was put on trial at the Old Bailey for returning early from transportation. She received a death sentence, but this was respited because she was pregnant.[9]

The primary concerns of magistrates about early returnees essentially regarded male criminals. Considering how many thousands of women were transported to both Maryland and Virginia, the numbers prosecuted for returning early was actually very small. Whether this means that few women returned before their sentences expired or that that those who did were able to successfully evade attention from the authorities is not evident. Data from both sides of the Atlantic suggest that the systems of surveillance in the colonies designed to detect and recapture escaping slaves, servants, and convicts were reasonably effective. American society was well organized to publicize and recapture those who overstepped the boundaries of their masters' tolerance, and it was particularly difficult for women convicts to stay invisible.[10] Between July 1718 and July 1776, only twelve women went on trial at the Old Bailey for returning early from transportation, with two trials being terminated owing to the difficulty of proving identity. Even Eleanor Connor, who *was* convicted, offered as her defense: "My name is not Connor, and I am not the person. Captain Lancey . . . said she [Connor] was drowned for she went in the ship *Nightingale*, of which he was captain." Whether Lancey was a witness of probity could not be tested. A few weeks earlier he had himself been capitally convicted in the Admiralty Courts and, being in Newgate, was unable to give evidence. The 1751 trial of Catherine Quin, alias Bulger, failed to proceed because the court found there was "no proof of the identity of her person."[11]

Nine of the women who were tried at the Old Bailey for returning early were convicted: three were executed, three were reprieved on condition of being retransported, and three had their death sentences respited for pregnancy.[12] Eleanor

Connor, Elizabeth Watson, and Sarah Wells can all be identified as early return-ees from Maryland who were prosecuted in London.

In 1765 in the northern jurisdiction of Durham, Mary Low, wife of John, was sentenced to transportation at St. Nicholas. She was back in England the following year and was convicted in summer 1766 of being "at large at St. Oswald, Durham." She was sentenced to death but reprieved following a heartfelt plea that she was "the mother of six children, the oldest not fourteen, and the rest under six years of age which are left to the charge of her disconsolate husband." She was again transported—for life.[13]

A convict woman who was bent on returning to Britain before the expiry of her sentence would need to have adequate funds. She would probably have had to pay out her contract upon arrival, to support herself before she could travel back across the Atlantic, and then to pay for her passage. She may also have had to pay bribes to sailors and others to keep quiet about her identity. In order to avoid attention she may have needed a male protector. If a woman had not bought out her contract upon arrival but had been sold and subsequently escaped, she would likely have attracted the early attention of a runaway catcher or alert residents—particularly if she had neither money nor an authentic pass issued by her master under the county seal. For all these reasons it is probable that not many of the women described in the last chapter remained at large for very long and thus were not able to return to Britain or Ireland. Hannah Boyer, Anne Griffith (Griffin), and Isabella Watson were the subject of multiple runaway advertisements over time, suggesting they were apprehended and returned to their owners—only to escape again on one or more occasions.

More successful fugitives did not have to look hard to find a vessel that might (potentially) take them back to Britain. The tobacco trade with England was conducted in a most direct fashion—from a planter's own landing wharves to the docks of Britain's seaports. Ships might actually stay anchored within sight of a planter's house for four or five months each year.[14] However, this proximity could act as a deterrent to escape because shippers and planters needed to maintain a satisfactory business relationship, and this would be damaged if shippers were to abet runaways and thus compromise the planter's economic investment. Runaway advertisements frequently forewarned the masters of vessels that if they carried off convicts, they would do so "at their peril."[15]

The most daring of the fugitives were more likely to make their way north or south to a port town where they had never been and where it was thus more likely they would not be recognized. They would then seek an opportunity to work their passage home—the men as sailors and the women as (possibly) washerwomen or cooks.[16] Traffic across the Atlantic fluctuated during the eighteenth century according to whether England was or was not at war. At the conclusion of the Seven

Years' War in 1763, the number of ships on the Atlantic increased steeply and this may have aided opportunities for return.[17]

If possessed of the funds to buy out their sentence upon arrival, women such as the incorrigible recidivist Catherine Davis would have found little point in remaining in Maryland where the scattered small towns provided few opportunities for professional shoplifters and pickpockets. In what was mainly a rural society, conduct was closely monitored, strangers stood out, and aberrant behavior quickly drew attention. This meant crimes were easier to detect and the courts were more easily able to deal with perpetrators. In other words, although there were wrong-doers in the colonial community, unlike in Britain these were not part of a large-scale criminal milieu supported by an extensive network of receivers. It was thus easier for women who actually wanted to put their criminal past behind them to do so. Maryland was, however, hardly free of criminality. On October 17, 1765, the *Maryland Gazette* reported on the activities of two receivers in Annapolis as follows:

> Several very considerable Traders (in the way of receiving Stolen Goods) have lately been found out in this Town and removed from their lodgings to the Prison. A man and his wife of the name Burt were discovered to have followed that business for a good while by a convict servant woman who lay at the point of death but, being very uneasy in her mind, she sent for her mistress, and confessed that she had often wronged her master and her, by the persuasion of those people, by stealing of pewter, candlesticks, pillows, sheets, pillow-cases, and that they wanted her to steal a bed, but she told them that she couldn't get it out of the window.[18]

From an examination of colonial county court records, it appears that the colonists' fear of convicts, particularly women, may have been unfounded. Of all the convicts transported to the Chesapeake, few were actually ever prosecuted for committing felonies or misdemeanors after their arrival. Women such as Martha Blacklock and Edith Street, who were tried for felonies, were unusual.[19] In Kent County on Maryland's Eastern Shore, the county court records reveal not only patterns of criminal activity but also the actual post-arrival crimes of convicts.[20] Between 1732 and 1746 bills of indictment were sought in the county court for 601 men and women, mainly for noncapital crimes such as assault, fornication, and nonviolent property theft, including grand larceny. Forty-one of these (less than 7 percent) involved convicts, but there were only twenty-seven individuals because nine were charged with more than one offense. Even this number might be too high, as some offenders had very common names (for example, John Jones) and may not have been convicts at all.[21] Of the twenty-seven individuals involved, possibly only two were women—Edith Street and Ann Farthing. Street was charged with a felony (theft), and Farthing with "mulatto bastardy."[22] The vast majority of all post-transportation prosecutions of women related to sexual transgressions such as "fornication," "bastardy," "mulatto bastardy," or "miscegenation." Between 1739 and 1757 in Charles County on the Western Shore, there were six prosecutions of four women who can be identified reliably as convicts. These prosecutions were all for moral offenses. In Baltimore County four women were prosecuted for mulatto bastardy between 1718 and 1783.[23]

There were some women convicts who returned from Maryland upon the expiry of their sentences and were accepted back into their families only "to renew their former malpractices," as William Eddis put it.[24] There is too little information available to know whether their recidivism was for economic, psychological, or other reasons. After her appalling experiences on John Sargent's ship, it is difficult to understand why Catherine Davis would risk a second term of transportation when her husband, a wigmaker, was presumably able to provide for her.

Nothing is known of the women who completed their sentences, returned to Britain or Ireland, and did not reoffend, though after seven or fourteen years away it is likely they experienced considerable difficulties in reconnecting with their families (if these were still alive) and their community. In the doggerel poem by "James Revel," he described a tearful reunion with his parents that owed much to the parable of the returning prodigal: "My mother and my father well I found / Who to see me with Joy did much abound. / My mother over me did weep with Joy / My father cried once more to see my boy."[25] Whether female prodigals were similarly welcomed by children or parents who may have had to endure a life of parish charity and institutionalization because of a woman's misdeeds can only be a matter for speculation. In any case, even if the idea of family and home drew women back, nothing would be the same after an absence of seven or more years. Some would find they had been replaced as partners, parents, and spouses. In 1768 a Northumberland man who had been sentenced to transportation for seven years at the quarter sessions in Hexham was told by his wife that, although she was sorry for his fate, she had replaced him with another man. Forsaken husbands are possibly even more likely to have taken new wives, having been effectively divorced by distance.[26]

Although sentiments cannot be satisfactorily ascribed to women who did not leave behind any letters or other documentary evidence relating to their exile and return, accounts by twentieth-century immigrant women going back to their homelands after years of absence suggest the sorts of emotions the convict women may have experienced, even if their families were still intact. One such modern account states: "Many of us live beyond the boundaries of our homeland, forever longing to recapture the security and warmth of our lost childhood home and of our own cultural group. Our home seems lost to us after the small and large cultural tran-

sitions we have made. Those transitions change us so deeply that when we do return 'home' we feel we no longer belong."[27]

In Maryland the convict women had a special (and low) status that dominated
almost every aspect of their relationship with the rest of society. Yet, although they
were perpetual outsiders, the length of time most of the women spent in America
meant they were bound to be affected by its norms and customs—at least to some
degree. The probable illiteracy of most of the women—about 64 percent of English women were illiterate at midcentury—meant few could maintain ties with
families and friends in Britain or Ireland and needed to adapt to their new situation to avoid the anguish of not belonging anywhere—of being "placeless."[28]

On April 11, 1771, John Orme of George-Town in Frederick County lodged
an advertisement in the *Maryland Gazette* for a female convict servant named Ann
Bailey who had run away more than two weeks previously. Bailey seems to have
been quite young (she was described at her trial as both "spinster" and "girl"). In
London she had led a floating life as a domestic servant. In December 1768, when
she was indicted and convicted for stealing clothes from Jane Kingston, her mistress, Bailey had been in the Kingston household for just one week. She claimed
she was "in liquor" when she committed the theft. She was transported on the
Thornton in February 1769 and probably arrived in America in May of that year.[29]
John Orme was a prosperous tavern keeper or innkeeper who provided accommodation for travelers, the operator of a ferry across the Potomac, and a sometime
organizer of horse races. In his application for a tavern license he had agreed not
to "suffer the loose and disorderly persons to tipple, game, or commit other disor-
ders or irregularities within his aforesaid house." This begs the question of why he
would hire a convict servant at all—especially one given to drinking. Anyway, in
his advertisement Orme stated: "Her [Bailey's] apparel *at home* was a checked stuff
gown but it's supposed she has taken some others."[30] Now, in April 1771, Bailey
had been in Maryland for about two years. She had another five years of her sentence to serve plus extra penalty time for running away—she had already clocked
up 150 penalty days when Orme advertised. It is unlikely Bailey viewed herself as
being "at home" in Georgetown—she did run away, after all—but was London still
home and, if so, where in London?

John Orme's reference to Bailey's being at home may not have meant very much
—as "keeper of the house" he may just have had his tavern in mind. Yet his phrase is
unusual. Advertisers for runaways were much more likely to refer to their runaway's
place of origin, thus making it explicit that they were not "country-born" and thus
very definitely not "at home." Seventeen advertisers mentioned that their servants
were English (six stating the original district or county from which their runaways
had come), nine mentioned Irish origins, three Welsh, and one German—a woman
who seems to have married in England and was thus doubly dislocated.

If the convict women did adjust successfully to their banishment and underwent a process of cultural transition, it would have lessened forever the likelihood of ever really "going home," even if they had the funds to travel back across the Atlantic or could work for their passage. It was once assumed that, after finishing their sentences, most of the convicts either returned to Britain or Ireland or settled somewhere in the colonies other than "their own neighbourhoods." William Eddis claimed that if "they had imbibed habits of modesty and industry, they removed to a distant situation where they may hope to remain unknown, and be enabled to pursue with credit every possible method of becoming useful members of society."[31] In 1765 a French traveler seemed to confirm this. In a letter home from Edenton in North Carolina he made the following observation: "This province is the asylum of the convicts that have served their time in Virginia and Maryland. When at liberty they all (or great part) come to this part where they are not known and settle here. It is a fine country for poor people but not for the rich."[32]

Not all former convicts moved to remote areas where their criminal past was unknown and where it could be put behind them. Recent research into probate, land, and other records by genealogists suggests that some of the convicts who served their time in Maryland stayed on after completing their sentences (even, in some cases, settling in the same counties).[33] Women such as Alice Carrington may have wanted to be with or near her offspring—Carrington had two daughters and a son. If the women's children were "mulatto bastards," like Henrietta, the daughter of Ann Farthing; Abigail, the daughter of Frances Humphreys; or James, one of Winifred Jones's five mixed-race children, they would remain the property of the women's former masters until they turned thirty-one. By then the women would be "elderly" by the standards of the time.[34]

Many of the women who remained in Maryland were destined for obscurity whether by their own design or not—particularly those who were not able to marry. If a woman stayed single, she was likely to remain a servant to others or a little-respected dependent in someone else's household. Some of the convict women had started their sentences when they were no longer young—Mary Ingram was fifty-three when transported in February 1720—and the subsequent years of toil must have taken a toll on their health and reduced their employment prospects. Some women apparently just stayed on the plantation where they had served their term which, in effect, replaced the parish in accepting responsibility for unproductive, disabled, and unemployable members of the laboring class.[35]

When those women who had supported themselves post-servitude could no longer do so, they became a charge on the community where they lived. In 1753, each county in Maryland was made an allowance for the support of the poor, who were frequently servants left to shift for themselves. The allowance was 647,027 pounds (293,487 kgs) of tobacco, which had a realizable value and was frequently used as a substitute for other currency. Fourteen years later, in 1767, each county established an almshouse to accommodate and protect the indigent.[36]

At the end of their sentences, even the younger and more able-bodied women found that their new freedom was the only thing they possessed. They had no property or capital with which to start a business, and unlike male convicts, who were more likely to have their skills recognized and rewarded, women had few options available to them in a largely wageless labor market—particularly without the economic attributes of literacy and numeracy. Some arranged new terms of indenture with their former masters (for up to seven years)—usually as domestic servants, an arena in which they competed with slaves and hired day labor. Although domestic service certainly provided the women with food and shelter, being a permanent, twenty-four-hour-a-day occupation, it effectively denied them the opportunity to marry and to form a household of their own—and marriage was really the only way by which a woman could fulfill societal and community expectations and provide a secure environment in which to raise children.[37]

In seventeenth-century Chesapeake it had been relatively easy for indentured female servants to make advantageous marriages at the end of their service period. This was because there was a significant shortage of women—at times men outnumbered women by a factor of three. However, during the transportation period—particularly after about 1750—the demographic picture had changed radically in ways that greatly affected the lives of all women and of female servants in particular. The gender ratio was now in balance, and the white population was predominantly native born. This population shared common beliefs and habits that provided the norm to which all immigrants had to adjust.

At every wealth level of society, white parents expected their daughters would eventually become wives, and thus their training was geared to child care, food preparation, gardening, poultry raising, and sewing. When young girls without means were orphaned and bound out by county courts, kinfolk expressed the wish that they be spared the drudgery of "working at the hoe," "tending corn and tobacco," and "pounding the mortar."[38] These gendered expectations are likely to have hobbled further the opportunities for adult convict women, who had spent years working at the hoe and tending corn and tobacco, to become accepted members of a society in which the roles of men and women were becoming increasingly sharply defined and differentiated. There was also a growing disparity between rich and poor. The absence of a thriving middle class left the convict women few options for social mobility.[39]

Yet, in spite of the difficulties faced by convict women in marrying, some did manage to do so—possibly around 10 percent of convict women wed within the

Marriage notice for former convicts Mary Passmore and John Dunnick, 1742. (*St. John's Parish Register*, Maryland Historical Society, Baltimore.)

province between 1730 and 1777. However, without birth dates, firmly establishing the number who did so is difficult, as many names are quite common. Some women contracted marriages with fellow convict servants. Such a one was Mary Passmore, who married John Dunnick in December 1742 in St. John's Parish, Baltimore County.

Passmore was a London thief who had been convicted in April 1733 for housebreaking—she had entered a house at eight o'clock in the morning and stolen multiple items of clothing belonging to the residents. She was found guilty to the value of 39 shillings and sentenced to transportation for seven years. She had to wait another nine months in Newgate before being carried to Maryland on the *Patapsco Merchant* in November 1733. Over four years later John Dunnick was convicted for the rather piratical crime of stealing "pieces of eight" (foreign silver) and was transported on the *Pretty Patsy* in September 1737. Judging from the date of their wedding, Passmore had probably completed her sentence but Dunnick may have had a further two years to serve.[40]

Those women who did have marketable skills were able to set themselves up in business—or at least use their craft skills to produce income. A woman who was neither convict nor servant advertised in the *Maryland Gazette* in July 1752 that she would "make and mend hoop petticoats," and Mary Anne March and her daughters advertised that they would teach embroidery and do quilting.[41] Yet a woman who ran her own business was more likely to be a widow who, upon her husband's death, continued to manage his business herself. In the *Maryland Gazette* there are many examples of women assuming responsibility for enterprises as various as block making, storekeeping, tavern keeping, and tailoring. Some women (widows) ran lodging houses, sold chocolates, or taught school as means of self-employment.[42]

Elizabeth Crowder was sentenced to transportation at the summer assizes in Yorkshire in 1744. She probably arrived in Maryland in 1745 and went to work for an Annapolis quilter named Sarah Monro, who advertised her as a runaway on April 1, 1746. Although Crowder's sentence would not normally have expired until around 1752, she appears to have finished her servitude in 1747 (at which time she may have been a servant to a Mrs. Carter rather than Sarah Monro). Although she had a husband named John back in Yorkshire and was no longer a young woman (she was about forty-three), she seems to have planned to stay in Maryland. In any case, on October 28, 1747, she placed the following advertisement in the *Maryland Gazette*:

ELIZABETH CROWDER, Quilter
(*who lately liv'd with Mrs* Carter, *in Annapolis*)
Is removed to Mr. *Carroll's* Quarter, about two Miles from Town where she performs all sorts of QUILTING in the best Manner, and at the most reasonable rates: Good Petticoats for *Eight* and *Ten shillings* a Piece, and coarse Petticoats for *Six Shillings.* Whoever may have occasion to employ her, may depend on being faithfully served by
Their humble servant
ELIZABETH CROWDER.[43]

Crowder's advertisement is of interest for more than its evidence of post-servitude employment because it is an example of a convict woman who had a high level of skill being able actually to use that skill in Maryland—there were probably others, but these have not come to notice. Making quilted petticoats involved first making a pattern and then cutting out two layers of fabric. The petticoat itself was cut from a light fabric such as wool, cotton, or silk and this was then sewn onto a worsted backing with patterned stitching. A decorative border might be attached at the bottom. Some quilting patterns were highly intricate—diamonds filled with floral, animal, or human motifs, including Adam and Eve, cupids shooting arrows, and the lion and the unicorn from the British coat of arms. Women of this period often quilted in their own homes either alone, with female family members, and/or with friends. However, because of the time-consuming work involved, some women bought ready-made petticoats from milliners or specialist quilters—such as Crowder and her former mistress, Sarah Monro.[44] Monro quilted not just petticoats but bed covers and gowns as well.[45] As Crowder's advertisement mentions "coarse Petticoats," she may have been trying to attract those interested in garments for everyday use without too much intricate patterning. "Coarse" was often a synonym for "plain," and in turn "plain" was often used to distinguish regular quilting from "fancywork" or embroidery, but Crowder's skills as a quilter were acknowledged and she was probably quite capable of the more elaborate sewing. It would be of interest to know whether she was deliberately setting herself up in competition with her former mistress.

As described in chapter 4, for much of the transportation period, the Maryland Assembly tried to restrict or control the convict trade because convicts were regarded as wretched, depraved, diseased, and fearsome undesirables. Through the pages of his *Pennsylvania Gazette*, Benjamin Franklin was a vocal and continual critic of the trade who believed that "instances of transported thieves advancing their fortunes in the colonies" were "extremely rare."[46] However, almost from the start, there were other voices approvingly asserting that the experience of servitude caused some convicts to reform.

As early as the 1740s, when the convict trade initiated by the act of 1718 had really been in place for only about twenty years, a contemporary observer of the Maryland scene, Edward Kimber, noted: "The Convicts that are imported here, sometimes prove very worthy Creatures, and entirely forsake their former Follies; . . . Several of the best planters, or their Ancestors, have, in the two colonies, been originally of the Convict-Class, and therefore are much to be prais'd and esteem'd for forsaking their old Courses."[47] Thomas Ringgold (who was a person of prominence in Maryland besides having a significant financial interest in the continuance of the convict trade) claimed that "the rigid discipline of colonial laws and seven years' labor converted the greater part into respectable and self-supporting citizens."[48]

In 1782 J. Hector St. John de Crèvecoeur, a French-born American agriculturalist, writer, and diplomat, published *Letters from an American Farmer*, a widely read collection of essays on American life. Surveying the newly created American republic, he asked what has become a famous and oft-cited question: "What then is the American, this new man?" In the course of answering that question he wrote: "What a strange compliment has our mother country paid to two of the finest provinces in America! England has entertained in that respect very mistaken ideas; what was intended as a punishment, is become the good fortune of several; many of those who have been transported as felons, are now rich, and strangers to the stings of those wants that urged them to violations of the law: they are become industrious, exemplary, and useful citizens."[49] De Crèvecoeur's opinion was similar to that of Thomas J. C. Williams, an early twentieth-century historian of Washington County and also a judge. He was of the opinion that many convicts in that county became "highly respected citizens and the progenitors of influential families."[50]

Such benign, approving, and optimistic estimates owe much not only to the well-worn Puritan tropes of sin, repentance, and redemption but also to that persistent narrative of American culture—the belief that transformation is always possible, even in the bleakest and most humble of lives. It is impossible to know the extent to which the estimates may have been based in fact. In the earliest years of the nineteenth century a woman named Sarah Thornton was transported to New South Wales in Australia for stealing lace. In 1820 she wrote a heartfelt letter to her family in England in which she said, "O that my voice could be heard by the young people in England to deter them from evil ways. For though I have by a regular line of good conduct, and great privations, arrived at a state of comfort, not one in twenty who is sent here obtains even the necessaries of life."[51] Although she served her sentence in a different country, her experience was probably not untypical of the post-servitude hardship of many transported convicts in Maryland—the fate of the marginal woman trying to establish personal and familial stability in a foreign land.

~

The convict women who remained in America had compelling reasons for concealing (or at least not drawing attention to) their criminal origins. If they were to become "exemplary, and useful citizens" rather than the "hussies" that they were often called, they needed to meet the behavioral and gender expectations of the colonial society and later the newly independent republic by becoming industrious wives and mothers. It appears that some (possibly most) did turn their backs on the past and their uncertain and isolated experience as servants and sought to blend into the population and put down roots. The difficulty involved today in tracing exactly what happened to the transported women suggests, in part, that whether by intention or circumstance, most were successful in the concealment of their origins.

8
Mary Nobody in the Republic of Virtue

Until just before the outbreak of the American War of Independence, Britain continued to rely heavily on transportation as a criminal punishment. The *Justitia*, under the command of Captain John Kidd, departed London in February 1776 with sixty-five convicts on board, including sixteen women.[1] The vessel probably arrived in Maryland in late April or early May 1776, although this seems to have been overlooked by the *Maryland Gazette*, no doubt preoccupied at the time with the more weighty matters of monarchical tyranny and taxation. The *Justitia*'s cargo of transportees was possibly the very last prewar shipment—occurring after the start of hostilities. The trade then ceased completely for the duration of the war. Yet Britain's county courts continued to make out transportation orders, and local jails, which were never intended to hold prisoners long term, started to run out of capacity.

Assuming that the need for prisoner accommodation was only temporary, the British government decided to provide relief to its county jails by housing convicts awaiting transportation in decommissioned ships. These usually had their masts and rigging removed and were thus termed "hulks." Initially the hulks were moored in the Thames River at Woolwich or at Deptford and later in the harbors of Plymouth and Portsmouth as well. The government contracted with convict shipper Duncan Campbell to manage all the hulks in the Thames. Campbell's ship the *Justitia* was one of the vessels adapted for the purpose. Soon "hulk after hulk, hung with bedding, clothes, weed and rotting rigging, lined the river like a floating shantytown."[2] In these makeshift prisons the mortality rate was appalling and the convicts, with nothing left to lose, posed a continuing and serious security risk. The government saw that a solution was needed and, before the peace treaty with the United States had even been signed, it had secured the services of a London merchant named George Moore for the purpose of recommencing the convict trade to America. Moore was promised 500 pounds from the Treasury in addition to whatever profits he might make from selling the convicts' labor in Maryland. An initial cargo of 143 prisoners was prepared for transportation on the *George*.[3]

In November 1783 the *Maryland Gazette* carried a "Report from London":

"On Saturday morning early about 90 convicts under sentence of transportation at Newgate, were put on a lighter at Black Friars which proceeded with and put them on board the *Swift*, captain Pump, lying at Blackwall, for their reception, and bound for Nova Scotia (the land of frost and freedom)."[4] In fact, this was a ruse; the *Swift* was actually the *George* renamed. It was bound for the United States and, after a disaster-ridden voyage, was shortly to arrive in Baltimore. However, owing to an extremely severe winter, the vessel became trapped in ice that was "thick enough to bear a hogshead of tobacco." On December 24, 1783, eighty-seven convicts were landed in Baltimore, but there was little seasonal cheer. George Moore's Maryland factor, George Salmon, found that the frigid weather kept buyers away, but there was little interest in the convicts anyway and sales were sluggish. By the middle of January only thirty had been sold and others had become ill—some close to death. Costs mounted for food, clothing, and medical care. Although Salmon (by offering credit) eventually disposed of all the convicts, a number of purchasers were highly dissatisfied; within a month their new servants had absconded. Salmon and Moore both lost a great deal of money.[5]

The *Swift* was destined to be the last transport ship to successfully land convicts in America, although there were two further attempts to do so.[6] In 1788, on the motion of Abraham Baldwin, the Continental Congress resolved: "That it be and is hereby recommended to the several states to pass proper laws for preventing the transportation of convicted malefactors from foreign counties into the United States." Maryland's government was urged "to take suit as may be necessary for the safety of citizens and the integrity of Government which we think most grossly insulted."[7] The twelve women on the *Swift*, including London thieves Mary Andrews, Mary Graves, Mary Walker, Mary Williams, and Mary White (a pickpocket), were thus the last female convicts to be sold into servitude in Maryland.[8] They were also the last of a line of involuntary exiles whose contribution to colonial Maryland was to be largely overlooked or forgotten by history—perhaps deliberately. This was not unconnected with the momentous political and philosophical questions that were intrinsic to the American Revolution.

Throughout the eighteenth century, but particularly in the decades leading up to the Revolution, reflective Americans became increasingly incensed at Britain's assumption that it could continue to dump its criminals in America regardless of local opinion. The legislatures of the colonies most affected by transportation—Maryland and Virginia—did all they could to restrict and regulate the convict trade but without much success. Yet protest was not restricted to Maryland and Virginia.

Benjamin Franklin who, among other things, was the publisher of the *Pennsylvania Gazette*, used this paper to say just what he thought about the mother country's bestowal of felons on its colonies. On May 9, 1751, under the name

Benjamin Franklin by
Joseph Siffred Duplessis.
(Copyright © National
Portrait Gallery, London.)

"Americanus," he wrote: "Our Mother knows what is best for us. What is a little
housebreaking, shoplifting, or highway robbing; what is a son now and then cor-
rupted and hanged, a daughter debauched and poxed, a wife stabbed, a husband's
throat cut, or a child's brains beat out with an axe, compared with this 'IMPROVE-
MENT and WELL PEOPLING of the Colonies!" He then made a reciprocal trade
proposal: "Rattlesnakes seem the most suitable returns for the human serpents sent
by our Mother Country. In this, however, as in every other branch of trade, she will
have the advantage of us. She will reap equal benefits without equal risk of the in-
conveniencies and dangers. For the rattlesnake gives warning before he attempts
his mischief; which the Convict does not."[9]

Two years later, on March 15, 1753, a correspondent signing himself "Publicus" wrote a long letter to the *Independent Reflector*, a newspaper published in New
York. In this he railed against transportation and its supposed impact on the level
of crime in the colonies. He said it was quite wrong that the "plagues of mankind"
should be removed from "one part of the [king's] dominion and cast ... upon another." He further suggested that potential settlers of good character were reluc-

tant to immigrate because they feared being in the company of "a herd of exiled malefactors."[10]

Some historians believe that transportation was responsible for helping to loosen the bonds of empire.[11] The antagonistic views of Americanus (Franklin) and Publicus certainly suggest this may have been the case, though the bonds were loosening anyway and would snap irreparably in 1776. By then the convict trade was just one grievance in a long list. The Declaration of Independence contained a litany of "oppressions" and "injuries" for which Britain and its king were alleged to be responsible.[12]

The Declaration of Independence expressed indignation at "absolute despotism," at "abuses and usurpations," at imminent military attack from "large armies of mercenaries," and at the imposition of economic burdens from taxes and limitations on trade. It asserted the legitimacy of rebellion and revolution and the need for government to be always at the "consent of the governed."[13] Its rhetorical language was intended to arouse and inspire large numbers of colonists to turn against Britain. It was not directed at the unfree or dependent members of society, such as women, Native Americans, slaves, free black people, servants, and probably the poor in general. Indeed, the Declaration implied that independence was a condition arrived at by *not* being dependent or enslaved.[14] Yet, inevitably, its assertions raised questions about citizenship, natural rights, and civic entitlements.

Between 1775 and 1777 statutory language in America moved quickly from "subject" to "inhabitant" to "member" and finally to "citizen." Initially, citizenship was conceived in highly gendered terms; it would apply to men who took up arms and exposed their lives for the defense of the new republic. Gradually allegiance—as demonstrated by physical presence and emotional commitment—came to be given equal weight with military service as a criterion for citizenship. By 1776 patriots were prepared to say that all loyal inhabitants, men and women, were citizens of the new republic and no longer subjects of the king.[15] Although the total number of convict women still serving out their sentences during the revolutionary years cannot have been very large, being female, unfree, servants, and poor they were outsiders on multiple counts. But what was their legal status? Not being "country born," were they subjects of the king in exile or "by location and volition" a part of the new citizenry?

When British convicts first started arriving in Maryland after 1718 they were definitely subjects. Those pardoned from execution on condition of transportation had reason to be grateful personally to the king. Their pardons supposedly gave them a "new credit and capacity."[16] Maryland's Assembly did not really buy that notion and, as discussed in chapter 4, made a number of legislative attempts (in 1719, 1723, 1728, 1751, and 1769) to draw a firm line around the convict population to ensure that imported felons were properly registered and identified so they could not pass as free "persons of character" and (the men) could not vote or testify in court proceedings (though after 1751 convicts were permitted to give testimony against other convicts in criminal prosecutions).[17]

Until about the middle of the century, the convicts shared a dual identity as both transported British criminals and indentured American servants (though their term was longer than other servants and, upon its completion, they may not have received freedom dues).[18] Once transportation started being considered as a polluting imperial imposition and the convicts actively resented as societal contaminants, their status became more like that of slaves—albeit term limited. In fact an act of Maryland's Assembly passed in December 1765 "to prevent the mischief Arising from the Multiplicity of Useless Dogs" declared that "any convict servant, Negro, or other *slave*" found abroad with a dog might receive up to fifteen lashes. "[19]

The convicts were always regarded as little more than tradeable and saleable chattels or commodities, and even when their crimes were "purged" by completion of their servitude, legal ambiguities remained; the "pathology" of crime was not easily forgiven.[20] A poem published in the *Maryland Gazette* put it cynically:

As well may Ethiopian Slaves,
Wash out the darkness of their skin;
As well the dead may leave their graves,
As old transgressors cease to sin.[21]

It seems likely that, at least until the Revolution, the convicts remained British subjects, though their civic rights and colonial status were circumscribed and limited by local legislation and regulatory measures. It is impossible to know whether, upon the onset of the Revolution, the women themselves ever questioned their status or their allegiance. Were their sympathies with the loyalists and the mother country from which they had been banished, or were they with the patriots in the land of their arduous and sometimes cruel servitude?

The convict women may have known nothing of the ideological debates that were raging among America's thinkers both before and after the onset of the Revolution or of the array of opinions being expressed, but they must have learned early of the colonies' fight for independence. The prerevolutionary boycott of British goods may have required them to assist with the accelerated production of homespun cloth, and upon the outbreak of war some of them may have come in contact with the fray itself. In Maryland, counties such as Cecil, Harford, and Baltimore were on the Continental army's line of march, and farmers found themselves having to supply the army with wagons, cattle, horses, grain, and other provisions. The town of Frederick was a powder depository and Hessian prisoner-of-war camp, Baltimore was a supply depot whose merchants and shipbuilders applied themselves to the business of naval warfare, and Annapolis was a mustering and shipment point with a hospital. It was also where military leatherwear was manufactured.[22] Some of the women may have become camp followers.

Did the women ever consider the opportunities presented by the Revolution to join with other bound servants and slaves—who shared a similar predicament—and stage their own rebellion? The likelihood of something like that happening was a common concern of Loyalist conservatives such as the Reverend Jonathan Boucher (1738–1804), who feared that talk of revolution would lead to Negro conspiracies and convict mutinies.[23] In the event Boucher's fears were not realized, and it is thus unknown whether any convicts ever actually plotted such uprisings.

The Revolution animated much philosophical debate and a dialectic on the nature of freedom and of individual rights. The debate tended to be influenced either by the ideas of the English philosopher John Locke (1632–1704) or by those of Scottish Enlightenment thinkers. Locke's ideas emphasized equality, individual autonomy, and the expansion of individual freedoms to those previously shut out of the political process (such as men without property, who were unfranchised)—but not to women. Scottish theorists emphasized rights (natural rights) as benefits conferred by God that should be expressed in the performance of duties to society. Conveniently, there was something for both sexes. While free women were acknowledged as citizens, certain expressions of civic equality, such as voting, political participation, and military service were to remain solely the preserve of men. Women were recognized as having rights—though these were of a fundamentally different character from male rights.[24]

Through the common law of coverture, wives were supposed to have a unity of purpose with their husbands. In most respects a wife—a *feme covert*—was not recognized as having legal rights and obligations distinct from those of her husband. Upon marriage these had been combined as one—the woman's legal rights were subsumed by those of her husband. An adult woman who was unmarried or widowed—a *feme sole*—even if materially independent, was not treated as such in political theory or practice. Most women's rights were thus not about liberty and choice. They were nonpolitical and derived from the obligations of being wives and mothers or fulfilling a gender-defined role.[25]

Yet if women did not have a separate economic interest, the practical requirements of their domestic roles gave some of them—though not slaves or servants—a certain status in the home and on the farm. It also gave them a moral authority that could be exercised to foster "civic virtue" in the new republic—the cultivation of community attributes and ethical values likely to sustain the republic, its liberty, and its laws. This was an essential element in the revolutionary generation's discussions of republicanism.[26] At the Constitutional Convention in 1787, John Dickinson, the delegate from Delaware and one of the most influential of the Founding Fathers, urged the convention to "endeavour with united Councils to establish a Government that not only may render our Nation great, respectable, free, and happy, but also VIRTUOUS."[27] Middle- and upper-class women seized the notion of civic virtue and made it their own. It would become for these women what military honor was for men, and they took on responsibility for trying to ensure that their menfolk lived up to the standards of the republican values they professed.[28]

In this Republic of Virtue no case could be made for the continued importation of the genuinely unvirtuous—the thieving lodgers and light-fingered servants, the pocket-picking prostitutes and housebreaking burglars, the shoplifters and the receivers, the vagrants and the merely poor. Moreover, as an independent nation that now regarded itself as an equal with other sovereign states, the United States could not risk a principal implication of transportation—that there was a continuing imperial power relationship, with that power still located in London.

It is highly unlikely that Thomas Jefferson would have had any tolerance for the recommencement of the convict trade. He was always wary of people he believed were incapable of defending republican liberty and might even be a means of destroying it. In fact, Jefferson wanted to bleach out the nation's convict stain completely.[29] On June 22, 1786, he wrote to M. de Meusnier: "The malefactors sent to America were not sufficient to merit enumeration. It was at a late period of their history that the practice began. I have no book by me which enables me to point out the date of its commencement. But I do not think the whole number would amount to 2,000 and being men principally eaten up with disease, they married seldom and propagated little."[30]

Jefferson's lofty, erroneous, and dismissive comments (like those of the nineteenth-century historian George Bancroft) were like an executive fiat. The history of the United States was to be centered on the idea that immigrants were people seeking freedom, economic opportunity, and the enlargement of individual rights. British convicts (identified as male) were to be regarded as an insignificant and unpleasant aspect of the colonial past who could have no place in a bright republican future. Their female counterparts were not even to be granted a place in the past.

Thus, when convict women completed their servitude after the Revolution, they had an ambiguous citizenship and neither economic status nor moral authority. These factors multiplied their marginality in a society that purported to value freedom—and, ironically, portrayed the new, independent republic as a woman in its civic iconography.[31] Yet these were not the only factors that contributed to their marginality and general invisibility—and to the invisibility of all the convict women who had arrived since 1718.

Despite the numbers of women transported to Maryland, they were treated in ways that made them easy to overlook. This was true from their initial indictment and prosecution to that time (usually) seven years later when they completed their sentence. This treatment was often a direct consequence of their gender. Being inexpensive (compared with the cost of slaves) and available at a discounted price (compared to male convicts), they were devalued both as servants and as women as soon as they were sold in America. They became people of consequence only when they ran away. Their owners were then faced with the loss or compromise of their investment and a challenge to their authority. This authority was sustained by a society in which planter power and patriarchy were defining characteristics.

In seeking to bring convict women out from obscurity, it is worth reviewing all the reasons for their being so little known—some of which have been canvassed in previous chapters. The most salient reason was their criminality; their convictions in Britain or Ireland meant they were inherently dubious. Their buyers were mistrustful of them, and colonial society, by and large, found them repugnant—particularly those suspected of having been prostitutes or characterized as prostitutes just because they broke the rules of civilized womanhood by drinking in public, swearing, fraternizing with sailors, and acting licentiously.[32] Yet the largest number of the convicted women—and there was not much regional variation in this profile—were petty thieves who were more likely to be first offenders than recidivists. Their often-opportunistic thefts were from shops or from their employers, landlords, masters and mistresses or, if prostitutes, from their clients. Some were only accessories to crime. But all came within the reach of an expanding array of statutes that prescribed capital sentences equally for murder and minor property theft—but were administered with a bewildering degree of judicial discretion. Crime made British society fearful and it made Maryland's colonists fearful as well—or at least apprehensive. This was partly because purchasers of convicts could never be sure of what they were actually getting—the sentencing discretion having blurred the gravity of criminality in individual cases. It is perhaps paradoxical that, despite their alleged faults, there was always a market for the convict women. Farmers, planters, merchants, tradesmen, and householders generally had diverse labor needs and the women were useful for meeting these needs.

Before their transportation the convict women were, as far as can be judged from their occupations, people of little account. They were predominantly unmarried and "people of the lower sort"—domestic servants, apprentices, street vendors, workers in the many categories of the clothing trades, and so on. In Maryland some were again engaged in domestic service. In urban centers (such as Annapolis), this meant a belowstairs grind of washing, scrubbing, cleaning, and polishing to ensure a standard of refinement in the homes of the elite and the upwardly mobile middle class. In rural and agricultural households, such service was likely to include tasks to do with food production and the processing of raw materials into items such as clothing, candles, soap, and cider. Many women were field laborers on tobacco plantations and some were assigned to do menial work in iron foundries.

In Britain and Ireland the women were members of a society whose ruling class believed rank and authority were divinely ordained and that disorderly conduct and social turbulence went against God's scheme for the world.[33] Members of the British ruling class had clear and highly gendered ideas about seemly female behavior. They expected their servants to be wholly devoted to the interests of their employers, to be passive and submissive. They did not appreciate it when servants demonstrated "loose manners of speech, romping rude behaviour and, especially, filching habits."[34] When social and economic change made the center of this world less secure and property owners felt beleaguered by a rising crime rate, transportation had an irresistible attraction as a means of reestablishing order and deference by excising those who offended, both by breaking the law and through their insubordination to society's norms. The sentiment briefly expressed in the Transportation Act—"In America, there is a great want of servants, who by their labour and industry might be the means of improving and making the said colonies and plantations more useful to this Nation"—was not much more than window dressing (see appendix 4). It was a means of making it seem as if transportation was specifically designed for the mutual benefit of the mother country and the colonies when it was actually to transfer a vexatious criminal problem.

There is not a great deal of information on the women's ages, but from the small number of instances where age was recorded (on a couple of shipping lists, at some trials, and in runaway advertisements), it would seem that most were in their midtwenties, though many were still in their teens. In the Maryland census of 1755, 5.44 percent of the female convicts then serving were under the age of sixteen. Mary Johnson, a girl of only ten, must have been one of the youngest, while the oldest on record was the fifty-three-year-old Mary Ingram. A few women may have been even older. Being young as well as female and felon, the convicts occupied a precarious position in Maryland's colonial society, which was acutely aware of the nuances of status.

The workings of the highly profitable convict trade were largely hidden from the general public on both sides of the Atlantic. Even the British government was said to stand "wholly aloof" from transportation arrangements.[35] Perhaps the trade was really understood properly only by the shippers and factors themselves—and to a lesser extent by those who paid the transportation subsidies, such as the British Treasury. The American factors were sufficiently savvy to know that, even if active hostility to the trade flared up only occasionally, the convicts were perennially unwelcome. The factors thus went about their business in a manner designed to attract little attention. Their newspaper advertisements of convict sales were euphemistic, brief, and to the point, and they tried to avoid disputes by meeting fully the needs of their clients. Once landed and sold, the convict women were not especially noticeable among the many other white female servants.

The colonists' resentment of the convict trade was motivated partly by fear of mayhem and disease but also because the trade offended their sense of amour propre. Like Thomas Jefferson, some were repelled by the taint conferred by the convicts and believed the peopling of the province "with the most abandoned profligates in the Universe" impugned its "Virtue."[36] Maryland was an established society; in 1734—fifteen years into the transportation period—it passed the centenary of its founding. It had a somewhat self-regarding elite and, as elegant Georgian buildings were erected and finely furnished, theaters opened, and literary clubs launched, there was talk of a "Golden Age."[37] The antagonism directed at convicts and at Lord Baltimore's veto of legislation designed to control their entry was actually part of a larger issue in Maryland regarding proprietary control versus local autonomy. Yet, despite this antipathy, Maryland's ruling and owner class maintained a high degree of control. Another of the Founding Fathers, John Adams, noted in his diary for February 23, 1777, "[T]he [Maryland] planters and farmers . . . assume the title of gentlemen, and they hold their negroes and convicts, that is all labouring people and tradesmen, in such contempt that they think themselves a distinct order of beings."[38]

That the convict women could be bought, sold, willed, and itemized as inventory for estate probate purposes reduced them even further than their crimes had already done; they were not only degendered but also dehumanized. Elizabeth Spriggs's letter and the dozens of runaway advertisements provide examples of the abuse to which some servant women were subjected—their inadequate food, clothing, and bedding, the whippings they received, and the iron collars and fetters they were sometimes forced to wear.

In the increasingly patriarchal society of the Chesapeake region, the roles of respectable women were believed to lie in the intimate domestic realm as wives, mothers, and daughters and as the focal point of (increasingly native-born) kin networks. It was these roles that established the moral authority of elite women and women "of the middling sort" and emphasized their status in fostering public virtue in the new republic, as discussed earlier in this chapter. During their servitude the convict women could not actively participate in this realm.[39] Even when they became pregnant (or married without permission), they had no opportunity to replicate these acceptable domestic roles. Conception, childbirth, and child rearing—uniquely female concerns—detracted from productivity and were thus vigorously punished. In this respect convict women were not alone—their experiences were akin to those of female indentured servants, who were similarly pun-

The house of Thomas Ringgold (1715–72), an Eastern Shore merchant and slave dealer who was a prominent member of Maryland's society and operated out of Chestertown. The photograph was taken in the early twentieth century. (*Maryland Period Rooms,* 18. Rephotographed by Mitro Hood. Courtesy of the Baltimore Museum of Art.)

ished, but male servants, whether convict or indentured, never had to face this perpetual risk to their eventual freedom unless they violated some other aspect of the moral law.

Almost the only evidence available of kindly expressions about female convicts are the occasional remarks in James Cheston's letterbooks, such as those concerning Sarah Webber—"a tidy looking girl." There is also the sale notice John Brice placed for his laundrywoman and the housekeeping skills sometimes mentioned in runaway advertisements.[40] But none of these comments were disinterested. The principal value of most of the convict women was in their contribution to the production of tobacco and other agricultural products—particularly as they were categorized as "nontaxable" and allowed poorer planters freedom from the risk of tobacco quotas based on the number of "taxables" owned.

The rapid growth of Maryland's population during the eighteenth century may have helped further to lessen the visibility of the convict women. Maryland's economy (as described in chapter 5) required a steady supply of bound workers to meet its chronic labor shortage. These included not only the much larger number of male convicts, who outnumbered the women by a factor of four, but also slaves, white indentured servants, and German "redemptioners." In 1755, when a census was taken in Maryland that measured the population under a number of categories, the 386 convict women then serving represented less than 2 percent of the female population over sixteen. They were outnumbered by 1,824 indentured servant women and 9,330 female slaves—that is, there were nearly five times as many white indentured servants and twenty-four times as many female slaves.[41]

Maryland was well served by shipping throughout the eighteenth century—better served than the future penal colony at Botany Bay in Australia—and the journey across the Atlantic was much shorter. Although it was difficult to pull off a successful escape from service, if this could be accomplished, a convict might readily find a vessel that would take her back to Britain or Ireland. Similarly, if she had the means and desire to do so (and her health had not been ruined), she was able to return home at the end of her term. This probably meant that a smaller percentage of the convict women remained in Maryland to settle permanently than would be the case in Australia. Those who did remain were apparently not eager to draw attention to their origins and, as was remarked by the French traveler quoted in chapter 7, many may have removed themselves to remoter regions where, unlike slaves, they could blend into the population without much notice.[42]

Only a tiny handful of firsthand convict memoirs remain, and these were all written by men, meaning that some aspects of the experiences of the women convicts have to be deduced from male accounts—which, of course, does not allow an understanding of how their experiences differed.[43] Based on known levels of female illiteracy in the eighteenth century, it is probable that most convict women were unable to read or write. The women's own voices are available only from a few trial records or petitions in which they occasionally spoke up in their own defense—most of what is known about individual convicts is from the observations and comments of others. None of the convict women who remained in Maryland after completing their sentence became notable for any entrepreneurial endeavor or other achievement (Elizabeth Crowder's single advertisement for her Annapolis quilting services is all there is). There are no individual examples of the reform that servitude was said to accomplish, and it is not possible to assess directly if or in what way the experience of having been a convict affected the women's lives after servitude. Much has to be surmised.

∽

In January 1751 a woman was sentenced to transportation at the quarter sessions in Surrey. She either did not know her surname or refused to give it, making one up for the record. In any case, the court listed her as "Mary Nobody alias Parsley, spinster of St. George's Parish, Southwark." In February she boarded the *Thames* under the command of Captain James Dobbins, reaching Annapolis on May 16, 1751.[44] The *Maryland Gazette* reported the frigate's arrival, stating it carried 120 convicts for sale.[45] From that point onward, nothing more is known of Mary Nobody. Her anonymity and circumstances are emblematic of all Maryland's convict women who, for a mixture of reasons—colonial distaste, their social insignificance, their gender, or their own self-effacement—have been obscured or neglected in the historical consciousness. Their story is part of the history of women in America and also the history of bound labor and unfree servitude in Maryland. For those reasons it deserves to be better known.

Appendix 1: Statistical Information on Convict Women

Table 1. Sentencing county or city in England or Wales for 7,957 transported women, 1720s–1776 and 1783

County or city where sentenced	Number of all convict women sent to America (%)	Number of convict women sent to Maryland (%)
Bedfordshire	52 (0.65)	3 (0.09)
Berkshire	10 (0.13)	0 (0.00)
Bristol	5 (0.06)	5 (0.15)
Buckinghamshire	31 (0.39)	9 (0.26)
Cambridgeshire	14 (0.18)	1 (0.03)
Cheshire	14 (0.18)	5 (0.15)
Cornwall	43 (0.54)	23 (0.67)
Cumberland	21 (0.26)	0 (0.00)
Derbyshire	44 (0.55)	12 (0.35)
Devon	260 (3.27)	76 (2.22)
Dorset	38 (0.48)	11 (0.32)
Durham	46 (0.58)	4 (0.12)
Essex	113 (1.42)	71 (2.07)
Flint	1 (0.01)	0 (0.00)
Gloucestershire	336 (4.22)	96 (2.81)
Hampshire	83 (1.04)	8 (0.23)
Herefordshire	62 (0.78)	6 (0.18)
Hertfordshire	38 (0.48)	20 (0.58)
Huntingdonshire	11 (0.14)	0 (0.00)
Kent	152 (1.91)	96 (2.81)
Lancashire	110 (1.38)	1 (0.03)
Leicestershire	12 (0.15)	3 (0.09)
Lincolnshire	29 (0.36)	2 (0.06)
London	1,415 (17.78)	744 (21.74)
Middlesex	3,419 (42.97)	1,731 (50.58)
Monmouthshire	39 (0.49)	3 (0.09)

County or city where sentenced	Number of all convict women sent to America (%)	Number of convict women sent to Maryland (%)
Norfolk	61 (0.77)	3 (0.09)
Northamptonshire	1 (0.01)	0 (0.00)
Northumberland	70 (0.88)	5 (0.15)
Nottinghamshire	22 (0.28)	0 (0.00)
Oxfordshire	34 (0.43)	5 (0.15)
Rutlandshire	1 (0.01)	0 (0.00)
Shropshire	116 (1.46)	12 (0.35)
Somerset	161 (2.02)	37 (1.08)
Staffordshire	53 (0.67)	7 (0.20)
Suffolk	31 (0.39)	0 (0.00)
Surrey	360 (4.52)	201 (5.87)
Sussex	31 (0.39)	16 (0.47)
Warwickshire	62 (0.78)	19 (0.56)
Westminster	1 (0.01)	1 (0.03)
Westmorland	7 (0.09)	0 (0.00)
Wiltshire	70 (0.88)	22 (0.64)
Worcestershire	80 (1.01)	8 (0.23)
Yorkshire	150 (1.89)	9 (0.26)
Unspecified	248 (3.12)	147 (4.30)
Total	7,957 (100.00)	3,422 (100.00)

Sources: Coldham, *The Complete Book of Emigrants in Bondage, Supplement to Complete Book of Emigrants in Bondage*, and *The King's Passengers to Maryland and Virginia*.

Table 2. Sentencing county or city in England or Wales for convict women sent to Maryland, by decade

County or city where sentenced	1720s	1730s	1740s	1750s	1760s	1770s, 1783	Total number (%)
Bedfordshire	0	0	0	0	0	2	2 (0.07)
Berkshire	1	0	0	0	0	0	1 (0.03)
Bristol	0	0	16	2	0	7	25 (0.82)
Buckinghamshire	2	0	1	3	2	1	9 (0.29)
Cambridgeshire	1	0	0	0	0	0	1 (0.03)
Cheshire	0	0	0	0	0	3	3 (0.10)
Cornwall	1	5	8	0	0	5	19 (0.62)
Cumberland	0	0	0	0	0	0	0 (0.00)
Derbyshire	1	0	0	0	0	0	1 (0.03)
Devon	3	24	9	6	1	10	53 (1.73)

County or city where sentenced	1720s	1730s	1740s	1750s	1760s	1770s, 1783	Total number (%)
Dorset	0	1	0	1	0	7	9 (0.29)
Durham	0	0	0	0	0	4	4 (0.13)
Essex	10	4	14	23	9	11	71 (2.32)
Flint	0	0	0	0	0	0	0 (0.00)
Gloucestershire	0	0	0	3	0	5	8 (0.26)
Hampshire	0	2	3	0	0	1	6 (0.20)
Herefordshire	0	0	2	1	0	3	6 (0.20)
Hertfordshire	12	2	4	7	0	2	27 (0.91)
Huntingdonshire	0	0	0	0	0	0	0 (0.00)
Kent	10	7	12	37	13	12	91 (2.94)
Lancashire	0	0	0	0	0	0	0 (0.00)
Leicestershire	2	0	0	0	0	0	2 (0.07)
Lincolnshire	1	0	0	0	0	0	1 (0.03)
London	142	81	110	199	97	60	689 (22.47)
Middlesex	321	208	287	454	234	176	1,680 (54.73)
Monmouthshire	0	0	0	1	0	1	2 (0.07)
Norfolk	0	0	1	0	0	0	1 (0.03)
Northamptonshire	0	0	0	0	0	0	0 (0.00)
Northumberland	0	0	0	0	0	4	4 (0.13)
Nottinghamshire	0	0	0	0	0	0	0 (0.00)
Oxfordshire	1	0	0	0	0	2	3 (0.10)
Rutlandshire	0	0	0	0	0	0	0 (0.00)
Shropshire	0	0	0	0	0	11	11 (0.36)
Somerset	1	7	0	0	0	10	18 (0.59)
Staffordshire	3	0	0	1	0	3	7 (0.23)
Suffolk	0	0	0	0	0	0	0 (0.00)
Surrey	30	13	16	73	26	20	178 (5.81)
Sussex	2	2	6	4	3	1	18 (0.59)
Warwickshire	0	0	0	0	0	19	19 (0.62)
Westminster	0	0	0	0	0	0	0 (0.00)
Westmorland	0	0	0	0	0	0	0 (0.00)
Wiltshire	0	2	3	0	1	7	13 (0.42)
Worcestershire	0	0	0	0	1	6	7 (0.23)
Yorkshire	5	0	0	0	0	2	7 (0.23)
Unspecified	46	12	0	0	0	13	71 (2.32)
Total	595	370	492	815	387	408	3,067 (100.00)

Source: Coldham, *The King's Passengers to Maryland and Virginia*, derived from surviving landing certificates.

Note: The discrepancy of 355 women between tables 1 and 2 is due to incomplete shipping records for all those sentenced to transportation in British courts.

Table 3. Crimes of 1,229 convict women sentenced at the Old Bailey, 1718–76

Crime	1720s[1]	1730s	1740s	1750s	1760s	1770–1776	Total number (%)
Theft—grand larceny	75	67	85	121	114	130	592 (48.17)
Theft from a specified place	71	31	30	30	18	15	195 (15.88)
Theft—other	24	61	34	10	13	2	144 (11.72)
Theft—shoplifting	26	19	14	9	11	8	87 (7.08)
Theft—pocket picking	21	14	8	12	8	5	68 (5.53)
Theft—receiving	6	12	6	12	3	10	49 (3.99)
Theft—burglary/ housebreaking	16	6	6	7	3	6	44 (3.58)
Violent theft— highway robbery	2	4	6	3	4	10	29 (2.36)
Theft—petty larceny	1	0	4	0	2	3	10 (0.81)
Theft—animals	0	2	0	1	0	0	3 (0.24)
Returning from transportation	2	0	0	0	0	1	3 (0.24)
Coining offenses	0	0	2	0	0	0	2 (0.16)
Murder	0	0	1	0	0	0	1 (0.08)
Deception—fraud	0	0	1	0	0	0	1 (0.08)
Infanticide	0	0	0	0	1	0	1 (0.08)
Total	244	216	197	205	177	190	1,229 (100.00)

[1]Includes 1718 and 1719.
Source: Compiled by the author from Old Bailey Session Papers, 1718–1776.

Table 4. Male/female composition of transport ships from England to Maryland, 1718–83

Decade	Men	Women	Total number (Female % of total)
1720s[1]	1,310	595	1,905 (31.23)
1730s	929	370	1,299 (28.48)
1740s	1,122	492	1,614 (30.48)
1750s	2,052	815	2,867 (28.42)
1760s	1,279	387	1,666 (23.22)
1770s, 1783	1,834	408	2,242 (18.2)
Total	8,526	3,067	11,593 (26.46)

[1]Includes 1718 and 1719.
Source: Compiled by the author from Peter Coldham, *The King's Passengers to Maryland and Virginia.*

Table 5. Items stolen by 1,174 convict women sentenced at the Old Bailey, 1718–76

Type of items stolen	1720s[1]	1730s	1740s	1750s	1760s	1770–76	Total number (%)
Clothing	72	79	73	78	62	51	415 (35.35)
Household items	58	32	38	55	39	25	247 (21.04)
Money	26	18	17	14	15	22	112 (9.54)
Fabric/ ribbons	22	27	11	14	17	18	109 (9.28)
Watches	5	10	6	17	12	26	76 (6.47)
Jewelry	12	7	4	8	8	3	42 (3.58)
Metal	0	7	5	0	1	1	14 (1.19)
Food	1	4	2	1	1	4	13 (1.11)
Animals	0	0	1	1	0	0	2 (0.17)
Other	3	4	0	2	2	2	13 (1.11)
Multiple categories	34	12	8	15	18	14	101 (8.60)
Unspecified	9	15	5	0	1	0	30 (2.56)
Total	242	215	170	205	176	166	1,174 (100.00)

[1]Includes 1718 and 1719.

Table 6. Marital status of 456 convict women sentenced at Old Bailey, 1718–76

Marital status	Number (%)
Single	241 (52.86)
Married	135 (29.60)
Widowed	80 (17.54)
Total	456 (100.00)

Note: Marital status not given routinely.
Source: Compiled by the author from trial information in Old Bailey Session Papers, 1718–1776.

Table 7. Ages of 86 convict women drawn from shipping or trial records and runaway advertisements, 1718–1776

Age	Trial/shipping records	Runaway advertisements	Total number (%)
15 or younger	3	0	3 (3.49)
16–20	10	5	15 (17.44)
21–25	17	6	23 (26.74)
26–30	14	7	21 (24.42)
31–35	7	2	9 (10.47)
36–40	4	6	10 (11.63)
41–50	2	2	4 (4.65)
Over 50	1	0	1 (1.16)
Total	58	28	86 (100.00)

Appendix 2: List of Convict Women's Occupations

The list is drawn from indictments, trial records, and runaway advertisements.

Apprentice
Breeches maker
Chapwoman (pedlar)
Children's nurse
Cook
Cook/storekeeper
Dairymaid
Dancing mistress
Farm servant
Glove maker
House servant
Journeyman quilter
Laundress
Leather dresser
Mantua maker
Milliner
Needlewoman (seamstress)
Quilter
Spinner
Spoon caster
Washerwoman
Weaver

Appendix 3: Privy Council Resolution, 1615

The Privy Council resolution of January 23, 1615, initiated transportation to the American colonies as a method of reprieving felons from execution.[1] The complete text follows.

Whereas it hath pleased his Majestie, out of his singular clemencie and mercie, to take into his princelie consideracion the wretched estate of divers of his subjectes, who by the lawes of the realme are adjudged to dye for sundrie offences, though heinous in themselves, yet not of the highest nature, so as his Majestie, both out of his gratious clemencie, as also for divers weightie consideracions, could wishe they might be rather corrected than destroyed, and that in their punishments some of them might live and yeald a proffitable service to the commonwealth in partes abroad, where it shal be found fitt to employe them; for which purpose his Majestie having directed his commission under the great Seale of England to us and the rest of his Privie Councell, giving full power, warrant, and authoritie to us or anie six or more of us whereof the Lord Chancelor, Lord Treasurer, Sir Ralph Winwood, his Majestie's Secretarie of State, the Lord Cheife Justice of England, to be two [*sic*] to reprive and stey from execucion suche persons as now stand convicted of anie robberie or fellonie (wilfull murther, rape, witchcraft or burglarie onelie excepted), who for strength of bodie or other abilities, shalbe thought fitt to be employed in forraine discoveries, or other services beyond the seas as shalbe certified unto us in writing by anie one or more of our judges, or serjeantes at lawe, before whom such felons have bene tried, or, in their absence, then by two suche principall Commissioners, before whom such fellons have bene convicted and the sayd parties, so reprived and certified as aforesaid, to appoint, bestowe and committ, to serve in such discoveries or other forraine employments, as wee, or anie six or more of us, shall assigne or appoint, and at the time to be prefixed by anie suche six of us as aforesayd, how long the sayd offenders or anie of them, shall remayne in such employments; willing and commanding, by vertue of the sayd commission, all his Majestie's judges, justices, sheriffes, gaolers and all other his Majestie's officers and loving subjectes, to whom it shall appertaine, to be ayding and assisting to the due performance of the premises with is spetiall proviso, that, if any of the sayd offenders shall refuse to goe, or yealding to goe, shall afterwards come back and retourne from those places where thay are or shalbe sent or employed before the time limmited by us, his Majestie's Comissioners, be fully expired, that then the sayd reprivall shall no longer stand, nor be of anie force, but the sayd offendor, or offenders, shall from thenceforthe be subject to the execucion of lawe, for the offence wherof hee was first convicted, as if nothing had bene donne by vertue of this commission. Theese are therefore to signifie unto all his Majestie's officers and other persons whome it may concerne, that, having received a certificat from Sir Henry Mountague, knight, his Majestie's Serjeant at Lawe, and recorder of the cyttie of London, that theese persons (viz.), Augustine Callis, Robert Everatt, William Clarke, Thomas Burrowes, John Duffeild, Raphe Bateman, Thomas Pitt, Andrewe Cole, John Crosse, John Honyard, Edward Caldecot, Thomas Kichin, Benjamine Eley, William Briggs, Abel Metcalfe, Edward Bland, and Humphry Skellicorne, being persons of able bodies and fitt to be employed beyond the seas, have had their tryall and were convicted before him for severall felonies, but not for any murther, rape, burglarie, or witchcraft; wee do by vertue of his Majestie's sayd commission, reprive the sayd persons from execucion of lawe, and do appoint them to be delivered unto Sir Thomas Smithe, knight, Gouvernor of the East India Companie or his assignees, to be conveyed into the East Indies or other partes beyond the seas where hee shall direct, with all convenient speed, and not to retourne agayne upon the payne before specified, without warrant first obteined under the hands of six of us of his Majestie's Privie Councell; and do will and in his Majestie's name commaund the Highe Sheriffe of the countie, where the sayd persons remayne, to deliver them accordingly to the sayd Sire Thomas Smithe, or those whom hee shall appoint to receive them. For doing wherof this, being according to his Majestie's commission, shalbe to him a sufficient warrant and discharge in that behalfe.

Lord Archbishop, Lord Treasurer, Lord Wotton, Mr Secretary Winwood, Mr Chancellor of the Exchequer, Master of the Rolls.

Appendix 4: Transportation Act of 1718

An Act for the Further Preventing Robbery, Burglary, and Other Felonies, and for the More Effectual Transportation of Felons, and Unlawful Exporters of Wool; and for Declaring the Law upon Some Points Relating to Pirates.[1]

1. Whereas it is found by experience, that the punishments inflicted by the Laws now in force against the offences of robbery, larceny and other felonious taking and stealing of money and goods, have not proved effectual to deter wicked and evil-disposed persons from being guilty of the said crimes; and whereas many offenders to whom Royal Mercy hath been extended, upon condition of transporting themselves to the West-Indies, have often neglected to perform the said condition, but returned to their former wickedness, and have been at least for new crimes brought to a shameful and ignominious death; and whereas in many of his Majesty's colonies and plantations in America, there is great want of servants, who by their labour and industry might be the means of improving and making the said colonies and plantations more useful to this Nation: Be it enacted by the King's most Excellent Majesty, by and with the advice and consent of the Lords Spiritual and Temporal, and the Commons, in this present parliament assembled, and by the authority of the same, that where any person or persons have been convicted of any offence within the benefit of clergy, before the 20th day of January, 1717 [18], and are liable to be whipt or burnt in the hand, or have been ordered to any workhouse, and who shall be therein on the said twentieth day of January; as also where any person or persons shall be hereafter convicted of grand or petit larceny, or any felonious stealing or taking of money or goods and chattels, either from the person or the house of any other, or in any other manner, and who by the law shall be entitled to the benefit of clergy, and liable only to the penalties of burning in the hand or whipping, (except persons convicted for receiving or buying stolen goods, knowing them to be stolen) it shall and may be lawful for the Court before whom they were convicted or any court held at the same place with the like authority,

if they think fit, instead, of ordering any such offenders to be burnt in the hand or whipped, to order and direct, that such offenders, as also such offenders in any workhouse as aforesaid, shall be sent as soon as conveniently may be, to some of his Majesty's colonies and plantations in America for the space of seven years; and that court before whom they were convicted, or any subsequent court held at the same place, with like authority as the former, shall have power to convey, transfer and make over such offenders by order of court, to the use of any person or persons who shall contract for the performance of such transportation, to him, or them, and his and their assigns, for such term of seven years; and where any persons have been convicted, or do now stand attainted of any offences whatsoever for which death by law ought to be inflicted, or where any offenders shall hereafter be convicted of any crimes whatsoever, for which they are by law to be excluded the benefit of clergy, and his Majesty, his Heirs or Successors shall be graciously pleased to extend Royal mercy to any such offenders, upon the condition of transportation to any part of America, and such intention of mercy be signified by one of his Majesty's Principal Secretaries of State, it shall and may be lawful to and for any court having proper authority to allow such offenders the benefit of a pardon under the Great Seal, and to order and direct the like transfer and conveyance to any person or persons (who will contract for the performance of such transportation) and to his and their assigns of any such before-mentioned offenders, as also of any person or persons convicted of receiving or buying stolen goods, knowing them to be stolen, for the term of fourteen years, in case such condition of transportation be general, or else for such other term or terms as shall be made part of such condition, if any particular time be specified by his Majesty, his Heirs and Successors, as aforesaid; and such person or persons so contracting, as aforesaid, his or their assigns, by virtue of such order of transfer, as aforesaid shall have a property and interest in the service of such offender for such terms of years.

2. And be it further enacted by the authority aforesaid that if any offender or offenders so ordered by any court to be transported for any term of seven years or fourteen years, or any other time or times as aforesaid, shall return into any part of Great Britain or Ireland before the end of his or their said term, he or she so returning as aforesaid, shall be liable to be punished as any person attainted of felony without the benefit of clergy, and execution may and shall be awarded against such offender or offenders accordingly; provided nevertheless that his Majesty, his Heirs and Successors, may at any time pardon and dispense with any such transportation and allow of the return of any such offender or offenders from America, he or they paying their owner or proprietor, at the time of such pardon, dispensation or allowance such sum of

money as shall be adjudged reasonable by any two justices of the peace residing within the province where such owner dwells; and where any such offenders shall be transported and shall have served their respective terms, according to the order of any such court as aforesaid, such services shall have the effect of a pardon to all intents and purposes as for that crime or crimes for which they were so transported and shall have so served as aforesaid.

3. And be it further enacted by the authority aforesaid that every such person or persons to whom any court shall order any such offenders to be transferred or conveyed as aforesaid, before any of them shall be delivered over to such person or persons, or his or their assigns, he or they shall contract and agree with any such person or persons as shall be ordered and appointed by such court as aforesaid and give sufficient security, to the satisfaction of such court, that he or they will transport, or cause to be transported, effectually such offenders so conveyed to him or them as aforesaid, to some of his Majesty's Colonies and Plantations in America as shall be ordered by the said court, and procure an authentick certificate from the governor, or the chief custom-house officer of the place (which certificate they are hereby required to give forthwith, without fee or reward, as soon as conveniently may be) of the landing of such offenders so transferred as aforesaid (death and casualties of the sea excepted) and that none of the said offenders shall be suffered to return from the said place to any part of Great Britain or Ireland by the willful default of such person or persons so contracting as aforesaid or by the willful default of his or her assigns.

4. And whereas there are several person who have secret acquaintance with felons and who make it their business to help persons to their stolen goods, and by that means gain money from them which is divided between them and the felons, whereby they greatly encourage such offenders, be it enacted by the authority aforesaid that wherever any person taketh money or reward directly or indirectly under pretence or upon account of helping any person or persons to any stolen goods or chattels, every person so taking money or reward as aforesaid (unless such person doth apprehend or cause to be apprehended such felon who stole the same and cause such felons to be brought to his trial for the same and give evidence against him) shall be guilty of felony and suffer the pains and penalties of felony according to the nature of the felony committed in stealing such goods, and in such and the same manner as if such offender had himself stole such goods and chattels, in the manner and with such circumstances as the same were stolen.

5. And whereas there are many idle persons who are under the age of one and twenty years lurking about in divers parts of London and elsewhere who want employment and may be tempted to become thieves, if not provided

for; and whereas they may be inclined to be transported and to enter into service in some of his Majesty's Colonies and Plantations in America, but as they have no power to contract for themselves, and therefore that it is not safe for merchants to transport them or take them into such services; be it enacted by the authority aforesaid that where any person of the age of fifteen years or more, and under the age of twenty-one, shall be willing to be transported and to enter into any service in any of his Majesty's Colonies or Plantations in America, it shall and may be lawful for any merchant or other to contract with any such person for any such service not exceeding the term of eight years, providing such person so binding him or herself do come before the Lord Mayor of London, or some other Justice of the Peace of the City, if such contract be made within the same or the liberties thereof, or before some other two Justices of the Peace of the place where such contract shall be made, if made elsewhere, and before such magistrate or magistrates acknowledge such consent and do sign such contract in his or their presence and with his or their approbation, and that then it shall be binding him or herself and to keep him or her within any of the said Plantations and or Colonies according to the tenor of such contract as aforesaid; and law or statute to the contrary in any wise notwithstanding; which said contract and approbation of such magistrate or magistrates, with the tenor of such contract, shall be certified by such magistrate or magistrates as to the next General Quarter Sessions of the Peace held for that county where such magistrate or magistrates shall reside, to be registered by the Clerk of the Peace without fee or reward.

6. And be it further enacted by the authority aforesaid that from and after the said twentieth day of January 1 1717 [18], if any person or persons shall be in prison for want of sufficient bail for unlawful exportation of wool or woolsels and shall refuse to appear or plead to a declaration or information to be delivered to such person or persons or to the gaoler, keeper or turnkey or the prison, at the said prison, for the said offence by the space of one term, judgement shall be entered against him by default; verdict or otherwise, and in case judgement shall be obtained against any such person or persons by default, verdict or otherwise, and such person or persons shall not pay the sum recovered against him or them for the said offence within the space of three months after entering up of such judgement, the court before whom such judgement shall be obtained shall, by order of court, cause such offender or offenders to be transported in the same manner as felons aforesaid for the term of seven years; and if such offender or offenders shall return to Great Britain or Ireland before the expiration of the said seven years, he or they shall suffer as felons and have execution awarded against them as persons attainted of felony without benefit of clergy.

7. [This clause, relating to the suppression of piracy, has not been included here.]

8. Provided always that nothing in this Act shall extend or be construed to extend to such persons as shall be convicted or attainted in that part of Great Britain called Scotland.

9. And be it also enacted that this Act shall extend to all his Majesty's dominions in America.

Appendix 5: Crimes Punished by Transportation at the Old Bailey, 1718–76

Convicts sentenced to transportation at the Old Bailey between 1718 and 1786 had committed the following offenses:

Breaking peace
Coining offenses
Damage to property
Deception—fraud
Infanticide
Manslaughter
Murder
Perverting justice
Receiving stolen goods
Royal Offences—Tax offences
Sexual Offences—Bigamy
Theft
    animals
    burglary/housebreaking
    embezzlement
    extortion
    from a specified place
    game law offences
    grand larceny
    housebreaking
    other
    Petit larceny
    petty larceny
    pocket picking
    receiving
    shoplifting
Violent highway robbery
Returning from transportation

Appendix 6: Colonial Legislation Regarding Convicts

1. An Act to Prevent the Great Evils Arising by the Importation of Convicts into This Province and for the Better Discovery of Such When Imported (1723). The preamble to the act states:

> Whereas the great number of convicts of late years imported into this province have not only committed several murders, burglaries and other felonies, but debauched the minds and principles of several of the ignorant and formerly innocent inhabitants thereof, so far as to induce them to commit several of the like crimes, the perpetration whereof are now become so common and frequent that honest people are very insecure in their lives or properties; and whereas the greater part of the magistrates' time is taken up in the trial and prosecution of the said convicts and their proselytes to the great delay of all civil business and the insupportable expense of the country which evils are in great measure occasioned by the masters, or owners of such convicts not taking care to keep them within due bounds and restraining them from injuring their neighbours, for remedy thereof...[1]

2. An Act to Prevent the Abuses of Concealing Convicted Felons and Other Offenders Imported into This Province and for the Better Discovery of Them (1728). The preamble to this act, after quoting those parts of 4 Geo. I, c. 11; and 6 Geo. I, c. 23 relating to the transportation of felons, states:

> Masters of vessels importing felons and offenders have neglected to bring testimonials of the offences whereof the said felons and offenders have been convicted whereby it might appear whether they were obliged to serve seven or fourteen years which hath already occasioned disputes between the persons entitled to the service of the felons and the felons themselves concerning their term of servitude; and several other masters of ships have imported felons and then made private contracts with them for less time of servitude than their sentence required and then disposed of these felons as people of

good repute . . . by which practices these felons and offenders, whose testimony ought not to be received in a court of record, or before any magistrate, because not known as such, may be received as witnesses to the manifest danger of the laws, liberties and properties of His Majestie's subjects of this Province.[2]

3. An Act to Make the Testimony of Convicted Persons Legal against Convicted Persons (1751). The preamble to this act stridently asserts:

Murders, burglaries and other felonies and offences have been so frequent of late that the lives and properties of His Majesty's subjects within this Province are become precarious: which offences have been generally committed by convicts imported into this Province and such as they induce to join with them in their wicked practices; and which crimes the said convicts are encouraged to perpetrate because they know that they are disabled from being witnesses against each other as the law now stands.[3]

Notes

Introduction

1. The phrase "His Majesty's Seven-year Passengers" was used in convict sale advertisements—for example, see the *Maryland Gazette*, December 10, 1761.

2. The quotation is a paraphrase of Bolingbroke's speech in William Shakespeare's *Richard II*, act III, scene 1. This play was written in about 1595 and thus offers a contemporary viewpoint on the harshness of exile.

3. Hakluyt, *A Discourse of Western Planting*, 28–32. (Spelling updated from original).

4. This wording is from the 1597 Vagabonds Act (39 Eliz. c.4), which introduced penal transportation as a punishment for the first time.

5. Sainsbury, *Calendar of State Papers, 1574–1660*, 11–12.

6. *Acts of the Privy Council of England*, 23–25.

7. Fogleman, "From Slaves, Convicts, and Servants to Free Passengers." See tables 1 and 2 on p. 44, where Fogleman estimates that 52,200 convicts and prisoners (including political exiles and kidnapping victims) were transported between 1700 and 1775. Peter W. Coldham has identified by name 45,000 convicts transported from England and Wales alone between 1614 and 1775; *More Emigrants in Bondage*, vii. See also Ekirch, *Bound for America*, 24–27. The actual number of convicts transported cannot be verified exactly due to missing records—particularly those destroyed when many of Ireland's public records were lost in a fire in 1922. See also note 20 below. The first census of the American population was not conducted until 1790, when the total population was 3,929,214. The nonwhite component of the population was 19.27 percent.

8. *Journals of the Continental Congress*, 528.

9. Sainsbury, *Calendar of State Papers, 1574–1660*, 447.

10. Sainsbury, *Calendar of State Papers, 1661–1668*, 101.

11. Abbot Emerson Smith, *Colonists in Bondage*, 99–109.

12. Radzinowicz, *A History of English Criminal Law*, 110–23.

13. This bill was enacted as the Transportation Act, 4 Geo. 1 c. 11. of 1718.

14. Jacobites were supporters of the Stuart dynasty's King James II, who had been ousted in the Glorious Revolution of 1688.

15. Beattie, *Crime and the Courts in England*, 503.

16. Throughout this book most dates will be based on the modern calendar, with the new year beginning on January 1 even though before 1752 Britain used March 25 as the legal start of the new year. Scotland had been observing January 1 as the start of the new year since 1600. The Transportation Act is sometimes described as being an act of 1717 rather than 1718 because it was passed in early March. The only exceptions to this convention will occur when citing pre-1752 cases from the March sessions of Maryland's county courts. In such citations the date will be shown as (for example) March 1743/44.

17. Raithby, *The Statutes at Large of England and Great Britain*, 399–402.

18. Abbot Emerson Smith, *Colonists in Bondage*, 117; Morris, *Government and Labor in Early America*, 323–47.

19. Defoe, *Moll Flanders;* [A] Creole, *The Fortunate Transport.*

20. Irish court records are significantly incomplete. A. Roger Ekirch in *Bound for America* estimates Irish convict numbers between 1718 and 1775 as thirteen thousand, with slightly more going to Virginia than Maryland. He also estimates the total number of Scottish convicts in the same period as seven hundred. Bernard Bailyn (*Voyagers to the West*) estimates Irish convict numbers at sixteen thousand and Scottish convict numbers at eight hundred. Women frequently comprised more than one-quarter of the passengers on convict ships and sometimes as many as one-third. This means that up to two thousand of Maryland's convict women may have been Irish and possibly up to one hundred may have been Scottish.

21. Grubb, "The Transatlantic Market for British Convict Labor," 94. See also Fogleman, "From Slaves, Convicts, and Servants to Free Passengers," 58.

22. *Gentleman's Magazine*, vol. 34, June 1764, 261. The counties were Baltimore, Charles, Anne Arundel, Charles, and Queen Anne's. There were 1,672 convicts (male and female) and 12,475 other bound laborers, including white indentured servants (male and female), "mulatto" slaves (male and female), and black slaves (male and female), making a total of 14,147 bound laborers.

23. Bancroft is quoted by Butler in "British Convicts Shipped to American Colonies."

24. Bancroft, *History of the United States*, 490–91.

25. Scharf, *History of Maryland*, 371–72. In 1904 Eugene McCormac produced a monograph entitled *White Servitude in Colonial Maryland* in which he devoted a whole chapter to convicts—immigrants whom he generally regarded as a regrettable and malign element.

26. Sollers, "Transported Convict Laborers in Maryland during the Colonial Period." Sollers's account of the fifty Newgate women is drawn from the *Calendar of State Papers, Colonial Series, America and the West Indies, 1696–1697*, ed. J. W. Fortescue, vol. 15, 1134. The objection from the West Indies was that women did not do field work in those colonies.

27. Morris, *Government and Labor in Early America*; Abbot Emerson Smith, *Colonists in Bondage.*

28. Ekirch, *Bound for America.*

29. Edmund S. Morgan, *American Slavery, American Freedom.*

30. See bibliography for articles by Kenneth Morgan and Farley Grubb. See also Gwenda

Morgan and Rushton, *Rogues, Thieves and the Rule of Law* and *Eighteenth-Century Criminal Transportation.*

31. Gordon S. Wood, *The Radicalism of the American Revolution*, 3–8, esp. 6. Wood's observation is quoted by Fogleman in "From Slaves, Convicts, and Servants to Free Passengers," 43.

32. Matthews, "Feminist History"; Scott, "Gender."

33. Brown, *Good Wives, Nasty Wenches and Anxious Patriarchs;* Carr and Walsh, "The Planter's Wife"; Isaacs, *The Transformation of Virginia;* Kulikoff, *Tobacco and Slaves;* Main, *Tobacco Colony;* Meyers, *Common Whores, Vertuous Women, and Loveing Wives;* Walsh, "The Experiences and Status of Women in the Chesapeake."

34. This summary of the principal direction of historical writing about the Chesapeake is based on comments in the introduction of Meyers and Perreault, *Colonial Chesapeake*, xx.

35. Barnes, "Where Did They Come From?"

36. Coldham, *The Complete Book of Emigrants in Bondage*, and *The King's Passengers to Maryland and Virginia.*

Chapter 1

1. All the women named in this first chapter and those that follow were transported to Maryland unless otherwise stated.

2. After the implementation of the Transportation Act, one of the first convict shipments was made by the *Sophia* (ex Bideford) under the command of Captain John Law. It carried forty-eight felons convicted in the summer assizes of 1718. Their arrival was registered in Queen Anne's County, Maryland, in March 1719. The last convicts carried to America before the outbreak of the War of Independence (which interrupted the trade) were transported in February 1776 on the *Justitia* under the command of Captain John Kidd. The convicts carried on the *Swift* in 1783 were the only felons actually landed in the former colonies after the war.

3. Wrigley and Schofield, *The Population History of England*, 208–9; Plumb, *England in the Eighteenth Century*, 11, 78; Razzell, "The Growth of Population in Eighteenth-Century England"; Johnston-Liik, *Ireland in the Eighteenth Century*, 15. The population of Scotland may have been approximately 1.3 million in 1755, and this increased to 1.6 million by 1801.

4. Plumb, *England in the Eighteenth Century*, 84–86.

5. The invention of the "flying shuttle" in 1733 (by John Kay), of the "spinning jenny" in about 1764 (generally attributed to James Hargreaves), and of Crompton's "mule" in 1775 (by Samuel Crompton) all enabled this trend.

6. These were the War of the Spanish Succession (1701–14), the War of Jenkins' Ear (1739–42)—which was subsumed by the War of the Austrian Succession (1740–48)—and the Seven Years' War (1756–63).

7. Hill, *Women Alone*, 22; Plumb, *England in the Eighteenth Century*, 82–83.

8. Edward P. Thompson, "Time, Work-Discipline and Industrial Capitalism," 84, 89.

9. Hay et al., *Albion's Fatal Tree*, 62 and (regarding letters sent warning of imminent criminal action) 274–79.

10. *Old Bailey Proceedings Online* (www.oldbaileyonline.org, version 6.0), trial of Sarah

Page, Catharine Goodwin, Mary Allaway, Elizabeth Talbot, April 1770 (t17700425-40); see also trial of Edward Holmes, Hannah Riddal, Elizabeth Soddi, April 1770 (t17700425-65) (accessed April 2, 2012). Page, Goodwin, Allaway, and Talbot as well as Riddal (Riddle) and Soddi were all transported to Maryland on the *Scarsdale* in July 1770.

11. Malcolmson, *Life and Labour in England*, 109; Langbein, "Albion's Fatal Flaws," 101.

12. Rule, *Albion's People*, 186–95.

13. Edward P. Thompson, *Customs in Common*, 102–3, 175.

14. Radzinowicz, *A History of English Criminal Law*, 77.

15. Coldham, *The Complete Book of Emigrants in Bondage*, 45, 93. Bartlett's conviction in 1722 was before the Waltham Black Act made poaching a capital offense.

16. Rule and Wells, *Crime, Protest and Popular Politics in Southern England*, 156.

17. Surrey Quarter Sessions Proceedings, 1763, Surrey History Centre, QS2/6, bundle 1, no. 37: Indictment of Lucy Osborn, December 19, 1763. The records do not show whether Osborn was sentenced to transportation.

18. Ibid., QS2/6, bundle 1, nos. 32 and 35: indictment of Judith Marshe and Diana Hudson.

19. Malcolmson, *Life and Labour in England*, 108–13.

20. Dobash, Dobash, and Gutteridge, *The Imprisonment of Women*, 27.

21. Rule, *Albion's People*, 106. See also Malcolmson, *Life and Labour in England*, 114–22.

22. *Gentleman's Magazine*, vol. 10, July 1740, 355–56.

23. Edward P. Thompson, *Customs in Common*, 310–13. Note 2 on p. 312 of this book contains the information on Crone and Withy. Information about the Newcastle transport contractors is from Gwenda Morgan and Rushton, *Rogues, Thieves and the Rule of Law*, 162.

24. Rule, *Albion's People*, 106.

25. Elizabeth Lloyd was sentenced in April 1767 and her crime is mentioned in Gwenda Morgan and Rushton's *Eighteenth-Century Criminal Transportation*, 112. Her transportation details are unknown, but in June 1768 she ran away from Thomas Johnson of Chestertown in Kent County, Maryland. *Maryland Gazette*, July 28, 1768. See also *Old Bailey Proceedings Online* (www.oldbaileyonline.org, version 6.0), trial of Elizabeth Foster and Hannah Lawrence, February 1736 (t17360225-19); trial of Mary Rock, June 1768 (t17680413-62) (accessed December 16, 2011). Elizabeth Foster and Hannah Lawrence were transported to Maryland on the *Patapsco Merchant* in 1736. Mary Rock was transported on the *Tryal* in June 1768. Elizabeth Giles of Staffordshire was sentenced in Lent 1768, though her transportation details are unknown. See listings for all women in Coldham, *The Complete Book of Emigrants in Bondage*, 289, 487, 684, 312.

26. Linebaugh, *The London Hanged*, 144.

27. Beattie, "The Criminality of Women in Eighteenth Century England," 100.

28. Ibid., 113n58.

29. Figure based on the names listed in Coldham's *The Complete Book of Emigrants in Bondage*, cross-checked with the passenger lists in the same author's *The King's Passengers to Maryland and Virginia*.

30. Wrigley, "A Simple Model of London's Importance in Changing English Society and Economy 1650–1750," 37, 44, 45, 47.

31. Picard, *Dr. Johnson's London*, 3–4.

32. Joan R. Kent, "The Centre and the Localities."

33. Hill, *Women, Work, and Sexual Politics*, 234–35.

34. Inwood, *A History of London*, 273, 277; quotation from Henry Fielding's *An Enquiry into the Causes of the Late Increase of Robbers &C.*

35. *Old Bailey Proceedings Online* (www.oldbaileyonline.org, version 6.0), trial of Elizabeth Stavenaugh, otherwise Elizabeth, the wife of Francis Howell, May 1745 (t17450530-8); trial of Anne Groves, July 1747 (t17470715-12) (accessed February 13, 2012). Stavenaugh was transported on the *Italian Merchant* in July 1745. Groves was transported on the *St. George* in January 1748.

36. Inwood, *A History of London*, 273–74.

37. Palk, "Private Crime in Public and Private Places," 136.

38. Lemire, "The Theft of Clothes and Popular Consumerism in Early Modern England," 267.

39. *Old Bailey Proceedings Online* (www.oldbaileyonline.org, version 7.0), trial of John Cox, Joseph Priestly, Eleanor Ogle, September 1775 (t17750913-68) (accessed June 25, 2012). Ogle was transported on the *Justitia* in February 1776.

40. Ibid., January 1734, trial of Grace Long (t17340116-42) (accessed June 25, 2012). Long was transported on the *Patapsco Merchant* in April 1734. Until 1808, the crime of pickpocketing involved "privately" (that is, without the victim's knowledge) stealing goods worth more than a shilling. The difficulty of proving that the victim had no knowledge of the crime made it difficult to convict defendants of this offense, though many were found guilty of lesser offenses.

41. Ibid., May 1737, trial of Ann Wilson and Mary Solomon (t17370526-39) (accessed June 25, 2012). Wilson was transported on the *Pretty Patsy* in September 1737.

42. William Hogarth's series of engravings entitled A Harlot's Progress was published in 1732. His Gin Lane was published in 1751 in support of a campaign directed against gin drinking among London's poor.

43. Hogarth, *The Complete Works of William Hogarth*, 19. The theme of A Harlot's Progress may have been suggested by Daniel Defoe.

44. Ibid., 97, 107. See also Linebaugh, *The London Hanged*.

45. *The Ordinary of Newgate: His Account of the Behaviour, Confessions and Dying Words of the Malefactors Who Were Executed on Wednesday the 3rd of This Instant August, 1726, at Tyburn*, 4, *Old Bailey Proceedings Online* (www.oldbaileyonline.org, version 6.0), August 1726 (OA17260803) (accessed December 15, 2011). Although the ordinary's accounts were explicitly moralistic and shaped for the purpose of demonstrating that, when faced with death, even the worst of criminals could be penitent about having abandoned (middle-class) righteousness and behavioral values, they were nevertheless based on actual testimony.

46. Hill, *Women, Work, and Sexual Politics*, 240–41.

47. Ibid., 238–39.

48. Inwood, *A History of London*, 262–63.

49. *Old Bailey Proceedings Online* (www.oldbaileyonline.org, version 7.0), trial of Elizabeth Deacon Mary Watson, February 1731 (t17310224-28); trial of Catherine Pollard, otherwise Parler, December 1736 (t17361208-42) (accessed June 26, 2013).

50. The remarks about the rookeries in St. Giles in the Fields are from a review of an

exhibition at London's Coningsby Gallery entitled *London's Underworld Unearthed: The Secret Life of the Rookery*; *Guardian*, May 16, 2011.

51. *Old Bailey Proceedings Online* (www.oldbaileyonline.org, version 6.0), trial of Margaret Ford, September 7, 1722 (t17220907-45) (accessed January 27, 2012). Ford was transported on the *Forward* in October 1722.

52. http://londonhistorians.wordpress.com/2010/10/27/compters-aka-counters (accessed April 7, 2012). The problem of debtors' prisons was addressed by James Oglethorpe, a member of the British Parliament who in 1728 chaired a committee to look into prison reform. This documented horrendous abuses in three debtors' prisons. As a result of the committee's actions, many debtors were released from prison with no means of support. Oglethorpe and a group of associates petitioned in 1730 to form the Trustees for the Establishment of the Colony of Georgia in America, which was envisaged as a place to which debtors might migrate and start over as landholding farmers. The petition was approved in 1732, and the first group of colonists, led by Oglethorpe, departed for the New World in November. The colony did not achieve Oglethorpe's objectives.

53. *Old Bailey Proceedings Online* (www.oldbaileyonline.org, version 6.0), trial of Mary Donoho, otherwise Davison, July 1742 (t17420714-21) (accessed April 6, 2012). Donoho was transported to Maryland on the *Forward* in September 1742.

54. Ibid., trial of Jane Knight and Ann Clements, February 1763 (t17630223-1) (accessed April 6, 2012). Clements was transported to Maryland on the *Neptune* in April 1763. Knight was acquitted.

55. Ibid., trial of Mary Harwood, February 1770 (t17700221-34) (accessed May 30, 2012). See also Styles, *The Dress of the People*, 272.

56. *Old Bailey Proceedings Online* (www.oldbaileyonline.org, version 7.0), trial of Martha Blaithwaite, alias Braithwait, June 1725 (t17250630-51) (accessed June 25, 2012). Blaithwaite was transported on the *Forward* in September 1725. She may have died on the passage as her name is not on the landing certificate. The offense of "privately stealing" 5 shillings or more worth of goods from a shop was defined separately as a capital offense in 1699.

57. Henry Fielding (novelist, playwright, journalist, and lawyer) was appointed as magistrate in 1748. After his death in 1754, he was succeeded by his half brother Sir John Fielding, who had worked as his brother's assistant since 1750. The Duke of Newcastle (the first Duke of Newcastle-upon-Tyne and the first Duke of Newcastle-under-Lyne) held a number of ministerial positions during the reign of George II, including secretary of state for the south (1724–48) and for the north (1748–54). He also played the roles of de facto foreign minister and defense minister between 1730 and 1754. When his brother Henry Pelham died in 1754, the duke followed him into the post of prime minister/first lord of the Treasury, holding this position from 1754 to 1756 and again from 1757 to 1762.

58. John Fielding, *A Plan for Reserving Those Deserted Girls Who Become Prostitutes from Necessity*, 44.

59. *Old Bailey Proceedings Online* (www.oldbaileyonline.org, version 6.0), trial of Ann Wilson and Mary Solomon, May 1737 (t17370526-39) (accessed April 12, 2012). Wilson was transported to Maryland on the *Pretty Patsy* in September 1737.

60. Rule, *The Experience of Labour in Eighteenth-Century Industry*, 41.

61. *Boswell's London Journal, 1762–1763*, quoted by Liza Picard in *Dr. Johnson's London*, 213.

62. *Old Bailey Proceedings Online* (www.oldbaileyonline.org, version 6.0), trial of

Margaret King, October 1752 (t17521026-7); trial of Catherine Haines and James Haines, January 1763 (t17630114-22) (accessed February 12, 2012). King was transported to Maryland on the *Greyhound* in December 1752. Catherine and James Haines were transported on the *Neptune* in April 1763.

63. Daniel Defoe, *A Tour through the Whole Island of Great Britain*, vol. 2, 251–52.

64. Gwenda Morgan and Rushton, *Eighteenth-Century Criminal Transportation*, 52–53.

65. Radzinowicz, *A History of English Criminal Law*, 77. See also Edward P. Thompson, *Whigs and Hunters*, 192–95.

66. In 1765 Sir William Blackstone identified no fewer than 160 criminal acts that had "been declared by act of parliament to be felonies without benefit of clergy; or in other words, to be worthy of instant death." *Commentaries on the Laws of England*, 18. In 1810 Sir Samuel Romilly, a prominent law reformer, estimated that there were actually 222 felonies for which the sentence was death. *Observations on the Criminal Law of England*, 3. See also Edward P. Thompson, *Whigs and Hunters*, 197.

67. In 1701 an anonymous pamphlet was published entitled *Hanging Not Punishment Enough* and George Ollyffe's 1731 tract *An Essay Humbly Offer'd for an Act of Parliament to Prevent Capital Crimes* urged the adoption of techniques such as disembowelling, breaking upon the wheel, drawing and quartering the hanged corpse, dissection, etc. In 1785, the Reverend Martin Madan published *Thoughts on Executive Justice*, in which he claimed the problem with punishment was that the severity of capital statutes was mitigated too often by judicial mercy, thus making penalties *uncertain*. See Radzinowicz, *A History of English Criminal Law*, vol. 1, 206–26, 239–41, 246–47.

68. Hay et al., *Albion's Fatal Tree*, 57.

69. Beattie, "The Criminality of Women in Eighteenth Century England," 81. Beattie's comprehensive analysis of the crimes of women appearing before the Surrey courts between 1663 and 1802 shows that the vast majority were charged with property crimes—theft in its multiple categories. See also King, "Female Offenders, Work, and Life-cycle Changes in Late Eighteenth Century London," 64.

70. Beattie, "The Criminality of Women in Eighteenth Century England," 92.

71. *Old Bailey Proceedings Online* (www.oldbaileyonline.org, version 6.0), trial of Mary Hewson, December 5, 1718 (t17181205-12) (accessed January 18, 2012). The *Worcester's* passengers are listed in Coldham, *The King's Passengers to Maryland and Virginia*, 1–2. The evidence shows the Julian calendar was still in use.

72. Beattie, "The Criminality of Women in Eighteenth Century England," 95. Beattie believes that pocket picking and shoplifting were underrepresented in the actual convictions. The offense of "privately stealing" 5 shillings or more worth of goods from a shop was defined separately as a capital offense in 1699, and the crime of pickpocketing involved "privately" stealing from the person of another goods worth more than a shilling.

73. *Old Bailey Proceedings Online* (www.oldbaileyonline.org, version 6.0), trial of Sarah Kingman, July 1739 (t17390718-18); trial of Margaret Newel, April 1740 (t17400416-7) (accessed February 15, 2012). Kingman was transported to Maryland on the *York* in February 1740 and Newel on the *Speedwell/Mediterranean* in April 1741.

74. Atkinson, "The Free-Born Englishman Transported," 97.

75. Gwenda Morgan and Rushton, *Eighteenth-Century Criminal Transportation*, 40–41, 49.

76. Gwenda Morgan and Rushton, *Rogues, Thieves and the Rule of Law*, 157.

77. *Handkerchief* was a broader term than it is today and could be a light muslin fichu, a triangular woolen scarf, or a folded square of light wool. Silk handkerchiefs seem to have been especially prized by thieves.

78. Friedrich August Wendeborn, *A View of England towards the Close of the Eighteenth Century*, 1786, quoted by Buck, *Dress in Eighteenth Century England*, 180.

79. Buck, *Dress in Eighteenth Century England*, 141.

80. Lemire, "The Theft of Clothes and Popular Consumerism in Early Modern England," 256–58, 270. See also *Old Bailey Proceedings Online* (www.oldbaileyonline.org, version 7.0), trial of Anne Monk, April 1755 (t17550409-23) (accessed May 27, 2012).

81. *Old Bailey Proceedings Online* (www.oldbaileyonline.org, version 6.0), trial of Mary Wade, July 1718 (t17180709-4); trial of Eleanor Middleditch, May 1761 (t17610506-12); trial of Catherine, wife of Nathaniel Wilks, otherwise Catherine Bolton, and Nathaniel Wilks, December 1765 (t17651211-10) (accessed April 10, 2012). There are no passenger lists for any of those sentenced to transportation in July 1718. Middleditch was transported on the *Maryland Packet* in October 1761. Wilks was transported on the *Tryal* in January 1766. In this period silk gauze was woven in western Scotland. The theft of "Scotch lawn" suggests that all the cloth stolen by the Wilkses may have been of Scottish manufacture.

82. Buck, *Dress in Eighteenth Century England*, 161–63.

83. *Old Bailey Proceedings Online* (www.oldbaileyonline.org, version 6.0). For examples of household theft, see the trials of Martha Barker, April 1719 (t17190408-29); Hannah White, January 1743 (t17430114-48); Ann Huntley, January 1727 (t17270113-12); Sarah Merchant, July 1754 (t17540717-50) (accessed December 18, 2011). Barker was transported on the *Margaret* in May 1719; White was transported on the *Justitia* in April 1743; Huntley was transported on the *Rappahannock Merchant* in March 1727.

84. The composite of three categories for these valuables is 19.59 percent of theft types.

85. Gwenda Morgan and Rushton, *Eighteenth-Century Criminal Transportation*, 53.

86. Items stolen in Newcastle-upon-Tyne shown in Gwenda Morgan and Rushton, *Rogues, Thieves and the Rule of Law*, 103 (table 5.5).

87. *Old Bailey Proceedings Online* (www.oldbaileyonline.org, version 6.0), trial of Margaret Fitchett, April 1725 (t17250407-28) (accessed April 6, 2012). Fitchett was transported to Maryland on the *Sukey* in April 1725.

88. The law governing infanticide was 21 James I, c. 27. of 1624.

89. Malcolmson, "Infanticide in Eighteenth Century England," 202.

90. David Kent, "Ubiquitous but Invisible," 125. See also Hill, *Servants*, 53.

91. Picard, *Dr. Johnson's London*, 58–59; *Old Bailey Proceedings Online* (www.oldbaileyonline.org, version 7.0), 1718–1737 (accessed April 6, 2012).

92. *Old Bailey Proceedings Online* (www.oldbaileyonline.org, version 6.0), trial of Ann Terry, May 1744 (t1744 t17440510-8) (accessed January 26, 2012). Terry was transported on the *Savannah* in October 1744. The legal definition of "non compos mentis" is also from this site.

93. Ibid., trial of Elizabeth Burton, October 1718 (t17181015-37) (accessed January 17, 2012). Burton was transported on the *Worcester* in February 1719. Sarah McCabe's crime is related in the *Gentleman's Magazine*, vol. 34, March 1764, 144.

94. *Old Bailey Proceedings Online* (www.oldbaileyonline.org, version 6.0), trial of Sarah Bibby (t17451204-15), December 1745 (accessed December 15, 2011). [Parks] *Virginia*

Gazette, May 29, 1746. Captain Dobbins's letter is dated March 7, 1745 (using the old calendar).

95. Beattie, "The Criminality of Women in Eighteenth Century England," 92. Morgan is listed among the passengers on the *Tryal* in August 1752. Coldham, *The King's Passengers to Maryland and Virginia*, 138.

96. Jenny Diver was executed on March 18, 1741, and Mary Cut and Come Again on March 15, 1745.

97. *Old Bailey Proceedings Online* (www.oldbaileyonline.org, version 6.0), trial of Mary Smith, July 1755 (t17550702-17) (accessed April 13, 2012). See also *Gentleman's Magazine*, vol. 25, July 5, 1755, 328.

98. The *Worcester*, which departed London in February 1719, was one of the first vessels to carry a sizeable number of convicts to Maryland after the act's implementation. On board were fifty-nine men and thirty-nine women who were from London or Middlesex and had been sentenced in the previous four months. Thirty (77 percent) of these women had been convicted of grand larceny or theft from a specified place or dwelling house. The remainder comprised five shoplifters, a pickpocket, a receiver of stolen goods, a housebreaker, and a woman who had been involved in a violent robbery. Four of the women (10.3 percent) were lodgers who had stolen from their landlords and ten (25.6 percent) were servants or apprentices who had stolen from their employers. The effectiveness of the law in punishing women who abused the trust of property owners or their masters and mistresses was evident. More than thirty years later, in December 1752, the *Greyhound* left London for Maryland with seventy-seven men and thirty-six women. The profile of the *Greyhound*'s female convicts was remarkably similar to that of the *Worcester* women. Thirty-five were from London or Middlesex and had been sentenced at the Old Bailey sessions of September, October, and December 1752. These included twenty-one thieves (of clothing, jewelry, and household goods), three receivers of stolen property (watches, watch chains, and household silver), one shoplifter, a pickpocket who had stolen a silver watch, and two burglars. Only one of the convicted women on the *Greyhound* was described specifically as a servant, but it is reasonably clear that another six or seven were servants as well (possibly 23 percent in all). The similarities in the convict cargoes of both ships, one at the beginning and one at the midpoint of the transportation period, indicate how quickly Britain's new punishment regime and shipment system became an established, routine, and reasonably stable feature of colonial labor-supply arrangements.

Chapter 2

1. Devon Record Office, QS 1/15 Order Book 1704–1718, f356 v. Easter, quoted by Gwenda Morgan and Rushton, *Eighteenth-Century Criminal Transportation*, 16.

2. Ibid., 18–19.

3. Hay et al., *Albion's Fatal Tree*, 27–28.

4. Howard, *The State of the Prisons in England and Wales*, 29–31.

5. See the introduction for a description of benefit of clergy and clergyable offenses.

6. Beattie, *Crime and the Courts in England*, 507–8. See also Radzinowicz, *A History of English Criminal Law*, 110–23.

7. Gwenda Morgan and Rushton, *Eighteenth-Century Criminal Transportation*, 38.

8. Ekirch, *Bound for America*, 31.

9. Oldham, *Britain's Convicts to the Colonies*, 12–13.

10. Morris, *Government and Labor in Early America*, 324.

11. *Old Bailey Proceedings Online* (www.oldbaileyonline.org, version 7.0), trial of Sarah Partridge, August 1725 (t17250827-53); trial of Mary Matthews, January 1726 (t17260114-34); trial of John Martin and Mary Mclaughlin, otherwise Mason, otherwise Thomas, September 1745 (t17450911-8); trial of Anne Boswell, January 1747 (t17470116-1) (accessed May 31, 2012).

12. Ibid., trial of Barbara Hensman, otherwise Harman, February 1744 (t17440223-1) (accessed June 23, 2012). Hensman was transported to Maryland on the *Neptune* in February 1744.

13. Hay et al., *Albion's Fatal Tree*, 42–43.

14. Beattie, *Crime and the Courts in England*, 509–10.

15. The comments about Rebecca Stones are mentioned in Coldham, *The Complete Book of Emigrants in Bondage*, 768.

16. Malcolmson, *Life and Labour in England*, 94.

17. Wrigley and Schofield, *The Population History of England*, 25.

18. *Old Bailey Proceedings Online* (www.oldbaileyonline.org, version 6.0), trial of Ann Blackerby, July 1735 (t17350702-20) (accessed December 14, 2011). Blackerby was transported to Maryland on the *John* in December 1735.

19. Ekirch, *Bound for America*, 64.

20. *Old Bailey Proceedings Online* (www.oldbaileyonline.org, version 6.0), trial of Elizabeth Curry, alias Giles, and Rose Curry, February 1732 (t17320223-3) (accessed February 6, 2012).

21. *Old Bailey Proceedings Online* (www.oldbaileyonline.org, version 6.0), trial of Elizabeth Deacon and Mary Watson, February 1731 (t17310224-28) (accessed February 6, 2011); trial of Mary Dew, Margaret Mackmasters, and Elizabeth Cole, alias Majesty Bess, February 1729 (t17290226-55) (accessed June 20, 2012).

22. This information was gathered by cross referencing Old Bailey trial records with the passenger lists contained in Coldham, *The King's Passengers to Maryland and Virginia*. Information on the Reverend Thomas Bray available from the website for London Lives, http://www.londonlives.org/static/StBotolphAldgate.jsp (accessed April 12, 2012).

23. *History of the Press Yard;* Howard, *The State of the Prisons in England and Wales*.

24. *Gentleman's Magazine*, vol. 23, January 1753, 21.

25. Howard, *The State of the Prisons in England and Wales*, section 1, 7–8, 15–16; section 2, 27.

26. Ibid., 2, 15,16. See also the introduction to section 2, 25–27.

27. *Gentleman's Magazine* vol. 27, June 1757, 268. [A] Creole, *The Fortunate Transport*, 29. Though this book is fiction, the details of prison and transportation have the same verisimilitude as Daniel Defoe's *Moll Flanders* and other convict narratives.

28. Coldham, *The Complete Book of Emigrants in Bondage*, 352, 579, 695, 22.

29. All the petitions quoted are from the State Papers Domestic for the reigns of George I, 1714–1727 (SP35), and George II, 1727–1760 (SP36), as indicated, the Public Record Office, Kew, UK.

30. Mary Earland to Duke of Newcastle, November 11, 1724, State Papers Domestic, SP35/53/131, Public Record Office, Kew, UK.

31. *Old Bailey Proceedings Online* (www.oldbaileyonline.org, version 6.0), trial of Catherine Floyd, alias Huggins, September 1739 (t17390906-36) (accessed December 14, 2011). See also Catherine Floyd to the king, September 18, 1739, State Papers Domestic, SP36/48/152, Public Record Office, Kew, UK.

32. See chapters 3 and 7 for more information on Catherine Davis.

33. Daniel and Mary Brown to the King, n.d., State Papers Domestic, SP36/149/19, Public Record Office, Kew, UK (original spelling); petition of Eleanor Connor to the archbishop of Canterbury, n.d. (possibly 1748), State Papers Domestic, SP36/109/45, Public Record Office, Kew, UK.

34. Gwenda Morgan and Rushton, *Rogues, Thieves and the Rule of Law*, 160.

35. Extracted from information listed in Coldham, *The Complete Book of Emigrants in Bondage* and *Supplement to Complete Book of Emigrants in Bondage*.

36. *Old Bailey Proceedings Online* (www.oldbaileyonline.org, version 7.0), trial of Margaret Annis, December 1724 (t17241204-51); trial of Mary Harvey, April 1725 (t17250224-49; trial of Rose Robinson, May 1745 (t17450530-4); trial of Catherine Herring, May 1745 (t17450530-12) (accessed June 23, 2012).

37. Bannet, "The Marriage Act of 1753," 234.

38. *Old Bailey Proceedings Online* (www.oldbaileyonline.org, version 7.0), trial of John Grierson, December 1755 (t17551204-39); trial of John Wilkinson, July 1756 (t17560714-29) (accessed November 23, 2012). Wilkinson died on the passage to Maryland.

39. *Old Bailey Proceedings Online* (www.oldbaileyonline.org, version 7.0), trial of Katherine Dunster and Ann Bowers, December 1725 (t17251208-4); see also trial of Mary Walker, January 1722 (t17220112-37) (accessed April 12, 2012). Bowers was transported to Maryland on the *Supply* in February 1726, and Walker was transported to Maryland on the *Gilbert* in July 1723.

40. Ibid., trial of Elizabeth Ricketts, April 1759 (t17590425-15) (accessed May 30, 2012). Ricketts was transported to Maryland on the *Phoenix* in December 1759.

41. Ibid., trial of Sarah Merchant, otherwise Sarah, wife of Jebus Merchant, otherwise Sarah Saunders, July 1754 (t17540717-50); punishment summary for July 1754 (s17540717-1) (accessed June 4, 2012). See also Sarah Marchant [*sic*] to the king, n.d. (at the end of the reign of George II), State Papers Domestic, SP36/128/112, Public Record Office, Kew, UK.

42. *Old Bailey Proceedings Online* (www.oldbaileyonline.org, version 6.0), trial of Mary Shirley, otherwise Catharine Davis, May 1744 (t17440510-26) (accessed December 15, 2011).

43. Kenneth Morgan, "Petitions against Convict Transportation," 112.

44. *The Ordinary of Newgate: His Account of the Behaviour, Confessions and Dying Words of the Malefactors Who Were Executed on Wednesday the 3rd of This Instant August, 1726, at Tyburn,* 4, *Old Bailey Proceedings Online* (www.oldbaileyonline.org, version 6.0), August 1726 (OA17260803) (accessed December 15, 2011). See also chapter 1.

45. Petition of Scottish prisoner Helen Mortimer, August 17, 1759, quoted in Ekirch, "The Transportation of Scottish Criminals to America during the Eighteenth Century," 372.

46. The results of the 1755 Maryland census were published nine years later in the *Gentleman's Magazine* vol. 34, June 1764, 261.

47. Ackroyd, *London*, 133.

48. *Old Bailey Proceedings Online* (www.oldbaileyonline.org, version 6.0), trial of Mary Johnson, December 1730 (t17301204-54); trial of Constance Buckle, December 1730 (t17301204-74); trial of Mary Smith, December 1730 (t17301204-51); trial of Mary Parsons and Honour Davis, December 1730 (t17301204-47) (accessed February 8, 2012).

49. *Gentleman's Magazine*, vol. 28, June 1758, 285, and vol. 41, October 1771, 470.

50. The information on the *Worcester* and the *Greyhound* was derived by cross-referencing shipping lists with the relevant Old Bailey trial records. Coldham, *The King's Passengers to Maryland and Virginia*, 1–2, 138–39.

51. The *Historical Register* (which ceased publication in 1738) and the *London Magazine* tended to provide more information on the convicts, but the *Gentleman's Magazine* was more regular in its reportage and reached a wider audience.

52. *Gentleman's Magazine*, vol. 2, April 1732, 720. These reports weren't always reliable. "Richard" Wentland was actually Edward Wentland, and neither of the two women who "pleaded their bellies" were found to be pregnant.

53. *Old Bailey Proceedings Online* (www.oldbaileyonline.org, version 6.0), trial of Dorothy Fosset, April 1732 (t17320419-8) and trial of Anne Wentland and Mary Harvey, alias Mackeg, April 1732 (t17320419-7); punishment summary for April 19, 1732 (s17320419-1) (accessed December 15, 2011). Fosset and Wentland were transported to Maryland on the *Caesar* in October 1732.

Chapter 3

1. Abbot Emerson Smith, *Colonists in Bondage*, 109–11. See also Ekirch, "The Transportation of Scottish Criminals to America during the Eighteenth Century," 371.

2. Hugh Thomas, *The Slave Trade*, 292.

3. William Stevenson to James Cheston, January 3, 1769, and December 30, 1769, James Cheston Incoming Letters, 1767–April 1771, Cheston-Galloway Papers, 1644–1888, box 9, Maryland Historical Society, Baltimore.

4. William Stevenson to James Cheston, January 2, 1768, James Cheston Incoming Letters, 1767–April 1771, Cheston-Galloway Papers, 1644–1888, box 9, Maryland Historical Society, Baltimore.

5. Just one example of many letters discussing cargoes of all types is that of Cheston to Stevenson, Randolph & Cheston, July 24, 1770, James Cheston Letterbooks for 1768–1771, Cheston-Galloway Papers, box 8, Maryland Historical Society, Baltimore.

6. William Stevenson to James Cheston, August 5, 1768. James Cheston Incoming Letters, 1767–April 1771, Cheston-Galloway Papers, box 9, Maryland Historical Society, Baltimore. See also Kenneth Morgan, "The Organization of the Convict Trade to Maryland," 207.

7. Kenneth Morgan, "The Organization of the Convict Trade to Maryland," 207.

8. Abbot Emerson Smith, *Colonists in Bondage*, 113–14, 123.

9. John Stewart to the Treasury, December 30, 1762, Treasury Papers, T/416 for 1762, Public Record Office, Kew, UK.

10. Stevenson, Randolph & Cheston to James Cheston, on August 17, 1769, James Cheston Incoming Letters, 1767–April 1771, Cheston-Galloway Papers, box 9, Maryland Historical Society, Baltimore. Comments about securing jailers are contained in letters from Stevenson to Cheston on August 5, 1768 and September 12, 1768.

11. James Cheston Incoming Letters, 1767–April 1771, May–December 1771, and James Cheston Letterbooks for 1768–1771 and 1772–June 1776, Cheston-Galloway Papers, boxes 8, 9 and 10, Maryland Historical Society, Baltimore.

12. Blumenthal, *Brides from Bridewell*, 24.

13. John Stewart to the Treasury, December 30, 1762, Treasury Papers, T/416 for 1762, Public Record Office, Kew, UK.

14. Browne, *Archives of Maryland*, 6:294.

15. Britton, *Historical Records of New South Wales*, 42, 44.

16. James Cheston Letterbook, 1772–June 1776, Cheston-Galloway Papers, box 8, Maryland Historical Society, Baltimore. Various letters in box 8 describe Stevenson's action.

17. Latimer, *Annals of Bristol in the Eighteenth Century*, 150–51. See also Gwenda Morgan and Rushton, *Eighteenth-Century Criminal Transportation*, 56.

18. Gwenda Morgan and Rushton, *Eighteenth-Century Criminal Transportation*, 17.

19. Horatio Sharpe to Hugh Hammersley, July 27, 1767, and Horatio Sharpe to Cecilius Calvert, Lord Baltimore, October 20, 1755, in Browne, *Archives of Maryland*, 9:413, 6:294.

20. *Historical Register*, July 1719. The women's crimes recorded in *Old Bailey Proceedings Online* (www.oldbaileyonline.org, version 6.0), trial of Susannah Cook, July 1719 (t17190708-55); trial of Elizabeth Curry, July 1719 (t17190708-19); trial of Elizabeth Dawson, July 1719 (t17190708-51) (accessed December 16, 2011).

21. Coldham, *The Complete Book of Emigrants in Bondage*, 426.

22. *Gentleman's Magazine*, vol. 6, May 1736, 290. See also Duncan Campbell to the Keeper of His Majesty's Gaol of Maidstone, July 16, 1772, Duncan Campbell Business Letterbook, vol. 1 (1772–1776), 37. Dixson Collection, State Library of New South Wales (Mitchell Library), Sydney.

23. Kenneth Morgan, "The Organization of the Convict Trade to Maryland," 213. Regarding Irish convicts, see Kenneth Morgan's review of Ekirch's *Bound for America*, "Convict Transportation to America," 30.

24. *Gentleman's Magazine*, vol. 36, May 1736, 290.

25. *The Ordinary of Newgate: His Account of the Behaviour, Confessions and Dying Words of the Malefactors Who Were Executed on Wednesday the 3rd of This Instant August, 1726, at Tyburn, Old Bailey Proceedings Online* (www.oldbaileyonline.org, version 6.0), March 18, 1741 (OA17410318) (accessed February 9, 2012). Jenny Diver was transported to Virginia as Mary Webb in June 1728 and as Jane Webb in June 1738. From the ordinary's (unreliable) account, it seems her story about being treated well on board relates to the 1728 transportation. See also Defoe, *Moll Flanders*, 396–97.

26. *London Magazine*, vol. 33, June 2, 1764, quoted in Oldham, *Britain's Convicts to the Colonies*, 17–18.

27. *Old Bailey Proceedings Online* (www.oldbaileyonline.org, version 6.0), trial of Mary Smith, Mary Parsons, John Duncumb, and Sarah Topham, June 1773 (T17730626-31) (accessed February 7, 2012). The evidence given at this trial provides a glimpse at the mob. The date given in the evidence was cross-referenced with shipping information in Coldham's

The King's Passengers to Maryland and Virginia, 242. All the offenders were sentenced to transportation and were carried to Virginia on the *Tayloe* in July 1773.

28. *Maryland Gazette*, August 20, 1752. This contains a report from Bristol datelined May 2, 1752.

29. Gwenda Morgan and Rushton, *Rogues, Thieves and the Rule of Law*, 130, 132.

30. Defoe, *Moll Flanders*, 386.

31. Quoted by Sollers in "Transported Convict Laborers in Maryland during the Colonial Period," 41. The visitor was a correspondent of a George Selwyn, who was Governor Horatio Sharpe's agent in London.

32. Shipping information is drawn from the *Maryland Shipping Returns, 1746–1775*, in Ekirch, *Bound for America*, 98. Information about the *Anne* in Blumenthal, *Brides from Bridewell*, 21. Information about the *Eagle* in Hugh Thomas, *The Slave Trade*, 660.

33. *Gentleman's Magazine*, vol. 38, May 1768, 241.

34. Duncan Campbell's evidence to a House of Commons committee looking into prisons, *Journals of the House of Commons* (November 26, 1778–August 24, 1780), 27:311.

35. There are several mentions of convict loads in James Cheston's correspondence. These examples are in letters from James Cheston to Stevenson, Randolph & Cheston on August 5, 1770, and August 22, 1770, James Cheston Letterbook, 1768–1771, Cheston-Galloway Papers, box 8, Maryland Historical Society, Baltimore. See also Gwenda Morgan and Rushton, *Eighteenth-Century Criminal Transportation*, 57.

36. James Cheston to Stevenson, Randolph & Cheston, October 10, 1770, James Cheston Letterbook, 1768–June 1771, Cheston-Galloway Papers, box 8, Maryland Historical Society, Baltimore; notice of sale of imported goods by James Houston, *Maryland Gazette*, December 8, 1757.

37. *Old Bailey Proceedings Online* (www.oldbaileyonline.org, version 7.0), trial of Mary Allen, April 1757 (t17570420-38); trial of Catherine Bourne, April 1757 (t17570420-51); trial of Rachel Dimsdale, April 1757 (t17570420-26); trial of Hannah Fordham, April 1757 (t17570420-41); trial of Sarah Gascoynek May 1757 (t17570526-12) (accessed June 5, 2012).

38. Defoe, *Moll Flanders*, 387.

39. The *Trial* may have been a different vessel from the *Tryal*, which was one of Duncan Campbell's ships. The *Tryal* deposited convicts in Maryland in June 1757 and could have been back in Britain by the end of the year, but there is no landing certificate connecting it with a voyage in December 1757.

40. Copy of letter from Goronwy Owen to Richard Morris, "Ar fwrdd y Trial yn Spithead, Rhagfyr 12, 1757" (December 12, 1757), manuscript NLW MS. 474E, National Library of Wales, Aberystwyth. Welsh translated by S. A. C Jones, April 2012. Original: "Dynion bawaidd aruthr yw Dynion y Môr. Duw fo'n geidwad, mae pob un o naddunt wedi cymeryd iddo gyffoden o fysg y Lladronesau ac nid ydynt yn gwneud gwaith ond cnuchio'n rhyferig ymhob congl o'r llong. Dyma 5 neu 6 o naddunt wedi cael y Clwy' tinboeth (na b'ond ei grybwyll!) oddiwrth y merched. Ac nid oes yma Feddyg yn y byd ond y fi sydd a Llyfr y Dr. Shaw genyf, ac yn ol hwnw y byddaf yn clyttio rhywfaint arnynt a'r hen Gyffiriau sydd yn y Gist yma."

41. Ibid. Original: "Y mae yma '(n y Caban) un o honynt, ond i weini pidyn y Gwr yma, nid i wasnaethu fy ngwraig i y deuwyd a hi yma."

42. Duncan Campbell to Dr. John Patterson, June 6, 1771, Duncan Campbell Private Letterbooks, vol. 7 (1766–1772), 93, Dixson Collection, State Library of New South Wales (Mitchell Library), Sydney. Somervell's name is also spelled "Somerville."

43. The account of Catherine Davidson is from the *Pennsylvania Gazette*, February 13, 1750, Kenneth Scott and Clarke, *Abstracts from the "Pennsylvania Gazette," 1748–1755. Old Bailey Proceedings Online* (www.oldbaileyonline.org, version 6.0), trial of Catherine Davidson and William Wilks, September 1748 (t17480907-53) (accessed 17 December 2011). Davidson was transported to Maryland on the *Thames* in August 1749.

44. Britton, *Historical Records of New South Wales*, 51.

45. *Old Bailey Proceedings Online* (www.oldbaileyonline.org, version 6.0), trial of Mary Cooper, May 1718 (t17180530-33); trial of Mary Hunt, October 1717 (t17171016-23); trial of Mary Jones, July 1717 (t17170717-20); trial of Mary Willoughby, July 1717 (t17170717-5); punishment summary for Mary Adsey, January 1718 (s17180110-1) (accessed January 15, 2012).

46. Shaw, *Calendar of Treasury Papers*, 591.

47. Abbot Emerson Smith, *Colonists in Bondage*, 128.

48. See chapter 1 for an account of the French interception of the *Plain Dealer* in 1745/46.

49. Abbot Emerson Smith, *Colonists in Bondage*, 126.

50. *Journals of the House of Commons* (November 26, 1778–August 24, 1780), 27:311.

51. Howard, *The State of the Prisons*, Section 1, 17; Coldham, *King's Passengers to Maryland and Virginia*, 131.

52. Beers and Berkow, *The Merck Manual of Diagnosis and Therapy*, section 2, no. 3.

53. Coventry City Records of Transportation, quoted in Coldham, *Emigrants in Chains*, 79.

54. James Cheston to Stevenson, Randolph & Cheston, October 1773, James Cheston Letterbook, 1772–June 1776, Cheston-Galloway Papers, box 8, Maryland Historical Society, Baltimore, 104.

55. *Gottlieb Mittelberger's Journey to Pennsylvania in the Year 1750 and Return to Germany on the Year 1754*, 20, http://archive.org/stream/gottlichmittelbe01mitt/gottlichmittelbe-01mitt_djvu.txt (accessed June 26, 2013).

56. Description of conditions on the *Rodney, Gentleman's Magazine*, vol. 38, May 1768, 241. See also Defoe, *Moll Flanders*, 386.

57. High Court of Admiralty: Oyer and Terminer Records, HCA 1/19, Public Record Office, Kew, UK: evidence in hearing of charges in relation to Captain John Sargent; High Court of Admiralty Oyer and Terminer Records, HCA 1/57, Public Record Office, Kew, UK: evidence in hearing of charges in relation to Captain Barnett Bond. See also Mittelberger, *Journey to Pennsylvania in the Year 1750 and Return to Germany on the Year 1754*, http://archive.org/stream/gottlichmittelbe01mitt/gottlichmittelbe01mitt_djvu.txt (accessed June 26, 2013), 23.

58. High Court of Admiralty: Oyer and Terminer Records, HCA 1/57, Public Record Office, Kew, UK: evidence in hearing of charges in relation to Captain Barnett Bond.

59. Meacham, "'They Will Be Adjudged by Their Drinke,'" 208.

60. Blumenthal, *Brides from Bridewell*, 23–24.

61. Copy of letter from Goronwy Owen to Richard Morris, "Ar fwrdd y Trial yn Spit-

head, Rhagfyr 12, 1757" (December 12, 1757), manuscript NLW MS. 474E, National Library of Wales, Aberystwyth. Original: "Y mae yn gorfod arnom erys pythefnos yfed Dwr drewllyd neu dagu (canys nid oes Diferyn o Ddiod fain yn y llong)."

62. *Maryland Gazette*, January 3, 1750.

63. Ibid.

64. *Maryland Gazette*, August 23, 1764, October 25, 1764.

65. *Old Bailey Proceedings Online* (www.oldbaileyonline.org, version 7.0), trial of Catherine Davis and Jane Canwell, September 1742 (t17420909-29) (accessed June 25, 2012). See also High Court of Admiralty: Oyer and Terminer Records, HCA 1/19: Criminal Papers, 1735–1744, Public Record Office, Kew, UK. Davis is an elusive character; a serial offender, she had multiple aliases and convictions. See chapter 7 for further details of her criminal career. There is no mention of Lewis Davis in the trial records, only in the Admiralty papers, but as both he and Henry Huggins were periwig makers, it is likely they were either one and the same person or close colleagues.

66. Steerage was the area of the after part of the quarterdeck in front of the main cabin from which the ship was originally steered. Contrary to modern usage, to travel in steerage was to have one of the best berths on a ship. Explanation included in the explanatory notes by David Blewett in Defoe, *Moll Flanders*, 453n430.

67. High Court of Admiralty: Oyer and Terminer Records, HCA 1/19, Public Record Office, Kew, UK: Evidence of John Johnstoun and Richard Gawdon in hearing of charges in relation to Captain John Sargent.

68. *Old Bailey Proceedings Online* (www.oldbaileyonline.org, version 6.0), trial of Hannah White, January 1743 (t17430114-48) (accessed December 17, 2011).

69. Ibid., trial of Dorothy Roberts, February 1743 (t17430223-1) (accessed December 17, 2011); trial of Margaret Robinson, October 1742 (t17421013-10) (accessed December 17, 2011).

70. High Court of Admiralty: Oyer and Terminer Records, HCA 1/57, Public Record Office, Kew, UK: Evidence of James Corrie, John Wright and William Warner in hearing of charges in relation to Captain Barnett Bond. Bond was acquitted after his jury trial at the Old Bailey.

71. Governor Horatio Sharpe to Hugh Hammersley, July 27, 1767, in Browne, *Archives of Maryland*, 9:411.

72. Ibid., 9:413.

73. Stevenson to Cheston, April 9, 1768, James Cheston Incoming Letters, 1767–April 1771, Cheston-Galloway Papers, box 9, Maryland Historical Society, Baltimore.

74. James Cheston to Stevenson, Randolph & Cheston, December 23, 1773, James Cheston Letterbook, 1772–June 1776, Cheston-Galloway Papers, box 8, Maryland Historical Society, Baltimore, 104.

75. In 1766 Maryland's Assembly passed *An Act to Oblige Ships Coming into This Province to Perform Quarantine*. This required captains to swear an oath that there was no illness on board.

76. Duncan Campbell Business Letterbook, vol. 1 (1772–1776), 665. Dixson Collection, State Library of New South Wales (Mitchell Library), Sydney.

77. Bailyn, *Voyagers to the West*, 326.

78. This is alluded to in a letter from William Stevenson to James Cheston dated No-

vember 21, 1769, James Cheston Incoming Letters, 1767–April 1771, Cheston-Galloway Papers, box 9, Maryland Historical Society, Baltimore.

79. Beattie, *Crime and the Courts in England*, 519.

Chapter 4

1. For a full description of the founding of Maryland and the settlement principles of Lord Baltimore, see Meyers, *Common Whores, Vertuous Women, and Loveing Wives*, 9–38.

2. In Britain, the Glorious Revolution of 1688 saw the overthrow of the Catholic king James II, the beginning of the joint reign of the staunchly Protestant monarchs William and Mary, and the onset of nearly sixty years of intermittent insurgent action by Jacobites.

3. Meyers, *Common Whores, Vertuous Women, and Loveing Wives*, 35.

4. Dunn, "Masters, Servants and Slaves in the Colonial Chesapeake and the Caribbean," 261–63.

5. Browne, *Archives of Maryland*, 6:329.

6. Oxley, *Convict Maids*, 198–201. See also derogatory epithets in runaway advertisements—e.g., *Maryland Gazette*, April 11, 1771 (Anne Bailey), July 2, 1767 (Mary Owens), and October 22, 1772 (Catherine Pardon).

7. Cecilius Calvert to Governor Horatio Sharpe, December 23, 1755, in Browne, *Archives of Maryland*, 6:329.

8. Browne, *Archives of Maryland*, 33:345, 349–50.

9. Jensen, *English Historical Documents*, 462; Bacon, *Laws of Maryland, 1723*, chapter 6, appendix 6.

10. Copy of Maryland census taken in 1755, *Gentleman's Magazine*, vol. 34, June, 261.

11. Jensen, *English Historical Documents*, 463.

12. Browne, *Archives of Maryland*, 35:213.

13. Ibid., 25:425–27.

14. Bacon, *Laws of Maryland, 1728*, chapter 23.

15. Browne, *Archives of Maryland*, 6:294–95, 328–29, 422.

16. Bacon, *Laws of Maryland, 1751*, chapter 11.

17. *Maryland Gazette*, August 21, 1751, October 16, 1751.

18. Bacon, *Laws of Maryland, 1743*, chapter 9.

19. *Maryland Gazette*, July 9, 1767, July 30, 1767, August 20, 1767.

20. A calculation made from information in Morris, *Government and Labor in Early America*, 315n, quoted in Kenneth Morgan, "Convict Runaways in Maryland," 254. Fogleman, "From Slaves, Convicts, and Servants to Free Passengers," 58, claims that, by the middle of the eighteenth century, convicts comprised at least one-quarter of all British migration to the American colonies and one-half of all English migration.

21. Browne, *Archives of Maryland*, 9:412.

22. *Maryland Shipping Returns, 1746–1775*, in Ekirch, *Bound for America*, 121.

23. Letter 1, September 1, 1769, in Eddis, *Letters from America*, 7–8.

24. James Cheston to Stevenson, Randolph & Cheston, June 21, 1774, James Cheston Letterbook, 1772–1776, Cheston-Galloway Papers, box 8, Maryland Historical Society, Baltimore.

25. Factors mentioned in Browne, *Archives of Maryland*, 25:435.

26. Ringgold's role as agent is mentioned in ibid., 9:421.

27. Report of the subcommittee that examined the ship *Johnston*, her papers, and log-book, at a meeting of the Committee of Observation for Talbot County, on Friday, the 7th of July, 1775, Maryland, Talbot County Committee; Bracco, John [S4-V2-p1104], http://lincoln.lib.niu.edu/cgi-bin/philologic/getobject.pl?c.3990:1.amarch (accessed April 21, 2012).

28. Goadby, *An Apology for the Life of Mr. Bampfylde-Moore Carew*, 107.

29. *Maryland Gazette*, April 29, 1756, December 10, 1761, November 18, 1762, July 21, 1757, June 30, 1768.

30. James Cheston to Stevenson, Randolph & Cheston, June 22, 1770, James Cheston Letterbook, 1768–1771, Cheston-Galloway Papers, box 8, Maryland Historical Society, Baltimore.

31. James Cheston to Stevenson, Randolph & Cheston, March 12, 1774. James Cheston Letterbook, 1772–June 1776, Cheston-Galloway Papers, box 8, Maryland Historical Society, Baltimore.

32. *Gentleman's Magazine*, vol. 34, June 1764, 261.

33. Kenneth Morgan, "The Organization of the Convict Trade to Maryland," 105.

34. Bailyn, *Voyagers to the West*, 324.

35. William Barker Jr. to John Palmer, December 16, 1758, quoted in Ekirch, *Bound for America*, 122.

36. This is a perceptive observation in Jordan and Walsh, *White Cargo*, 252. See also Grubb, "The Market Evaluation of Criminality," 300n28.

37. Rind's *Virginia Gazette*, July 26, 1770. This was a comment in a runaway advertisement for four servants placed by Charles Hammond Jr. and Ephraim Howard, son of Henry.

38. Abbot Emerson Smith, *Colonists in Bondage*, 221; Goadby, *An Apology for the Life of Mr. Bampfylde-Moore Carew*, 107.

39. Butler, "British Convicts Shipped to American Colonies."

40. Advertisement for James Griffiths, *Maryland Gazette*, July 21, 1757.

41. Revel, *The Poor Unhappy Felon's Sorrowful Account*. Although a real James Revel was transported to America in 1771 on the *Thornton*, Peter Rushton and Gwenda Morgan have proposed *(Eighteenth-century Criminal Transportation*, 89–92) that the narrative may have been a fictional fabrication by someone hoping to replicate the success of other tales of "notorious transported felons" such as *Moll Flanders*. Nevertheless, most of the details in the verses are sufficiently realistic to suggest they were informed by actual reports of transportation and the circumstances of post-arrival servitude.

42. Elizabeth B. Anderson, *Annapolis*, 17.

43. Ibid.; letter 2, October 1, 1769, in Eddis, *Letters from America*, 13. See also Papenfuse, *In Pursuit of Profit*, 14.

44. Land, *Colonial Maryland*, 120–21. See also http://www.chestertown.com/places (accessed April 18, 2012) and the photograph of Ringgold's house in chapter 8.

45. Letter 6, September 20, 1769, in Eddis, *Letters from America*, 36.

46. Defoe, *Moll Flanders*, 381.

47. James Cheston Letterbook, 1772–June 1776, Cheston-Galloway Papers, box 8, Maryland Historical Society, Baltimore.

48. Coldham, *The King's Passengers to Maryland and Virginia*, 255–57, cross-referenced with Coldham, *The Complete Book of Emigrants in Bondage*, 394, 666.

49. Coldham, *Emigrants in Chains*, 144.

50. James Cheston to Anthony Stewart, April 5, 1773, and James Cheston to John Chapman, April 5, 1773, James Cheston Letterbook, 1772–April 1776, Cheston-Galloway Papers, box 8, Maryland Historical Society, Baltimore.

51. Thomas Smyth to James Cheston, November 1774, James Cheston Incoming Letters, July–December 1774, Cheston-Galloway Papers, box 14, Maryland Historical Society, Baltimore.

52. Dunn, "The Recruitment and Employment of Labor," 171.

53. Harrower, "Diary of John Harrower," entry for May 16, 1774 (spelling original).

54. Coldham, *The King's Passengers to Maryland and Virginia*, 255–61. Bolton and Williams may have been unconvicted indentured servants.

55. Williams, *A History of Washington County*, 11.

56. Bailyn, *Voyagers to the West*, 346–49.

57. James Cheston to Stevenson, Randolph & Cheston, June 21, 1774, James Cheston Letterbook, 1772–June 1776, Cheston-Galloway Papers, box 8, Maryland Historical Society, Baltimore.

58. Kenneth Morgan, "The Organization of the Convict Trade to Maryland," 219. A Maryland law of 1715 specified that freedom dues of clothing and tools for male servants and clothing for women had to be paid to indentured servants upon completion of their terms. It is not clear whether this applied to convict servants after 1718.

59. Grubb, "The Market Evaluation of Criminality," 298. See also Atkinson, "The Free-Born Englishman Transported," 97.

60. Grubb, "The Market Evaluation of Criminality," 302.

61. Duncan Campbell's evidence to a House of Commons committee looking into prisons, *Journals of the House of Commons* (November 26, 1778–August 24, 1780), 27:311.

62. See Moale's advertisements in the *Maryland Gazette*, July 3, 1760, July 9, 1761.

63. James Cheston to Stevenson, Randolph & Cheston, 2 April 1774, James Cheston Letterbook, 1772–June 1776, Cheston-Galloway Papers, box 8, Maryland Historical Society, Baltimore.

64. These examples are drawn from the letterbooks of James Cheston, Matthew Ridley, and George Woolsey and are quoted by Bailyn, *Voyagers to the West*, 333–34.

65. Ibid. See also Grubb, "The Market Evaluation of Criminality," 300.

66. All occupations derived from court records or runaway advertisements in the *Maryland Gazette*.

67. Wilstach, *Tidewater Maryland*, 90.

68. James Cheston to Stevenson, Randolph & Cheston, April 2, 1774, James Cheston Letterbook, 1772–June 1776, Cheston-Galloway Papers, box 8, Maryland Historical Society, Baltimore.

69. Kenneth Morgan, "The Organization of the Convict Trade to Maryland," 219.

70. James Cheston to Stevenson, Randolph & Cheston, June 28, 1775, James Cheston Letterbook, 1772–June 1776, Cheston-Galloway Papers, box 8, Maryland Historical Society, Baltimore.

71. Cole, "A White Woman, of Middle Age, Would Be Preferred," 83. Cole discusses

the qualities (revealed by advertising) sought by women when selecting a nursemaid where there were multiple servant options—slave, mulatto, white—available.

72. Galenson, *White Servitude in Colonial America*, 272; Land, "Economic Base and Social Structure," 644; Kellow, "Indentured Servitude in Eighteenth Century Maryland," 239–40.

73. Coldham, *The King's Passengers to Maryland*, 2–5 (sale information for the *Margaret*, September 1719), 255–58 (sale information for the *Elizabeth*), 260–61 (sale information for the *Isabella*). The owners have been identified in the *Maryland Gazette*, in Coldham, *Settlers of Maryland*, in wills and estate inventories, and in histories such as Land, *Colonial Maryland*.

74. Elizabeth B. Anderson, *Annapolis*, 36; Land, *Colonial Maryland*, 158–60.

75. Advertisement for Mary Rider, *Maryland Gazette*, April 19, 1749.

76. Flanagan, "The Sweets of Independence," 297–300.

77. *Old Bailey Proceedings Online* (www.oldbaileyonline.org, version 7.0), trial of Winifred Haynes, April 1719 (t17190408-31); trial of Martha Barker, April 1719 (t17190408-29) (accessed June 20, 2012). Carter and Welch are mentioned in Coldham, *Settlers of Maryland*, 111, 707.

78. Information on Joseph Pettibone from Cotton, *Maryland Calendar of Wills*.

79. Surrey Quarter Sessions Proceedings, 1718, Surrey History Centre, QS2/6. Indictment for Abigail Green alias Harvey, October 5, 1718.

80. Land, *Colonial Maryland*, 158–60.

81. Gustavus Hesselius (1682–1755) was a Swedish portrait painter who had migrated to America.

82. Hoffman, *Princes of Ireland, Planters of Maryland*, 109, 231–32, 258.

83. Advertisement for Anna Norman, *Pennsylvania Gazette*, October 23, 1746; advertisement for Frances Barret, *Maryland Journal*, November 4, 1780, November 11, 1780.

84. Hoffman, *Princes of Ireland, Planters of Maryland*, 235–39; *Maryland Gazette*, August 9, 1759, June 11, 1761.

85. Advertisement for Ann Wilson, *Maryland Gazette*, November 2 and December 21, 1775; advertisement for William Manly, *Maryland Gazette*, May 9 and May 30, 1776.

86. Information on Francis and William Deakins derived from the following publications: Patricia A. Anderson, *Frederick County Maryland Land Records*, 55 (abstracted from land records in Maryland State Archives, microfilm rolls CR37, 515, and CR 37,516, January 2003); Bowie, *Across the Years in Prince George's County*, 737; Gude, *Where the Potomac Begins*, 20; James W. Thomas and Williams, *History of Allegany County*, 4–7, 102, 178; Tracey and Dern, *Pioneers of Old Monocacy*, 126, 261; Williams and McKinsey, *History of Frederick County*, 85–86; U.S. Government, *First Census of the United States, Montgomery County, MD*, 90.

87. Coldham, *The King's Passengers to Maryland and Virginia*, 255–58. See also Coldham, *Settlers of Maryland*, 174–75.

88. Brugger, *Maryland*, 103; James Cheston to Stevenson, Randolph & Cheston, July 24, 1770, James Cheston Letterbook, 1768–1771, Cheston-Galloway Papers, box 8, Maryland Historical Society, Baltimore.

89. Coldham, *The King's Passengers to Maryland and Virginia*, 256–57.

90. Purchaser information gathered from the *Maryland Gazette*, August 28, 1760, May

28, 1752, October 6, 1757, October 17, 1768, August 23, 1745, January 21, 1768, April 20, 1748, and November 8, 1764.

91. Landholding information on Owings and Hamilton from Coldham, *Settlers of Maryland*, List of Settlers, 500, 288. See chapter 5, notes 87 and 89 for details of Ellis and Humphreys.

92. Land, "Economic Base and Social Structure," 644.

93. Kimber, "Itinerant Observations in America," 329; Revel, *The Poor Unhappy Felon's Sorrowful Account*, 191.

94. Kellow, "Indentured Servitude in Eighteenth Century Maryland," 247.

95. Atkinson, "The Free-Born Englishman Transported," 97.

96. Bacon, *Laws of Maryland, 1715*, chapter 40, 21.

Chapter 5

1. Atkinson, "The Free-Born Englishman Transported, 97.

2. Papenfuse, *In Pursuit of Profit*, 5.

3. Carr, "Diversification in the Chesapeake," 356–57.

4. Headlam, *Calendar of State Papers, 1720–1721*, 129–31, 420–21. Also James Brooks to the Lords of Trade and Plantations, June 1, 1774.

5. Skaggs, *Roots of Maryland Democracy*, 39–46.

6. Newton, *Calendar of State Papers, 1732–1733*, 49. On March 1, 1733, Sir William Janssen, principal secretary to the lord proprietor, submitted *A Short Account of the Province of Maryland* to the Council of Trade and Plantations. See also Carr, "Diversification in the Chesapeake," 342.

7. Governor John Seymour to the Board of Trade, quoted in Land, *Colonial Maryland*, 106.

8. The figures for 1720 and 1770 are given in Land, *Colonial Maryland*, 120, 274. The figures for 1755 were based on a formal census, the results of which were published in the *Gentleman's Magazine*, vol. 34, June 1764, 261.

9. Skaggs, *Roots of Maryland Democracy*, 35.

10. Ibid., 50.

11. Thomas Hughes, *History of the Society of Jesus in North America*, vol. 2, 551.

12. Quoted by Kulikoff, *Tobacco and Slaves*, 47–48.

13. Clemens, "The Operation of an Eighteenth Century Chesapeake Tobacco Plantation," 524. See also Robert, *The Story of Tobacco in America*, 17–18.

14. Land, "Economic Base and Social Structure," 644.

15. Bacon, *Laws of Maryland, 1715*, chapter 15, paragraph 5.

16. Kellow, "Indentured Servitude in Eighteenth Century Maryland," 247–50. See also *Proposals for a Tobacco Law in the Province of Maryland*.

17. Main, *Tobacco Colony*, 108.

18. McCormac, *White Servitude in Colonial Maryland*, 72, 75–76.

19. Elizabeth Sprigs to John Sprigs, September 22, 1756, High Court of Admiralty: Oyer and Terminer Records, HCA/30/258, no. 106, Public Record Office, Kew, UK. See also Revel, *The Poor Unhappy Felon's Sorrowful Account*, 194.

20. http://www.nationalarchives.gov.uk/pathways/blackhistory/culture/representing.htm (accessed December 30, 2011).

21. *Old Bailey Proceedings Online* (www.oldbaileyonline.org, version 7.0), trial of Elizabeth Jones, April 1735 (t17350416-29) (accessed June 12, 2012).

22. Advertisement for Elizabeth Willoughby, *Maryland Gazette*, October 17, 1750; advertisement for Anne Sayer, *Maryland Gazette*, October 6, 1757.

23. Advertisement for Anna Maria Norman, *Pennsylvania Gazette*, October 23, 1746.

24. Defoe, *A Tour through the Whole Island of Great Britain*, vol. 1, 218–19.

25. Marshall, *The Rural Economy of Yorkshire*, 303.

26. Letter 5, June 8, 1770, in Eddis, *Letters from America*, 36.

27. Advertisements for runaways, *Maryland Gazette*, September 30, 1746, September 21, 1752; advertisement for Grace Jones, *Maryland Journal*, October 5, 1779, October 26, 1779.

28. Advertisements for Sarah Davis, *Maryland Gazette*, April 27, 1758, May 11, 1758.

29. Mount Harmon at Earleville in Cecil County overlooks the Sassafras River and preserves three buildings from a medium-sized eighteenth-century tobacco plantation.

30. Coldham, *The King's Passengers to Maryland and Virginia*, 261; advertisement for John and Mary McCreary, *Maryland Gazette*, May 11, 1758; advertisement for Jacksons, *Pennsylvania Gazette*, July 19, 1750.

31. Quoted from a letter written by Talbot County planter Henry Hollyday, in Daniel Blake Smith, *Inside the Great House*, 251. See also Main, *Tobacco Colony*, 111n27.

32. Lieutenant Governor Hart to Council of Trade and Plantations (London), August 25, 1720, in Headlam, *Calendar of State Papers, 1720–1721*, 129.

33. Letter 9 December 24, 1771, in Eddis, *Letters from America*, 57.

34. Main, *Tobacco Colony*, 197.

35. *Old Bailey Proceedings Online* (www.oldbaileyonline.org, version 6.0), trial of Joseph Rashfield and Elizabeth Field, October 1726 (t17261012-3) (accessed April 19, 2012). See also Peden, *St. John's and St. George's Parish Registers*, 28.

36. *Maryland Gazette*, January 24, 1750 ("winter fever"), January 16, 1752 (smallpox), July 9, 1767, July 30, 1767, August 20, 1767 (jail fever).

37. Lieutenant Governor Ogle to Council of Trade and Plantations (London), in Headlam, *Calendar of State Papers, 1734–1735*, 254.

38. Brown, *Good Wives, Nasty Wenches and Anxious Patriarchs*, 354.

39. Advertisement placed by James MacGill, *Maryland Gazette*, December 12, 1757.

40. Beers and Berkow, *The Merck Manual of Diagnosis and Therapy*, 1242; Carter, *Diary*, 627.

41. Breslaw, "From Edinburgh to Annapolis," 409, 414; advertisements for Jesuit's Bark, *Maryland Gazette*, May 3, 1745, May 10, 1745.

42. Berkin, *Revolutionary Mothers*, 6–7.

43. When convict servant Winifred Jones was prosecuted in Baltimore County Court in August 1725, in June 1728, and in November 1733, she was described as a "servant to Thomas Sheredine in Annapolis." She also worked at his Baltimore County property. See note 91 below for further details of Jones. See also (regarding Thomas Sheredine) *Maryland Gazette*, April 26, 1745, May 22, 1751, May 28, 1752; and Scharf, *History of Western Maryland*, 456.

44. For a discussion of urban and rural households in the eighteenth century, see Wulf, *Not All Wives*, 88–102.

45. Runaway advertisement for Hannah Boyer placed by Catherine Jenings, *Maryland Gazette*, May 28, 1752.

46. Revel, *The Poor Unhappy Felon's Sorrowful Account*, 191.

47. Meacham, "'They Will Be Adjudged by Their Drinke,'" 212–13. See also Boydston, *Home and Work*, 12–14.

48. Clemens, "The Operation of an Eighteenth Century Chesapeake Tobacco Plantation," 525. See also Daniel Blake Smith, *Inside the Great House*, 59; Miller, "An Archaeological Perspective on Diet."

49. Coldham, *The King's Passengers to Maryland and Virginia*, 4, 261. McCarty may have been an unconvicted indentured servant.

50. Advertisements placed by Alice Davis, Ann Milton, Sarah Monro, Rachel Pottenger, and Catharine Jenings, *Maryland Gazette*, November 15, 1764, November 22, 1764, October 6, 1757, April 1, 1746, May 6, 1746, July 19, 1753, August 23, 1753, November 13, 1751; advertisement for Elizabeth Crowder, *Maryland Gazette*, April 1, 1746, May 6, 1746.

51. Brown, *Good Wives, Nasty Wenches and Anxious Patriarchs*, 299.

52. *Maryland Gazette*, January 19, 1764.

53. Land, "Economic Base and Social Structure," 642.

54. Kalman, *The Kitchen*, 13–25, 31.

55. Inventory of William Wood, appraised by Richard Caswell and Thomas Dulany, Baltimore County Inventories 6:26, Maryland State Archives, Annapolis; *Old Bailey Proceedings Online* (www.oldbaileyonline.org, version 7.0), trial of Barbara Black, February 21, 1733 (t17330221-16) (accessed June 2, 2012).

56. Land, *Colonial Maryland*, 74. See also Williams, *A History of Washington County*, 12.

57. Deetz, *In Small Things Forgotten*, 33.

58. Land, "Economic Base and Social Structure," 644.

59. Cotton, *Maryland Calendar of Wills, 1726 to 1732.*

60. Main, *Tobacco Colony*, 115.

61. Hammond, *Leah and Rachel*, 11.

62. Dunn, "Masters, Servants and Slaves in the Colonial Chesapeake and the Caribbean," 262; Yentsch, *A Chesapeake Family and Their Slaves*, 166.

63. Coldham, *Settlers of Maryland*, 157.

64. Elizabeth Sprigs to John Sprigs, September 22, 1756, High Court of Admiralty: Oyer and Terminer Records, HCA/30/258, no. 106, Public Record Office, Kew, UK.

65. Thomas Hughes, *History of the Society of Jesus in North America*, vol. 1, 342.

66. [A] Creole, *The Fortunate Transport*, 32.

67. Letter 6, September 20, 1770, in Eddis, *Letters from America*, 38.

68. Ibid.

69. Ibid., 37.

70. Main, *Tobacco Colony*, 202.

71. Ellefson, *The Private Punishment of Servants and Slaves in Eighteenth-Century Maryland*, 26. See also Bacon, *Laws of Maryland, 1715*, chapter 19, paragraphs 12–13.

194 / Notes to Pages 98–100

72. Ellefson, *The Private Punishment of Servants and Slaves in Eighteenth-Century Maryland*, 9.

73. Bacon, *Laws of Maryland, 1715,* chapter 44, paragraph 31. This clause gave the provincial and county courts the authority to determine complaints between masters and servants. Atkinson, "The Free-Born Englishman Transported," 104; *Old Bailey Proceedings Online* (www.oldbaileyonline.org, version 6.0), trial of Elizabeth Whitney, alias Dribray, February 1740 (accessed December 26, 2011); Baltimore County Court (Proceedings), Liber 1742–1743: TB D 1, MSA C400-19:122, Liber 1728–1730: HWS 6, MSA C400-13:93, Maryland State Archives, Annapolis.

74. *Maryland Gazette,* August 4, 1747.

75. Bacon, *Laws of Maryland, 1715,* chapter 27, paragraphs 2–6; and *1749,* chapter 12, paragraph 6. For a discussion of sexual norms in Maryland at this time, see Cardno, "'The Fruit of Nine, Sue Kindly Brought.'"

76. Genealogists such as (for example) Robert Andrew Oszakiewski have carefully cross-matched transportation records with some of Maryland's county court records to produce illustrative examples of convict servants who were indicted in Maryland after transportation. Peden, *Bastardy Cases.*

77. Ibid. Seven of these women were convicted on more than one occasion. See also Baltimore County Court (Proceedings), Liber 1742–1743: TB D 1, MSA C400-19:74, and Liber 1743–1745, MSA C400-20:293, Maryland State Archives, Annapolis; *Old Bailey Proceedings Online* (www.oldbaileyonline.org, version 7.0), trial of Elizabeth Earle and Hannah Howard, February 1733 (t17330221-42) (accessed December 7, 2012). Ann or Anne Ambrose was transported in 1725. A person of that name was indicted and prosecuted in Queen Anne's County on the Eastern Shore in 1728/29. She may or may not have been the Ann Ambrose who was indicted and prosecuted in Baltimore County in both 1730/31 and 1737/38 when she was a servant to John Parrish. Ellefson, "Prosecutions in Queen Anne County," 117; Baltimore County Court (Proceedings), Liber 1730–1732: HWS 7, MSA C400-14:156, 166 and Liber 1736–1739: HWS IA, MSA C400-16 129, 160, Maryland State Archives, Annapolis.

78. Trial of indentured servant Elizabeth Rennals (not a convict), Kent County Criminal Court Records, 1728–1734, 567:127–28, Maryland State Archives, Annapolis.

79. Bacon, *Laws of Maryland, 1715,* chapter 27, paragraphs 2–6; and *1749,* chapter 12, paragraph 6.

80. Ibid., *1715,* chapter 27, paragraph 5.

81. Ibid., *1727,* chapter 2, paragraphs 4–6.

82. Carr and Walsh, "The Planter's Wife," 549n21. The length of extra service required as restitution varied from county to county and from time to time.

83. Russo and Russo, "Court Treatment of Orphans and Illegitimate Children in Colonial Maryland," 156–57.

84. Often termed "mollatto" or "mullatto" bastardy in court records. The law governing this offense is listed in Bacon, *Laws of Maryland, 1715,* chapter 44, paragraph 26.

85. Maryland State Archives, Charles County Court Records, Liber 1755–1756: E 3, MSA C658-41:127 and Liber 1755–1756: E 3, MSA C658-41:180; in Oszakiewski, "Index to Convict Servants in Charles County Court Records, 1718–1778," 54–59. See

also *Old Bailey Proceedings Online* (www.oldbaileyonline.org, version 6.0), trial of Maria Newman June 1752, (t17520625-56) (accessed June 2, 2012). Maria Newman was transported on the *Tryal* in August 1752.

86. Kent County Criminal Court Records, 1738–39, 668:178–81, Maryland State Archives, Annapolis. Ann Farthing was from Somerset in England and had been convicted at the quarter sessions there in October 1732.

87. Baltimore County Court (Minutes), 1755–1763 (no page given), Maryland State Archives, Annapolis. See also *Old Bailey Proceedings Online* (www.oldbaileyonline.org, version 7.0), trial of Jane Ellis, October 1747 (t17471014-9) (accessed December 15, 2012). Ellis was convicted of grand larceny and was transported on the *St. George*. The arrival of this vessel was registered in Annapolis in March 1748.

88. Her conviction being in March, the date was March 5, 1744/45, owing to the old calendar.

89. Bacon, *Laws of Maryland, 1715,* chapter 44, paragraph 27. Frances Humphreys was convicted at the Old Bailey (along with two co-conspirators) for assault and robbery in February 1740. See *Old Bailey Proceedings Online* (www.oldbaileyonline.org, version 7.0), trial of Elizabeth Hales, Elizabeth Jarvis, Frances Humphryes [*sic*], February 1740 (t17400227-5) (accessed December 28, 2012). It seems likely from the trial evidence that Humphreys was a London prostitute. She was transported in June 1740. Her first conviction for bastardy was in November 1743. Baltimore County Court (Proceedings), liber 1743–1745:71, 168, 471, 481.

90. Maryland State Archives, Charles County Court Records, Liber 1755–1756: E 3, MSA C658-41:179; also Liber 1757–1758: H 3, MSA C658-43:1; listed in Oszakiewski, "Index to Convict Servants in Charles County Court Records, 1718–1778," 54–59. See also *Old Bailey Proceedings Online* (www.oldbaileyonline.org, version 6.0), trial of Ann Nelson, February 1742 (t17420224-32) (accessed June 2, 2012). Nelson was convicted of theft and was transported on the *Bond* in April 1742.

91. *Old Bailey Proceedings Online* (www.oldbaileyonline.org, version 7.0), trial of Winifred Jones, May 1723 (t17230530-3) (accessed December 29, 2012). Winifred Jones was transported from London to Maryland on the *Alexander* in July 1723 (*King's Passengers to Maryland and Virginia,* 17–18). She was charged with mulatto bastardy at the Baltimore County Court at the August 1725 court, the June 1728 court, and the November 1733 court. At the last session her son James Jones was bound out to serve her master. Baltimore County Court (Proceedings), Liber 1723–1725: IS TW 3, MSA C400-11:14, 31, 32; Liber 1728–1730: HWS 6, MSA C400-13:16; and Liber 1733–1734: HWS 9, MSA C400-15: 142–43; Maryland State Archives, Annapolis. See also Prerogative Court (Inventories), 1718–1777, MSA S534, liber 50, folio 174.

92. Bacon, *Laws of Maryland, 1715,* chapter 44, paragraph 26.

93. *Old Bailey Proceedings Online* (www.oldbaileyonline.org, version 6.0), trial of Margaret Lewis, December 4, 1730 (t17301204-50) (accessed December 24, 2011); Anne Arundel County Court (Judgment Record), Court Minutes, August 1741: 252, Maryland State Archives, Annapolis.

94. Russo and Russo, "Court Treatment of Orphans and Illegitimate Children in Colonial Maryland," 156–65.

95. Walsh, "The Experiences and Status of Women in the Chesapeake," 1. Walsh ascribes this trend to the changing composition of the population; there was no longer a shortage of women.

96. Brown, *Good Wives, Nasty Wenches and Anxious Patriarchs*, 331–34.

97. Grubb, "The Market Evaluation of Criminality," 300–301.

98. Jean Astruc, *A Treatise of the Venereal Disease,* quoted by Grubb, "The Market Evaluation of Criminality," 302.

99. Main, *Tobacco Colony*, 110.

100. *Gentleman's Magazine,* vol. 21, September 1751, 426. The trial was in Lancaster on August 30, 1751.

101. Hill, *Women Alone*, 138–39.

102. Advertisement for Sarah Knox, *Maryland Gazette,* January 25, 1753. According to the advertisement, Sarah Knox was convicted in summer 1750 and transported to Virginia on the *Duke of Cumberland* that same year.

103. Advertisement for "Elizabeth," *Pennsylvania Gazette,* September 21, 1758; advertisement for Francis Burrowes, *Maryland Gazette,* August 28, 1760, October 9, 1760.

104. Advertisement for Margaret Cane, *Maryland Gazette,* November 15, 1764. See also the issue for January 14, 1765, in which Philpott advises that he intends to cease keeping a public house.

105. Earle, *The Evolution of a Tidewater Settlement*, 162.

106. Kimber, "Itinerant Observations in America," 324.

107. Advertisement for Mary Owens, *Maryland Gazette,* July 2, 1767. Mary Owens was sentenced at Shropshire's summer quarter sessions in 1764. Her transportation details are unknown.

108. Robert Malcolmson explores the types and significance of recreation available to eighteenth-century rural workers in *Life and Labour in England*, 98–99. See also Dunn, "Masters, Servants and Slaves in the Colonial Chesapeake and the Caribbean," 243.

109. Advertisements for Elisha Bond, *Maryland Gazette,* October 21, 1747, November 11, 1747; advertisement for Jackson (in which the bagpipes are mentioned) *Maryland Gazette,* May 11, 1758.

110. Meacham, "'They Will Be Adjudged by Their Drinke,'" 202–5.

111. Brown, *Good Wives, Nasty Wenches and Anxious Patriarchs*, 276. While Brown is writing about next-door Virginia, similar social conventions applied throughout the Chesapeake.

112. Earle, *The Evolution of a Tidewater Settlement*, 157–58, 161. Earle is quoting a document in the Archives of Maryland, 44:647.

113. Revel, *The Poor Unhappy Felon's Sorrowful Account*, 191.

114. *An Act for Reviving an Act for Raising a Supply towards the Defraying the Public Charge of This Province and to Prevent Too Great a Number of Irish Papists Being Imported into This Province* in Bacon, *Laws of Maryland, 1704,* chapter 9. *An Act for Reviving an Act for Raising a Supply towards the Defraying the Public Charge of This Province and to Prevent Too Great a Number of Irish Papists Being Imported into This Province*; Thomas Hughes, *History of the Society of Jesus in North America*, 1:342, 2:553–54.

115. The Jewish women's names are all listed in Coldham, *The Complete Book of Emigrants in Bondage*, 2, 429, 434, 569.

Chapter 6

1. Bacon, *Laws of Maryland, 1715*, chapter 44, paragraph 6.

2. Advertisement for Margaret Tasker, *Maryland Gazette,* January 19, 1764. Tasker arrived in about November 1762 and ran off in January 1764. Advertisements for Hannah Boyer, *Maryland Gazette,* November 13, 1751, May 28, 1752. Boyer ran away from Catharine Jenings in November 1751 and from Daniel Wells in May 1752. Advertisements for Isabella Watson, *Maryland Gazette,* June 21, 1764, July 14, 1768. Watson ran away from John Frederick Augustus Priggs in 1764 and again in 1768.

3. Ridgely Account Books, Maryland Historical Society, Baltimore, MS. 691, microfilm roll 11, quoted by Rushton and Morgan, "Running Away and Returning Home." George Washington also kept such notes about his slaves. Bailyn, *Voyagers to the West,* 351.

4. Kenneth Morgan, "Convict Runaways in Maryland," 255.

5. Descriptions of female servant clothing in Copeland, *Working Dress in Colonial and Revolutionary America,* 160. Sometimes the sleeve ruffle was actually attached to the shift but revealed at the elbow. See also Baumgarten, *What Clothes Reveal,* 219.

6. Advertisement for Sarah Davis, *Maryland Gazette,* April 27, 1758; advertisement for Isabella Pierce, *Maryland Gazette,* June 21, 1745.

7. Advertisement for Margaret Tasker, *Maryland Gazette,* January 19, 1764. See also Ellefson and Ellefson, *Runaway Convict Servants in Maryland,* chart 106. This is a source document for vol. 822 of *Archives of Maryland On-line,* http://www.aomol.net/megafile/ msa/speccol/sc2900/sc2908/000001/000822/pdf/chart105.pdf (accessed January 3, 2012).

8. Advertisement for Mary Owens, *Maryland Gazette,* July 2, 1767; advertisement for Hannah Boyer, *Maryland Gazette,* May 23, 1752; advertisement for Mary Brady, *Maryland Gazette,* November 22, 1764; advertisement for Frances Burrowes, *Maryland Gazette,* August 28, 1760; advertisement for Anne Pervis, *Maryland Gazette,* August 14, 1755; reprinted advertisement for Sarah Wilson, *Rivington's New-York Gazeteer; or, The Connecticut, New-Jersey, Hudson's-River and Quebec Weekly Advertiser,* May 13, 1773.

9. Advertisement for Mary Osbourn, *Maryland Gazette,* January 5, 1764; advertisement for Mary Jackson, *Maryland Gazette,* May 11, 1758; advertisement for Elizabeth Lloyd, *Maryland Gazette,* July 28, 1768.

10. Advertisement for Mary Rider, *Maryland Gazette,* April 19, 1749.

11. Reprinted advertisement for Sarah Wilson, *Rivington's New-York Gazeteer; or, The Connecticut, New-Jersey, Hudson's-River and Quebec Weekly Advertiser*, May 13, 1773; advertisement for Mary Osbourn, *Maryland Gazette,* January 5, 1764; advertisement for Elizabeth Crowder or Crowther, *Maryland Gazette,* April 1, 1746; advertisement for Margaret Vyans, *Maryland Gazette,* June 14 and July 19, 1753.

12. Advertisement for Anne Bailey, *Maryland Gazette,* April 11, 1771; advertisement for Elizabeth Hawkins, *Maryland Gazette,* July 19, 1753; advertisement for Sarah Robbins, *Pennsylvania Gazette,* April 14, 1773; advertisement for Sarah Davis, *Maryland Gazette,* April 27, 1758; advertisement for Sarah Plint, alias Merchant, *Maryland Gazette,* March 19 and 26, 1767; advertisement for Mary Owens, *Maryland Gazette,* July 2, 1767; advertisement for Catherine Pardon, *Maryland Gazette,* October 22, 1772. *Artful* was allied by Dr. Johnson to "artificial"—i.e., "made with art; not natural" or "contrived with skill."

13. Advertisement for Mary Rider, *Maryland Gazette,* April 19, 1749; advertisement for Catherine Pardon, *Maryland Gazette,* October 22, 1772; advertisement for Mary Owens, *Maryland Gazette,* July 2, 1767; advertisement for Margaret Cane, *Maryland Gazette,* November 15, 1764; advertisement for Catherine Pardon, *Maryland Gazette,* October 22, 1772.

14. Kulikoff, *Tobacco and Slaves,* 177n19. The incidence of the adjectives in the notices is as follows: agreeable, affable, amenable, amiable (33); charitable, benevolent, esteemed (13); virtuous (14); well accomplished (15), of which 12 also listed agreeable; pious, Christian (7); sensible, "every quality to make a man happy" (5).

15. Advertisement for Hannah Boyer, *Maryland Gazette,* May 28, 1752 (emphasis added); earlier advertisement for Boyer in *Maryland Gazette,* November 13, 1751.

16. Styles, *The Dress of the People,* 57.

17. Some eighteenth-century fabric names are now either obsolete or their meaning has changed. Where this is the case, a definition is provided in parentheses. Baumgarten, *What Clothes Reveal,* 113, 115. Advertisement for Catherine Miller, *Maryland Gazette,* September 12, 1771.

18. Advertisement for Margaret Vyans, *Maryland Gazette,* June 14, 1753; advertisement for Ann Wilson, *Maryland Gazette,* November 2, 1775; advertisement for Isabella Watson, *Maryland Gazette,* December 1, 1768. Information on John Priggs from Luce Foundation for American Art, http://wc.rootsweb.ancestry.com/cgi-bin/igm.cgi?op=GET&db=mrmarsha&id=I66006 (accessed May 1, 2012).

19. Clemens, "The Operation of an Eighteenth Century Chesapeake Tobacco Plantation," 519.

20. Prude, "To Look upon the 'Lower Sort,'" 155.

21. Baumgarten, *What Clothes Reveal,* 113–15.

22. Advertisement for Mary Osbourn, *Maryland Gazette,* January 5, 1764; advertisement for Mary Barrington, *Maryland Gazette,* May 21, 1761.

23. Kulikoff, *Tobacco and Slaves,* 179; advertisement for Elizabeth Edwards, alias Redding, alias Kay, *Maryland Gazette,* April 20, 1748; advertisement for Elizabeth Crowder (newly soled shoes), *Maryland Gazette,* April 6, 1746; advertisement for Elizabeth Bryan, *Maryland Gazette,* May 10, 1764; advertisement for Margaret Tasker, *Maryland Gazette,* January 19, 1764; advertisement for Hannah Boyer, *Maryland Gazette,* May 28, 1752.

24. Advertisement for Elizabeth Hawkins, *Maryland Gazette,* July 19, 1753; advertisement for Margaret Tasker, *Maryland Gazette,* January 19, 1764; advertisement for Mary Rider, *Maryland Gazette,* April 19, 1749; advertisement by John Copithorn, *Maryland Gazette,* July 14, 1757. See also Baumgarten, *What Clothes Reveal,* 93.

25. Advertisement for Mary Owens, *Maryland Gazette,* July 2, 1767; advertisement for Nell Fitzgerald, *Maryland Gazette,* October 6, 1767; *Representation of the Transports Going from Newgate to Take Water at Blackfriars,* engraving from 1735, in Rayner and Crook, *The Complete Newgate Calendar.*

26. Advertisement for Isabella Watson, *Maryland Gazette,* June 21, 1764.

27. White and White, *Stylin',* 22–23.

28. Advertisement for Anne Griffith (or Griffin), *Maryland Gazette,* May 2, 1765; advertisement for Elizabeth Hawkins, *Maryland Gazette,* July 19, 1753; advertisement for

Nancy Partington (or Partinton), *Maryland Gazette,* December 22, 1763; advertisement for Catherine "O'Bryan," *Maryland Gazette,* October 10, 1750; reprinted advertisement for Sarah Wilson, *Rivington's New-York Gazeteer; or, The Connecticut, New-Jersey, Hudson's-River and Quebec Weekly Advertiser,* May 13, 1773; advertisement for Elizabeth Lloyd, *Rivington's New-York Gazeteer; or, The Connecticut, New-Jersey, Hudson's-River and Quebec Weekly Advertiser,* July 28, 1768.

29. Advertisement for Elizabeth Bryan, *Maryland Gazette,* May 10, 1764. By 1740 Bladensburg had four taverns and two stores. Kulikoff, *Tobacco and Slaves,* 227. Chamier advertised that he was holding Bryan on January 1768.

30. Advertisement for Anne Griffith (or Griffin), *Maryland Gazette,* August 13, 1767. This was three months after she ran away for a second time.

31. Advertisement for Anne Sayer, *Maryland Gazette,* October 6, 1757; advertisement for Nell Fitzgerald *Maryland Gazette,* October 6, 1774; advertisement for Catherine Davidson *Pennsylvania Gazette,* February 13, 1750.

32. Advertisements for William Manly, *Maryland Gazette,* May 9, 1776, May 30, 1776; advertisement for Moses Dykes and John Burrows, *Maryland Gazette,* June 11, 1761. This mentions these two convicts ran away with Burrows's wife. Two years earlier (*Maryland Gazette,* August 8, 1759), Dykes had absconded with *his* wife from John Ireland and a white servant belonging to John Worthington.

33. Advertisements for Sarah Plint, alias Powell, alias Merchant, *Maryland Gazette,* March 19, 1767, March 26, 1767; advertisements for Elizabeth Willoughby, *Maryland Gazette,* October 10, 1750, October 17, 1750.

34. Advertisements for Ann Wilson, *Maryland Gazette,* November 2, 1775, December 21, 1775; advertisements for William Manly, *Maryland Gazette,* May 9, 1776, May 30, 1776.

35. Advertisement for Frances Burrows, *Maryland Gazette,* August 28, 1760; advertisement for the unnamed wife of Moses Dykes, *Maryland Gazette,* August 9, 1759.

36. McCormac, *White Servitude in Colonial Maryland,* 51–55. McCormac's comments are based on the law of 1715. See Bacon, *Laws of Maryland, 1715,* chapter 44, paragraph 6.

37. Kenneth Morgan, "Convict Runaways in Maryland," 264.

38. Advertisement for Isabella Pierce, *Maryland Gazette,* June 21, 1745; advertisement for Nancy Partinton (or Partington), *Maryland Gazette,* December 22, 1763; advertisement for Nell Fitzgerald, *Maryland Gazette,* October 6, 1774.

39. The term *self-fashioning* is used by David Waldstreicher in "Reading the Runaways." See also advertisement for Mary Rider, *Maryland Gazette,* April 19, 1749. Dr. Carroll's advertisement spells seamstress "sempstress." The emphasis is added.

40. Advertisement for Sarah Knox, *Maryland Gazette,* January 25, 1753; extract of a letter dated July 13, 1752, from Chester, Pennsylvania, *Maryland Gazette,* August 13, 1752. See also *Virginia Gazette,* July 3, 1752.

41. Coldham, *Settlers of Maryland,* 204. The item about Sarah Wilson in the *London Magazine* mentions she was imported into Maryland in the fall of 1771, though in view of the date of her trial it is more likely to have been sometime in 1768. However, she is not listed (as Wilson) on any of the convict ships that are on record as having left London in

that year. Gwenda Morgan and Peter Rushton have suggested that little about the Wilson story is reliable, that it gained traction only because it was irresistible to the press, and that it should be treated with great caution. *Eighteenth-Century Criminal Transportation*, 85–89.

42. *Gentleman's Magazine,* vol. 43, July 1773, 357; *London Magazine,* May 1773, 311 quoted by Butler, "British Convicts Shipped to American Colonies."

43. *Rivington's New-York Gazeteer; or, The Connecticut, New-Jersey, Hudson's-River and Quebec Weekly Advertiser*, May 13, 1773.

44. Listing for Sarah Wilson, 6/203 of June 1767, MJ/CJ Calendars of Indictments, London Metropolitan Archives; *Gentleman's Magazine,* vol. 38, January 1768, 44.

45. Coldham, *The Complete Book of Emigrants in Bondage*, 351; *Gentleman's Magazine,* vol. 43, November 1773, 574.

46. Advertisement for Nancy Partington (or Partinton), *Maryland Gazette,* December 22, 1763; advertisement for Mary Price, *Maryland Gazette,* September 14, 1769.

47. Abbot Emerson Smith, *Colonists in Bondage,* 267. A former convict, William Green, claimed that for a month's absence a runaway would have to serve an extra year. *The Sufferings of William Green*, 7.

48. Bacon, *Laws of Maryland, 1715,* chapter 44, paragraph 6.

49. Advertisement for Nell Fitzgerald, *Maryland Gazette,* October 6, 1774; advertisement for Sarah Davis, *Maryland Gazette,* May 4, 1758.

50. *Old Bailey Proceedings Online* (www.oldbaileyonline.org, version 6.0), trial of Mary Wall, August 28, 1725 (t17250827-79); trial of Margaret Pew, December 8, 1725 (t17251208-11); trial of Barbara Black, February 21, 1733 (t17330221-16) (accessed 21 December 2011). See also Prerogative Court (Inventories), 1718–1777, MSA S534, 11:325 (Mary Wall), 15:1 (Margaret Pew); Baltimore County Inventories, liber 6, folio 26 (Barbara Black), Maryland State Archives, Annapolis.

51. *Maryland Gazette,* June 21, 1745.

52. Papenfuse, *In Pursuit of Profit*, 18; John Brice's advertisements appeared in 1765 in the *Maryland Gazette* issues for March 28, April 4, April 11, April 25, May 2, May 9, May 16, May 23, May 30, June 6, June 13, and June 27.

53. *Maryland Gazette,* September 20, 1770. This contains an advertisement for the sale of a convict servant at public vendue. Martha Anderson, alias Blacklock—sale to Day, Baltimore County Court (Proceedings), Liber 1728–1730: HWS 6, MSA C400-13:275; sale to Higginson, Baltimore County Court (Proceedings), Liber 1730–1732: HWS 7, MSA C400-14:98; running away, Baltimore County Court (Proceedings), HWS 9, MSA C400-14:131; Maryland State Archives, Annapolis. Martha Anderson alias Blacklock was not advertised when she ran away.

Chapter 7

1. Letter 6, September 20, 1770, in Eddis, *Letters from America,* 37.

2. Oldham, *Britain's Convicts to the Colonies,* 30.

3. *Old Bailey Proceedings Online* (www.oldbaileyonline.org, version 7.0), ordinary of Newgate's Account, March 1741 (OA17410318) (accessed April 30, 2012). Mary Young (as Mary Webb) was transported to Virginia on the *Elizabeth* in June 1728 and (as Jane Webb) on the *Forward* in June 1738.

4. *Old Bailey Proceedings Online* (www.oldbaileyonline.org, version 7.0), trial of Catherine Floyd, alias Huggins, September 1739 (t17390906-36); trial of Mary Young and Catherine Davis, January 1741 (t17410116-15); trial of Mary Shirley, July 1742 (t17420714-18); trial of Catherine Davis and Jane Canwell, September 1742 (t17420714-18); trial of Mary Shirley, May 1744 (t17440510-26) (accessed April 30, 2012). Mary Shirley was transported to Virginia on the *Justitia* in May 1744.

5. Ekirch, *Bound for America*, 220.

6. *The Discoveries of John Poulter, Alias Baxter: A Full Account of All the Robberies He Had Committed and the Surprising Tricks and Frauds He Has Practised for the Space of Five Years Last Past in Different Parts of England.* This 1753 tract is included in Rawlings, *Drunks, Whores and Idle Apprentices*, 139–77.

7. Ibid., 170.

8. Petition of Eleanor Connor to the archbishop of Canterbury, n.d., State Papers Domestic, SP36/109/45, Public Record Office, Kew, UK.

9. *Old Bailey Proceedings Online* (www.oldbaileyonline.org, version 7.0), trial of Eleanor, wife of John Connor, otherwise Tobin, otherwise Woods, and John Conner, February 1754 (t17540227-9) (accessed April 29, 2012). In the trial transcript the name of the transport ship's captain's name is spelled "Whitare" and no destination is given, but Captain Whitepair is mentioned in the *Maryland Gazette*'s shipping notices and Maryland was the destination of most vessels ex Bideford. See State Papers Domestic, Petition of Eleanor Connor to the Archbishop of Canterbury, n.d. (possibly 1748), Public Record Office, Kew, UK.

10. Rushton and Morgan, "Running Away and Returning Home."

11. Ibid. (Connor). See also *Old Bailey Proceedings Online* (www.oldbaileyonline.org, version 7.0), trial of Mary Quin, alias Bulger, September 1751 (t17510911-21) (accessed December 16, 2011).

12. The Old Bailey verdicts for returning early from transportation, 1718–76, are as follows. Executed: Mary Barter, Mary Coulston, Elizabeth Doyle; reprieved for transportation for fourteen years: Elizabeth Doyle (first return penalty), Mary North, Alice Walker; respited for pregnancy: Eleanor Connor, Elizabeth Watson, Sarah Wells; acquitted: Mary Quin, Elizabeth Birmingham, Catherine Wigmore.

13. Coldham, *The Complete Book of Emigrants in Bondage*, 511. See also Gwenda Morgan and Rushton, *Rogues, Thieves and the Rule of Law*, 166.

14. Gould, *Money and Transportation in Maryland*, 154.

15. Kenneth Morgan, "Convict Runaways in Maryland," 262.

16. Rawlings, *Drunks, Whores and Idle Apprentices*, 169.

17. Hay, "War, Dearth and Theft in the Eighteenth Century," 134.

18. *Maryland Gazette,* October 17, 1765.

19. Baltimore County Court (Proceedings), Martha Anderson, alias Blacklock, Liber 1728–1730: HWS 6, MSA C400-13:14; Kent County Court (Bonds and Indentures), 1694–1782, Liber JS 17: MSA C1028-5:20–22, Edith Street. However, the county courts did not hear charges connected with murder, robbery, and burglary, and the records for these courts are patchy. Beginning in the 1720s serious criminal cases were often tried by circuit courts, for which the minutes have not survived.

20. Ekirch, *Bound for America*, 171–73. Prosecution figures are drawn from table 12 on

p. 173: "Distribution of Kent County Criminal Prosecutions by Social Standing or Occupation 1732–1746." The criminal prosecutions did not include slaves. If they did, the percentage would be even lower.

21. Ibid., 172, note 2.

22. Kent County Court (Bonds and Indentures), 1694–1782, Liber JS 17: MSA C1028-5:20–22, Edith Street. Kent County Criminal Court Records (Trial of Ann Farthing), Maryland State Archives, Annapolis, 668: 178–181 (accessed November 25, 2012).

23. Oszakiewski, "Index to Convict Servants in Charles County Court Records, 1718–1778"; Peden, *Bastardy Cases.*

24. Letter 6, September 20, 1779, in Eddis, *Letters from America*, 38.

25. Revel, *The Poor Unhappy Felon's Sorrowful Account*, 194.

26. *Newcastle Courant*, July 23, 1768, quoted by Rushton and Morgan, "Running Away and Returning Home."

27. Garcia, "Exploring Cultural Homelessness," 57.

28. Malcolmson, *Life and Labour in England*, 95.

29. Advertisement for Ann Bailey, *Maryland Gazette*, April 11, 1771, April 18, 1771; *Old Bailey Proceedings Online* (www.oldbaileyonline.org, version 7.0), trial of Ann Bailey, December 1768 (t17681207-23) (accessed May 4, 2012).

30. Emphasis added to Orme's wording of his advertisement for Ann Bailey. Information on Orme from Ecker, *A Portrait of Old George Town*, 25–26.

31. Letter 6, September 20, 1770, in Eddis, *Letters from America*, 37.

32. "Journal of a French Traveller in the Colonies," 738.

33. Oszakiewski, "Index to Convict Servants in Charles County Records: A Further Study," 284.

34. Alice Carrington was transported from Kent to Maryland on the *Loyal Margaret* in June 1726. In August 1729 and again in November 1733, when she was a servant of Hezekiah Balch, she was indicted and tried for "Bastardy." Baltimore County Court (Proceedings), Liber 1728–1730, HWS 6 MSA C-400:277. Carrington was mother to Mary, born by August 1729 and bound to Hezekiah Balch; to Johanna (by William Beezley), born September 2, 1731; and to James Hogg, born by November 1733 and bound to James Lee. Information drawn from Barnes, *Baltimore County Families;* and Peden, *St. John's and St. George's Parish Registers*, 75. For details of Ann Farthing, Frances Humphreys, and Winifred Jones, see chapter 5, notes 86, 89, 91.

35. Edmund S. Morgan, *American Slavery, American Freedom*, 339–40. Although Morgan deals explicitly with Virginia, it is likely that this situation prevailed in other parts of the Chesapeake where there were similar servant arrangements and plantation economies.

36. Frederick Robertson Jones, *The Colonization of the Middle States and Maryland*, 444.

37. Matthaei, *An Economic History of Women in America*, 57; Walsh, "The Experiences and Status of Women in the Chesapeake," 1–4.

38. Walsh, "The Experiences and Status of Women in the Chesapeake," 3.

39. Ibid., 6, 15.

40. *Old Bailey Proceedings Online* (www.oldbaileyonline.org, version 7.0), trial of Mary Parsmore or Passmore, April 4, 1733 (t17330404-35); trial of John Dunnick, May 26, 1737

(t17370526-38) (accessed April 29, 2012); Peden, *St. John's and St. George's Parish Registers*, 238.

41. *Maryland Gazette*, July 9, 1752, March 27, 1751.

42. Editions of the *Maryland Gazette* with the relevant items or advertisements are those of May 27, 1756 (block making); August 16, 1749 (storekeeping); November 13, 1755, August 16, 1749, March 6, 1755, April 4, 1761 (tavern keeping); April 26, 1759 (tailoring); May 27, 1756, August 25, 1757 (lodgings keeping); May 22, 1760 (chocolate retailing); February 21, 1754, and May 22, 1760 (teaching).

43. Runaway advertisement for Elizabeth Crowder, *Maryland Gazette*, April 1, 1746; advertisement for sewing services, *Maryland Gazette*, October 28, 1747.

44. Baumgarten, *What Clothes Reveal*, 89.

45. Advertisement for quilting services by Sarah Monro, *Maryland Gazette*, July 26, 1745.

46. Benjamin Franklin to the *Pennsylvania Gazette*, May 9, 1751, in Labaree and Bell, *The Papers of Benjamin Franklin*, 130–33.

47. Kimber, "Itinerant Observations in America," 329.

48. *Maryland Gazette*, July 30, 1767. The comment is in a letter from A.B. (assumed to be Thomas Ringgold).

49. Letter 111, in de Crèvecoeur, *Letters from an American Farmer*, 64.

50. Williams, *A History of Washington County*, 21.

51. Letter from Sarah Thornton dated 1820, quoted by Daniels, *Convict Women*, 221.

Chapter 8

1. Coldham, *The King's Passengers to Maryland and Virginia*, 262–63.

2. National Maritime Museum, "Prison Hulks on the River Thames."

3. Ekirch, *Bound for America*, 233–34.

4. *Maryland Gazette*, November 13, 1783.

5. Ekirch, "Great Britain's Secret Convict Trade to America," 1289–90.

6. The *Mercury* was another of George Moore's ships that was refused entry to U.S. ports in 1784 and eventually landed its convicts in British Honduras. A final effort was made in 1787, but the *Prince William Henry*, with twenty-two convicts, was refused entry in Baltimore. Coldham, *The King's Passengers to Maryland and Virginia*, iv–v.

7. *Journals of the Continental Congress*, vol. 34 (Washington, DC: Library of Congress, 1904–37), 494–95, 528, quoted in Abbot Emerson Smith, *Colonists in Bondage*, 124.

8. Ekirch, A, "Great Britain's Secret Convict Trade to America"; Coldham, *The King's Passengers to Maryland and Virginia*, iv–v, 264.

9. *Pennsylvania Gazette*, May 9, 1751, letter included in Labaree and Bell, *The Papers of Benjamin Franklin*, 131. Some modifications made to the original spelling and use of capitalization.

10. Livingston, *The Independent Reflector*.

11. Oldham, *Britain's Convicts to the Colonies*, 32.

12. The list of injustices in the Declaration of Independence did not mention the convict trade explicitly.

13. The full text of the Declaration of Independence is available at www.archives.gov /exhibits/charters/declaration_transcript.html (accessed December 3, 2012).

14. Gundersen, "Independence, Citizenship, and the American Revolution," 77. Neither the Declaration of Independence nor the new Constitution mentioned women at all.

15. Hoffman and Albert, *Women in the Age of the American Revolution*, 29–35.

16. Atkinson, "The Free-Born Englishman Transported," 108.

17. Bacon, *Laws of Maryland, 1751*, chapter 11, paragraph 2.

18. Ibid., chapter 44, paragraph 9. This law of 1715 specifies freedom dues of clothing and tools for male servants and clothing for women. Whether this applied to convict servants after 1718 is not clear.

19. *Proceedings and Acts of the General Assembly of Maryland 1764–1765*, quoted by Atkinson, "The Free-Born Englishman Transported," 106–7 (emphasis added).

20. Atkinson, "The Free-Born Englishman Transported," 107–8.

21. *Maryland Gazette*, August 20, 1752.

22. Brugger, *Maryland*, 125–26.

23. Ibid., 116.

24. Zagarri, "The Rights of Man and Woman in Post-revolutionary America," 204–5. Thomas Jefferson equated citizenship with political rights, and because he did not support women's right to vote, he presumed either that women were not citizens or (and this is more likely) that women were dependent citizens. Gundersen, "Women and the Political Process in the United States," 64.

25. Wulf, *Not All Wives*, 89–90. Curiously, in 1776 New Jersey adopted a constitution that ignored gender barriers in its suffrage law and defined voters as adult inhabitants "worth fifty pounds." As married women's property ownership was invariably limited, however, only single women could vote. In 1807 a new law defined voters solely as adult white male taxpaying citizens. Klinghoffer and Elkis, "'The Petticoat Electors,'" 159–60.

26. Zinn, *A People's History of the United States*, 73. See also Hoffman and Albert, *Women in the Age of the American Revolution*, 39. See also Gundersen "Independence, Citizenship, and the American Revolution," 59–60, 76, 77.

27. Ahern, "The Spirit of American Constitutionalism," 19.

28. Hoffman and Albert, *Women in the Age of the American Revolution*, 39.

29. Edmund S. Morgan, *American Slavery, American Freedom*, 383–85. Morgan discusses Jefferson's fears.

30. Jefferson, *Writings*, 158.

31. From about the middle of the eighteenth century, Columbia was the poetic name used for America. With the birth of the Republic, a goddesslike Columbia became its female personification. By the end of the nineteenth century Columbia was, to some extent, replaced by personifications of liberty based on the Roman goddess of freedom—Libertas. The most notable is the female Statue of Liberty in New York Harbor.

32. Grubb, "The Market Evaluation of Criminality," 300–301.

33. Malcolmson, *Life and Labour in England*, 108.

34. [A] Creole, *The Fortunate Transport*, 21.

35. Latimer, *Annals of Bristol in the Eighteenth Century*, 150.

36. Letter from Philanthropos, *Maryland Gazette*, August 20, 1767.

37. Land, *Colonial Maryland*, 179–205.

38. Adams, *Diary and Autobiography*, 261. The capitalization of nouns in the original document has been replaced with lower case.

39. Daniel Blake Smith, *Inside the Great House*, 226–27.

40. Brice placed twelve advertisements in separate editions of the *Maryland Gazette* between March 1765 and June 1765.

41. *Gentleman's Magazine*, vol. 34, June 1764, 261.

42. "Journal of a French Traveller in the Colonies," 738.

43. These were written by James Annesley, David Benfield, Bamfylde Moore Carew, William Green, William Parsons, and "James Revel."

44. Coldham, *The Complete Book of Emigrants in Bondage*, 585; Coldham, *The King's Passengers to Maryland and Virginia*, 130.

45. *Maryland Gazette*, May 22, 1751.

Appendix 3

1. *Acts of the Privy Council of England, in the Reign of James I*, vol. I, 1614–15 (London: His Majesty's Stationery Office, 1925).

Appendix 4

1. Raithby, John, ed. *The Statutes at Large of England and Great Britain, from Magna Carta to the Union of the Kingdoms of Great Britain and Ireland*, vol. 4 (1708–1726), 399–402.

Appendix 5

1. Compiled by the author from Old Bailey trial information 1718–1776.

Appendix 6

1. Bacon, *Laws of Maryland, 1723*, chapter 6.

2. Ibid., *1728*, chapter 23. Supplements to this legislation were passed in 1729 and 1769. ·

3. Ibid., *1751*, chapter 11.

Bibliography

Primary Sources

Manuscripts

LONDON METROPOLITAN ARCHIVES
MJ/CJ Calendars of Indictments
MJ/SP/T Transportation Contracts
WJ/SR Session of the Peace Rolls, 1620–1785

MARYLAND HISTORICAL SOCIETY, BALTIMORE
Carroll-Maccumbin Papers, 1644–1888, manuscript 000219
Cheston-Galloway Papers, 1644–1888, manuscript 1994
Maryland Gazette, 1727–1733, 1745–1787

MARYLAND STATE ARCHIVES, ANNAPOLIS
Anne Arundel County Court (Judgment Record), 1703–1844, MSA C91
Baltimore County Court (Minutes), 1755–1851, MSA C386
Baltimore County Court (Proceedings), MSA C400
Baltimore County Inventories
Charles County Court (Court Record), 1658–1780, MSA C658
Kent County Criminal Court Records (via *Archives of Maryland Online*)
Kent County Court (Bonds and Indentures), 1694–1782, MSA C1028
Maryland Gazette (via *Archives of Maryland Online*)
Prerogative Court (Inventories), 1718–1777, MSA S534, vol. 11, 15, 50

NATIONAL LIBRARY OF WALES, ABERYSTWYTH
Manuscript NLW MS. 474E

OLD BAILEY SESSION RECORDS
Ordinary's Accounts 1676–1772 (via Old Bailey Online)
Proceedings of the Old Bailey, 1674–1913 (via Old Bailey Online)

PUBLIC RECORD OFFICE, KEW, UK
High Court of Admiralty: Oyer and Terminer Records
State Papers Domestic
Treasury Papers

STATE LIBRARY OF NEW SOUTH WALES (MITCHELL LIBRARY), SYDNEY
Duncan Campbell Business Letterbooks, vols. 1 and 2
Duncan Campbell Private Letterbooks, vol. 7

SURREY HISTORY CENTRE WOKING, U.K.
Surrey Quarter Sessions Proceedings, 1718
Surrey Quarter Sessions Proceedings, 1763

Printed Material

[A] Creole, *The Fortunate Transport; or, The Secret History of the Life and Adventures of the Celebrated Polly Haycock, the Lady of the Gold Watch*. London: T. Taylor, [1750?]. Eighteenth Century Collections Online. Gale. State Library of New South Wales Public (accessed January 4, 2012).

Acts of the Privy Council of England, in the Reign of James I. Vol. I, *1614–15*. London: His Majesty's Stationery Office, 1925.

Adams, John. *Diary and Autobiography of John Adams*. Vol. 2. Edited by L. Butterfield. Cambridge, MA: Belknap Press of Harvard University Press, 1961.

Bacon, Thomas, ed. *Laws of Maryland—Session Laws: 1637–1763*. Annapolis: Jonas Green, 1765.

Britton, Alexander, ed. *Historical Records of New South Wales*. Vol. 1, part 2. Sydney: NSW Government Printer, 1879.

Brooks, James, to the Lords of Trade and Plantations, June 1, 1774. *Maryland Historical Magazine* 2 (1907): 354–62.

Browne, William Hand, ed. *Archives of Maryland*. Vols. 6, 9, 25, 33, and 35. Baltimore: Maryland Historical Society, 1895.

Carter, Landon. *The Diary of Colonel Landon Carter of Sabine Hall, 1752–1778*. Edited by Jack B. Greene. Charlottesville: University Press of Virginia, 1965.

de Crèvecoeur, J. Hector St. John. *Letters from an American Farmer*. 1782; Oxford: Oxford University Press, 1998.

Defoe, Daniel. *A Tour through the Whole Island of Great Britain*. Vols. 1 and 2. 1724; London: Dent Everyman's, 1962.

Eddis, William. *Letters from America*. Edited by A. Land. Cambridge, MA: Belknap Press of Harvard University Press, 1969.

Fielding, Henry. *An Enquiry into the Causes of the Late Increase of Robbers & C: With Some Proposals for Remedying this Growing Evil*. London: A. Millar, 1751.

Fielding, John. *A Plan for Reserving Those Deserted Girls Who Become Prostitutes from Necessity*. London: A. Millar, 1751.

Gentleman's Magazine. Vols. 1–46 inclusive (1731–76).

Goadby, Robert. *An Apology for the Life of Mr. Bampfylde-Moore Carew, Commonly Called the King of the Beggars*. . . . London: W. Owen, 1775. Eighteenth Century Collections Online. Gale. State Library of New South Wales Public (accessed January 4, 2012).

Gove, Philip P. "An Oxford Convict in Maryland." *Maryland Historical Magazine* 37 (1942): 193–98. (Letter to Mr. David Whitton in Oxford dated 1772 from David Benfield, a convict from Oxford transported to Maryland in 1771.)

Green, William. *The Sufferings of William Green, Being a Sorrowful Account, of His Seven Years Transportation.* . . . London, 1775? Eighteenth Century Collections Online. Gale. State Library of New South Wales Public (accessed January 4, 2012).

Hakluyt, Richard, the Younger. *A Particuler Discourse concerning the greate necessitie and manifolde commodyties that are like to grow to this realme of Englande by the Westerne discoveries lately attempted, known as Discourse of Western Planting.* 1584; London: Hakluyt Society, 1993.

Hammond, John. *Leah and Rachel; or, The Two Fruitfull Sisters, Virginia and Mary-Land: Their Present Condition, Impartially Stated and Related.* London: T. Mabb, 1656. *Early English Books Online* (accessed June 16, 2012).

Harrower, John. "Diary of John Harrower." *American Historical Review* 6 (1904): 75–77.

Headlam, Cecil, ed. *Calendar of State Papers (Colonial)—America and West Indies for 1719–1720.* London: His Majesty's Stationery Office, 1932.

———. *Calendar of State Papers (Colonial)—America and West Indies for 1720–1721.* London: His Majesty's Stationery Office, 1932.

———. *Calendar of State Papers (Colonial)—America and West Indies for 1730.* London: His Majesty's Stationery Office, 1937.

Headlam, Cecil, and Arthur Percival Newton, eds. *Calendar of State Papers (Colonial)—America and West Indies for 1731–1733.* London: His Majesty's Stationery Office, 1938.

History of the Press Yard; or, A Brief Account of the Customs and Occurrences That Are Put into Practice. London: T. Moor, 1717.

Historical Register. Vols. 4, 5, 6 (1719, 1720, 1721).

Hogarth, William. *The Complete Works of William Hogarth in a Series of One Hundred and Fifty Superb Engravings on Steel.* London: Murdoch, n.d., 73–80.

Maryland Period Rooms in the Baltimore Museum of Art. Baltimore: Hollow Press for the Baltimore Museum of Art, 1987.

Mittelberger, Gottlieb. *Journey to Pennsylvania in the Year 1750 and Return to Germany on the Year 1754.* http://archive.org/stream/gottlichmittelbe01mitt/gottlichmittelbe01mitt _djvu.txt (accessed November 21, 2013).

Newton, Arthur Percival, ed. *Calendar of State Papers (Colonial)—America and West Indies for 1732–1733.* London: Her Majesty's Stationery Office, 1939.

———. *Calendar of State Papers (Colonial)—America and West Indies for 1734–1735.* London: Her Majesty's Stationery Office, 1953.

———. *Calendar of State Papers (Colonial— America and West Indies for 1735–1736.* London: Her Majesty's Stationery Office, 1953.

Ollyffe, George. *An Essay Humbly Offer'd for an Act of Parliament to Prevent Capital Crimes, and the Loss of Many Lives: And to Promote a Desirable Improvement and Blessing in the Nation.* London: J. Downing, 1731.

Pennsylvania Gazette. 1740, 1745, 1746, 1749, 1750, 1751, 1754, 1758, 1764, 1766, 1767, 1768, 1772, 1773, 1775.

Proposals for a Tobacco Law in the Province of Maryland, Humbly Offered to the Considera-tion of the Legislature and all Lovers of Their Country. Annapolis, 1726.

Raithby, John, ed. *The Statutes at Large of England and Great Britain, from Magna Carta to the Union of the Kingdoms of Great Britain and Ireland, in Ten Volumes, vol. 4 from 7 Anne A.D. 1708 to 13 George I A.D. 1726.* London: G. Eyre & A. Strahan, 1811.

Rayner, J., and G. Crook, eds. *The Complete Newgate Calendar.* London: Navarre Society, 1926.

Revel, James. *The Poor Unhappy Felon's Sorrowful Account of His Fourteen Years Transporta-tion at Virginia, America.* Dublin: B. Corcoran, n.d. Edited by J. Jennings and reprinted in *Virginia Magazine of History and Biography* 56 (1948): 181–94.

Rivington's New-York Gazeteer; or, The Connecticut, New-Jersey, Hudson's-River and Quebec Weekly Advertiser, May 13, 1773, July 28, 1768.

Sainsbury, W. Noel, ed. *Calendar of State Papers, Colonial Series.* Vols. 1, 5, 7 (1574–1660, 1661–1668, 1669–1674), *America and West Indies, 1574–1660.* 1860; Vaduz: Her Majesty's Stationery Office, Kraus Reprint, 1964.

Shaw, William Arthur, ed. *Calendar of Treasury Papers, 1729–1730.* 1897; Vaduz: Her Majesty's Stationery Office, Kraus Reprint, 1964.

"Transportation of Felons to the Colonies." *Maryland Historical Magazine* 27 (December 1932):263–74. Reprints miscellaneous primary documents.

U.S. Government. *First Census of the United States, Montgomery County, MD. [1790]* Washington, Government Printing Office, 1907.

Virginia Gazette, [Parks] 1746; [Rind's] 1770.

Secondary Sources

Articles

Adams, Donald R. "Prices and Wages in Maryland, 1750–1850." *Journal of Economic His-tory* 46 (September 1986): 625–45.

Ahern, Gregory S. "The Spirit of American Constitutionalism: John Dickinson's Fabius Letters." *Humanitas* 11 (1998):57–76.

Atkinson, Alan. "The Free-Born Englishman Transported: Convict Rights as a Measure of Eighteenth Century Empire." *Past and Present* 144 (August 1994): 88–115.

Bannet, Eve Tavor. "The Marriage Act of 1753: 'A Most Cruel Law for the Fair Sex.'" *Eight-eenth Century Studies* 30 (Spring 1997): 233–54.

Barnes, Robert. "Where Did They Come From?" *Bulldog*, February 28, 2000. www.msw.md.gov/msa/refserv/html/bull00html (accessed April 17, 2012).

Beattie, John M. "The Criminality of Women in Eighteenth Century England." *Journal of Social History* 8 (Summer 1975): 80–116.

Breslaw, Elaine G. "From Edinburgh to Annapolis: Dr. Alexander Hamilton's Colonial Maryland Practice." *Maryland Historical Magazine* 9 (Winter 2001): 409–14.

Butler, James D. "British Convicts Shipped to American Colonies." *American Historical Review* 7 (October 1896): 12–33.

Carr, Lois, and Lorena Walsh. "The Planter's Wife: The Experience of White Women in 17th Century Maryland." *William and Mary Quarterly*, 3rd ser., 34 (1977): 130–56.

Clemens, Paul G. E. "The Operation of an Eighteenth Century Chesapeake Tobacco Plantation." *Agricultural History* 49 (July 1975): 517–31.

Ekirch, A. Roger. "Bound for America: A Profile of British Convicts Transported to the Colonies, 1718–1775." *William and Mary Quarterly*, 3rd ser., 42 (1985): 184–200.

———. "Great Britain's Secret Convict Trade to America, 1783–1784." *American Historical Review* 89 (1984): 1285–91.

———. "The Transportation of Scottish Criminals to America during the Eighteenth Century." *Journal of British Studies* 24 (July 1985): 366–74.

Ellefson, C. "Prosecutions in Queen Anne County by Crime Charge between 1728 and 1748." http://aomol.net/megafile/msa/speccol/sc2900sc2908/000001/000819/pdf/chart102.pdf (accessed January 3, 2012).

Fogleman, Aaron S. "From Slaves, Convicts, and Servants to Free Passengers: The Transformation of Immigration in the Era of the American Revolution." *Journal of American History* 85 (June 1998): 43–76.

Galenson, David. "The Rise and Fall of Indentured Servitude in the Americas: An Economic Analysis." *Journal of Economic History* 44 (March 1984): 1–14.

Grubb, Farley. "The Market Evaluation of Criminality: Evidence from the Auction of British Convict Labor in America, 1767–1775." *American Economic Review* 91 (March 2001): 295–304.

———. "The Transatlantic Market for British Convict Labor." *Journal of Economic History* 60 (March 2000): 94–122.

Gundersen, Joan. "Independence, Citizenship, and the American Revolution." *Signs* 13 (1987–88): 59–77.

Hay, Douglas. "War, Dearth and Theft in the Eighteenth Century." *Past and Present* 95 (1982): 117–60.

Hufton, Olwen. "Women without Men: Widows and Spinsters in Britain and France in the Eighteenth Century." *Journal of Family History* 9, no. 4 (1984): 355–76.

Johnson, Keach. "The Baltimore Iron Works Seeks English Subsidies for the Colonial Iron Industry." *Maryland Historical Magazine* 46 (1951): 27–43.

Kellow, Margaret M. R. "Indentured Servitude in Eighteenth Century Maryland." *Histoire sociale—Social History* 17 (November 1984): 229–55.

Kent, David. "Ubiquitous but Invisible: Female Domestic Servants in Mid-Eighteenth Century London." *History Workshop* 28 (July 1989): 111–29.

Kent, Joan R. "The Centre and the Localities: State Formation and Parish Government in England, circa 1640–1740." *Historical Journal* 38 (June 1995): 363–404.

King, Peter. "Female Offenders, Work, and Life-Cycle Changes in Late Eighteenth Century London." *Continuity and Change* 11 (1996): 61–90.

Klinghoffer, Judith A., and Lois Elkis. "'The Petticoat Electors': Women's Suffrage in New Jersey, 1776–1807." *Journal of the Early Republic* 12 (1992): 159–93.

Land, Aubrey C. "Economic Base and Social Structure: The Northern Chesapeake in the Eighteenth Century." *Journal of Economic History* 25 (December 1965): 639–54.

Langbein, John H. "Albion's Fatal Flaws." *Past and Present* 98 (1983): 96–120.

Lemire, Beverly. "The Theft of Clothes and Popular Consumerism in Early Modern England." *Journal of Social History* (1990): 255–76.

Mackay, Lynn. "Why They Stole: Women in the Old Bailey, 1779–89." *Journal of Social History* 32 (Spring 1999): 623–40.

Matthews, Jill. "Feminist History." *Labour History* 50 (1986): 147–53.

Morgan, Gwenda, and Peter Rushton. "Print Culture, Crime and Transportation in the Criminal Atlantic." *Continuity and Change* 22 (May 2007): 49–71.

Morgan, Kenneth. "Convict Runaways in Maryland, 1745–1775." *Journal of American Studies* 23 (August 1989): 253–67.

———. "Convict Transportation to America." *Reviews in American History* (March 1989): 29–34.

———. "English and American Attitudes towards Convict Transportation, 1718–1775." *History* 72 (1987): 416–30.

———. "The Organization of the Convict Trade to Maryland." *William and Mary Quarterly*, 3rd ser., 42 (1985): 201–27.

———. "Petitions against Convict Transportation, 1725–1735." *English Historical Review* (1989): 111–13.

Oszakiewski, Robert Andrew. "Index to Convict Servants in Charles County Records: A Further Study." *Maryland Genealogical Bulletin* 32 (Summer 1991): 284–87.

———. "Index to Convict Servants in Charles County Records, 1718–1778." *Maryland Genealogical Bulletin* 32 (Winter 1991): 54–59.

———. "Index to Convict Servants in Kent County, 1719–1769." *Maryland Genealogical Bulletin* 36 (Summer 1995): 43–84.

———. "Index to Convict Servants in Queen Anne's County Court Records." *Maryland Genealogical Bulletin* 31 (Winter 1990): 46–58.

Price, Jacob M. "The Economic Growth of the Chesapeake and the European Market, 1697–1775." *Journal of Economic History* 24 (December 1964): 496–511.

Prude, Jonathan. "To Look upon the 'Lower Sort': Runaway Ads and the Appearance of Unfree Laborers in America, 1750–1800." *Journal of American History* 78 (June 1991): 124–59.

Razzell, Peter E. "The Growth of Population in Eighteenth-Century England: A Critical Reappraisal." *Journal of Economic History* 53 (December 1993): 743–71.

Rushton, Peter, and Gwenda Morgan. "Running Away and Returning Home: The Fate of English Convicts in the American Colonies." *Crime, Histoire and Sociétés/Crime, History and Societies* 7, no. 2 (2003): 61–80.

Scott, Joan W. "Gender: A Useful Category of Historical Analysis." *American Historical Review* 91, Number 5 (1986): 1053–75.

Sollers, Basil. "Transported Convict Laborers in Maryland during the Colonial Period." *Maryland Historical Magazine* 2 (March 1907): 17–47.

Thompson, Edward P. "Time, Work-Discipline and Industrial Capitalism." *Past and Present* 38 (December 1967): 56–97.

Waldstreicher, David. "Reading the Runaways: Self-fashioning, Print Culture, and Confidence in Slavery in the Eighteenth Century Mid-Atlantic." *William and Mary Quarterly* 3rd ser., 56 (April 1999): 243–72.

Wright, F. Edward. "Kent County Criminal Records, 1723–1728." *Maryland Genealogical Society Bulletin* 36 (Summer 1995): 392–418.

Wrigley, Edward A. "A Simple Model of London's Importance in Changing English Society and Economy, 1650–1750." *Past and Present* 37 (July 1967): 44–70.

Zagarri, Rosemarie. "The Rights of Man and Woman in Post-revolutionary America." *William and Mary Quarterly* 3rd ser., 55 (1998): 203–30.

Dissertations and Theses

Dedrick, Craig R. "The Economic Authority of Widows: Middling, Lesser Elite, and Elite Testation Patterns in Kent County, Maryland, 1660–1775." MA thesis, Lehigh University, 1994.

Flanagan, Charles M. "The Sweets of Independence: A Reading of the James Carroll Daybook, 1714–1721." PhD diss., University of Maryland, 2005.

Books

Ackroyd, Peter. *London: The Biography*. London: Chatto & Windus, 2000.

Anderson, Elizabeth B. *Annapolis: A Walk through History*. Centreville, MD: Tidewater, 1984.

Anderson, Patricia A. *Frederick County Maryland Land Records, Liber N Abstracts, 1770–1772*. Gaithersburg, MD, Gen Law Resources, 2003. (Abstracted from land records in Maryland State Archives, microfilm rolls CR37, 515 and CR 37,516, January 2003.)

Bailyn, Bernard. *Voyagers to the West: A Passage on the Peopling of America on the Eve of the Revolution*. New York: Vintage Books, 1988.

Bancroft, George. *History of the United States from the Discovery of the American Continent to the Declaration of Independence*. Vol. 1. London: Routledge, Warne, & Routledge, 1862.

Barnes, Robert. *Baltimore County Families, 1659–1759*. Baltimore: Genealogical Publishing, 1975.

———. *Maryland Marriages, 1634–1777*. Baltimore: Genealogical Publishing, 1975.

Battestin, Martin C., with Ruthe R. Battestin. *Henry Fielding: A Life*. London: Routledge, 1989.

Baumgarten, Linda. *What Clothes Reveal: The Language of Clothing in Colonial and Federal America*. New Haven: Colonial Williamsburg Foundation in association with Yale University Press, 2002.

Beattie, John M. *Crime and the Courts in England, 1660–1800*. Princeton: Princeton University Press, 1986.

———. "Crime and the Courts in Surrey." In *Crime in England, 1550–1800*, edited by J. Cockburn. Princeton: Princeton University Press, 1977.

———. *Policing and Punishment in London, 1660–1720: Urban Crime and the Limits of Terror*. Oxford: Oxford University Press, 2001.

Beers, Mark H., and Robert Berkow, eds. *The Merck Manual of Diagnosis and Therapy*. Whitehouse, NJ: Merck Research Laboratories, 1999.

Berkin, Carol. *Revolutionary Mothers: Women in the Struggle for America's Independence*. New York: Knopf, 2005.

Blackstone, William. *Commentaries on the Laws of England*. 13th ed. Vol. 4. London: T. Cadell, 1825.

Blumenthal, Walter. *Brides from Bridewell: Female Felons Sent to Colonial America.* 2nd ed. Westport, CT: Greenwood, 1973.

Bowie, Effie Gwynn. *Across the Years in Prince George's County: Genealogical and Biographical History of Some Prince George's County Maryland and Allied Families.* 1947; Baltimore: Genealogical Publishing for Clearfield, 1997.

Boydston, Jeanne. *Home and Work: Housework, Wages, and the Ideology of Labor in the Early Republic.* New York: Oxford University Press, 1990.

Brewer, John, and John Styles, eds. *An Ungovernable People: The English and Their Law in the Seventeenth and Eighteenth Centuries.* London: Hutchison, 1980.

Brown, Kathleen M. *Good Wives, Nasty Wenches and Anxious Patriarchs: Gender, Race and Power in Colonial Virginia.* Williamsburg: University of North Carolina University Press, 1996.

Browne, William Hand. *Maryland: The History of a Palatinate.* Boston: Houghton Mifflin, 1888.

Brugger, Robert J. *Maryland: A Middle Temperament, 1634–1988.* Baltimore: Johns Hopkins University Press in association with Maryland Historical Association, 1988.

Buck, Anne. *Dress in Eighteenth Century England.* London: B. T. Batsford, 1979.

Cardno, Catherine. "'The Fruit of Nine, Sue Kindly Brought': Colonial Enforcement of Sexual Norms in Eighteenth Century Maryland." In *Colonial Chesapeake: New Perspectives,* edited by Debra Meyers and Melanie Perreault. Lanham, MD: Lexington Books, 2006.

Carr, Lois Green. "Diversification in the Chesapeake: Somerset County Maryland in Comparative Perspective." In *Colonial Chesapeake Society,* edited by Lois Green Carr, Philip D. Morgan, and Jean B. Russo. Chapel Hill: University of North Carolina Press, 1988.

Carr, Lois Green, Philip D. Morgan, and Jean B. Russo, eds. *Colonial Chesapeake Society.* Chapel Hill: University of North Carolina Press, 1991.

Cockburn, James Swanston, ed. *Crime in England, 1550–1800.* Princeton: Princeton University Press, 1977.

Coldham, Peter Wilson. *The Complete Book of Emigrants in Bondage, 1614–1775.* Baltimore: Genealogical Publishing, 1988.

———. *Emigrants in Chains: A Social History of Forced Emigration to the Americas of Felons, Destitute Children, Political and Religious Non-conformists, Vagabonds, Beggars, and Other Undesirables, 1607–1776.* Baltimore: Genealogical Publishing, 1992.

———. *The King's Passengers to Maryland and Virginia.* Westminster, MD: Heritage Books, 2006.

———. *More Emigrants in Bondage, 1614–1775.* Baltimore: Genealogical Publishing, 2002.

———. *Settlers of Maryland, 1679–1783.* Vol. 1. Baltimore: Genealogical Publishing, 2002.

———. *Supplement to Complete Book of Emigrants in Bondage, 1614–1775.* Baltimore: Genealogical Publishing, 2001.

Cole, Stephanie. "A White Woman, of Middle Age, Would Be Preferred: Children's Nurses in the Old South." In *Neither lady nor Slave: Working Women in the Old South,* edited by Susanna Delfino and Michele Gillespie. Chapel Hill: University of North Carolina Press, 2002.

Copeland, Peter. *Working Dress in Colonial and Revolutionary America.* Westport, CT: Greenwood, 1977.

Cotton, Jane Balwin, ed. *Maryland Calendar of Wills, 1726 to 1732*. Vol. 6. Baltimore: Kohn & Pollock, 1904.

Daniels, Kay. *Convict Women*. Sydney: Allen & Unwin, 1998.

Deetz, James. *In Small Things Forgotten: An Archaeology of Early American Life*. New York: Anchor Books, Doubleday, 1996.

Defoe, Daniel. *Fortunes and Misfortunes of the Famous Moll Flanders*. 1722; Harmondsworth, UK: Penguin Classics, 1989.

Delfino, Susanna, and Michele Gillespie, eds. *Neither Lady Nor Slave: Working Women of the Old South*. Chapel Hill: University of North Carolina Press, 2002.

The Dictionary of Welsh Biography, 1941–1970: Together with a Supplement to the Dictionary of Welsh Biography Down to 1940. London: Honourable Society of Cymmrodorion, 2001.

Dobash, Russell P., R. Emerson Dobash, and Sue Gutteridge. *The Imprisonment of Women*. Oxford: Basil Blackwell, 1986.

Dunn, Richard S. "Masters and Servants in the Colonial Chesapeake and the Caribbean." In *Early Maryland in a Wider World*, edited by David Quinn. Detroit: Wayne State University Press, 1982.

———. "The Recruitment and Employment of Labor." In *Colonial British America: Essays in the New History of the Early Modern Era*, edited by Jack P. Greene and Jack Richon Pole. Baltimore: Johns Hopkins University Press, 1984.

Earle, Carville. *The Evolution of a Tidewater Settlement: All Hallows Parish, Maryland, 1650–1783*. Chicago: University of Chicago Press, 1975.

Ecker, Grace Dunlop. *A Portrait of Old George Town*. Richmond, VA: Dietz, 1951. Project Gutenberg, EBook #27716, 2009.

Ekirch, A. Roger. *Bound for America: The Transportation of British Convicts to the Colonies, 1718–1775*. Oxford: Oxford University Press, 1987.

Ellefson, C. Ashley. *The Private Punishment of Servants and Slaves in Eighteenth-Century Maryland*. 2010. This is a source document for vol. 822 of *Archives of Maryland Online*, http://www.aomol.net/megafile/msa/speccol/sc2900/sc2908/000001/000822/pdf/am822.pdf (accessed January 3, 2012).

Ellefson, C. Ashley, and Beverly Ellefson. *Runaway Convict Servants in Maryland, 1734–1775*, chart 106. This is a source document for vol. 822 of *Archives of Maryland Online*, http://www.aomol.net/megafile/msa/speccol/sc2900/sc2908/000001/000822/pdf/chart105.pdf (accessed January 3, 2012).

Emmer, Piet C., ed. *Colonialism and Migration: Indentured Labor Before and After Slavery*. Higham MA: Dordrecht, M. Hijhoff, 1986.

Everstine, Carl Nicholas. *The General Assembly of Maryland, 1634–1776*. 1909; Charlottesville, VA: Michie, 1980.

Fraser, Walter J., R. Frank Saunders Jr., and Jon L. Wakelyn, eds. *The Web of Southern Social Relations: Women, Family, and Education*. Athens: University of Georgia Press, 1985.

Galenson, David. *White Servitude in Colonial America*. New York: Cambridge University Press, 1981.

Garcia, Mercedes Morris. "Exploring Cultural Homelessness: At Home Here, There, and Nowhere." In *Women in Cross Cultural Transitions*, edited by Jill M. Bystydzienski and Estelle P. Resnik. Bloomington, IN: Phi Delta Kappa Educational Foundation, 1994.

Gee, Joshua. *The Trade and Navigation of Great-Britain Considered.* London: A. Bettesworth, C. Hitch & S. Birt, 1738.

Gemery, Henry A. "Markets for Migrants: English Indentured Servitude and Emigration in the Seventeenth and Eighteenth Centuries." In *Colonialism and Migration: Indentured Labor Before and After Slavery,* edited by Piet C. Emmer. Higham, MA: Dordrecht, M. Hijhoff, 1986.

Gould, Clarence P. *The Land System in Maryland, 1720–1765.* Baltimore: Johns Hopkins University Press, 1913.

———. *Money and Transportation in Maryland, 1720–1765.* Baltimore: Johns Hopkins University Press, 1915.

Green, Karen M. *The Maryland Gazette, 1727–1761: Genealogical and Historical Abstracts.* Galveston: Frontier, 1990.

Gude, Gilbert. *Where the Potomac Begins: A History of the North Branch Valley.* Washington, DC: Seven Locks, 1984.

Gundersen, Joan. *To Be Useful to the World: Women in Revolutionary America, 1740–1790.* New York: Twayne, 1996.

Hay, Douglas. "Property Authority and the Criminal Law." In *Albion's Fatal Tree: Crime and Society in Eighteenth Century England,* edited by Douglas Hay et al. London: Allen Lane, 1975.

Hay, Douglas et al., eds. *Albion's Fatal Tree: Crime and Society in Eighteenth Century England.* London: Allen Lane, 1975.

Hay, Douglas, and Francis Snyder. *Policing and Prosecution in England, 1750–1850.* Oxford: Oxford University Press, 1989.

Herndon, Ruth Wallis, and John E. Murray. *Children Bound to Labor: The Pauper Apprentice System in Early America.* Ithaca: Cornell University Press, 2009.

Hill, Bridget. *Servants: English Domestics in the Eighteenth Century.* New York: Oxford University Press, 1996.

———. *Women Alone: Spinsters in England, 1660–1850.* New Haven: Yale University Press, 2001.

———. *Women, Work and Sexual Politics in Eighteenth Century England.* Oxford: B. Blackwell, 1989.

Hitchcock, Tim, and Heather Shaw, eds. *The Streets of London: From the Great Fire to the Great Stink.* London: Rivers Oram, 2003.

Hoffer, Peter Charles, ed. *Colonial Women and Domesticity: Selected Articles on Gender in Early America.* New York: Garland, 1988.

Hoffman, Ronald. *Princes of Ireland, Planters of Maryland: A Carroll Saga, 1500–1782.* Chapel Hill: University of North Carolina Press, 2000.

Hoffman, Ronald, and Peter J. Albert, eds. *Women in the Age of the American Revolution.* Charlottesville: University Press of Virginia, 1989.

Hughes, Robert. *The Fatal Shore: A History of the Transportation of Convicts to Australia, 1787–1868.* London: Collins Harvill, 1987.

Hughes, Thomas. *History of the Society of Jesus in North America, Colonial and Federal.* Vols. 1 and 2. New York: Burrows Brothers, 1907.

Ignatieff, Michael. *A Just Measure of Pain: The Penitentiary in the Industrial Revolution, 1750–1850.* New York: Pantheon Books, 1978.

Inwood, Stephen. *A History of London.* London: Macmillan, 1998.

Isaacs, Rhys. *The Transformation of Virginia*. Chapel Hill: University of North Carolina Press, 1999.

Johnston-Liik, Edith Mary. *Ireland in the Eighteenth Century*. Dublin: Gill & Macmillan, 1974.

Jones, Frederick Robertson. *The Colonization of the Middle States and Maryland*. Vol. 4 of *The History of North America*. Philadelphia: George Barrie & Sons, 1904.

Jones, Jacqueline. "Race, Sex, and Self-evident Truths: The Status of Slave Women during the Era of the American Revolution." In, *Women in the Age of the American Revolution*, edited by Ronald Hoffman and Peter J. Albert. Charlottesville: University Press of Virginia, 1989.

Jordan, Don, and Michael Walsh. *White Cargo: The Forgotten History of Britain's White Slaves in America*. New York: New York University Press, 2008.

Kalman, Bonnie. *The Kitchen*. New York: Crabtree, 1993.

Kermode, Jenny, and Garthine Walker, eds. *Women, Crime and the Courts in Early Modern England*. London: UCL, 1994.

Kessler-Harris, A. *Out to Work: A History of Wage Earning Women in the United States*. New York: Oxford University Press, 2003.

King, Peter. *Crime, Justice and Discretion in England, 1740–1820*. Oxford: Oxford University Press, 2000.

Kulikoff, Allan. *Tobacco and Slaves: The Development of Southern Cultures in the Chesapeake, 1680–1800*. Chapel Hill: University of North Carolina Press for the Institute of Early American History and Culture, Williamsburg, Virginia, 1986.

Land, Aubrey C. *Colonial Maryland: A History*. Millwood, NY: KTO, 1981.

Latimer, John. *Annals of Bristol in the Eighteenth Century*. Bristol: J. Frome, 1893.

Linebaugh, Peter. *The London Hanged–Crime and Civil Society in the Eighteenth Century*. Harmondsworth, UK: Allen Lane, Penguin Press, 1991.

Madaras, Larry, and James SoRelle, eds. *Taking Sides: Clashing Views in United States History*. 13th ed. Vol. 1. New York: McGraw-Hill Higher Education, 2009.

Main, Gloria. *Tobacco Colony: Life in Early Maryland, 1650–1720*. Princeton: Princeton University Press, 1982.

Malcolmson, Robert W. "Infanticide in Eighteenth Century England." In *Crime in England, 1550–1800*, edited by James S. Cockburn. Princeton: Princeton University Press, 1977.

———. *Life and Labour in England, 1700–1780*. London: Hutchison, 1981.

Marks, Shula, and Peter Richardson. *International Labour Migration: Historical Perspectives*. Hounslow, UK: M. Temple Smith for the Institute of Commonwealth Studies, 1984.

Marshall, William. *The Rural Economy of Yorkshire, Comprising the Management of Landed Estates and the Present Practice of Husbandry in the Agricultural Districts of That County. Vol*. 2. London: T. Cadell, 1788.

Matthaei, Julie A. *An Economic History of Women in America*. New York: Schocken Books, 1982.

McCormac, Eugene. *White Servitude in Colonial Maryland, 1634–1820*. Baltimore: Johns Hopkins University Press, 1904.

Meacham, Sarah Hand. "'They Will Be Adjudged by Their Drinke, What Kind of Housewives They Are': Gender, Technology, and Household Cidering in England and the

Chesapeake, 1690–1760." In *Colonial Chesapeake: New Perspectives*, edited by Debra Meyers and Melanie Perreault. Lanham, MD: Lexington Books, 2006.

Meyers, Debra. *Common Whores, Vertuous Women, and Loveing Wives: Free Will Christian Women in Colonial Maryland*. Bloomington: Indiana University Press, 2003.

Meyers, Debra, and Melanie Perreault, eds. *Colonial Chesapeake: New Perspectives*. Lanham, MD: Lexington Books, 2006.

Miller, Henry M. "An Archaeological Perspective on Diet." In *Colonial Chesapeake Society*, edited by Lois Green Carr, Philip D. Morgan, and Jean B. Russo. Chapel Hill: University of North Carolina Press, 1991.

Morgan, Edmund S. *American Slavery, American Freedom: The Ordeal of Colonial Virginia*. New York: Norton, 1995.

Morgan, Gwenda. *The Debate on the American Revolution*. Manchester: Manchester University Press, 2007.

Morgan, Gwenda, and Peter Rushton. *Eighteenth-Century Criminal Transportation: The Formation of the Criminal Atlantic*. New York: Palgrave Macmillan, 2003.

———. *Rogues, Thieves and the Rule of Law: The Problem of Law Enforcement in Northeast England, 1718–1800*. London: UCL, 1998.

Morgan, Gwenda, and Peter Rushton, eds. *The Justicing Notebook (1750–1764) of Edmund Tew, Rector of Boldon*. Woodbridge, Suffolk, UK: Boydell [for] the Surtees Society, 2000.

Morris, Richard B. *Government and Labor in Early America*. New York: Columbia University Press, 1946.

National Maritime Museum. "Prison Hulks on the River Thames: Life on Board." In *Port Cities, London*. http://www.portcities.org.uk (accessed June 10, 2012).

O'Brien, Eris. *The Foundation of Australia, 1786–1800: A Study in English Criminal Practice and Penal Colonisation in the Eighteenth Century*. London: Sheed & Ward, 1937.

Oldham, Wilfrid. *Britain's Convicts to the Colonies*. Sydney: Library of Australian History, 1990.

Oxley, Deborah. *Convict Maids*. Melbourne: Cambridge University Press, 1996.

Palk, Deidre. "Private Crime in Public and Private Places: Pickpockets and Shoplifters in London, 1780–1823." In *The Streets of London: From the Great Fire to the Great Stink*, edited by Tim Hitchcock and Heather Shaw. London: Rivers Oram, 2003.

Papenfuse, Edward C. *In Pursuit of Profit: The Annapolis Merchants in the Era of the American Revolution, 1763–1805*. Baltimore: Johns Hopkins University Press, 1975.

Peden, Henry. *Bastardy Cases in Baltimore Co., 1673–1783*. Westminster, MD: Willow Bend Books, 2001.

———. *St. John's and St. George's Parish Registers (Baltimore and Harford Counties), 1696–1851*. Westminster, MD: Family Line, 1987.

Picard, Liza. *Dr. Johnson's London: Life in London, 1740–1770*. London: Weidenfeld & Nicolson, 2000.

Plumb, John H. *England in the Eighteenth Century*. Harmondsworth, UK: Penguin Books, 1981.

Pringle, Patrick. *Hue and Cry: the Birth of the British Police*. London: Museum Press, 1956.

Quinn, David, ed. *Early Maryland in a Wider World*. Detroit: Wayne State University Press, 1982.

Radzinowicz, Leon. *A History of English Criminal Law and Its Administration from 1750.* Vol. 1. London: Stevens & Sons, 1948.

Rawlings, Philip. *Drunks, Whores and Idle Apprentices: Criminal Biographies of the Eighteenth Century.* New York: Routledge, 1992.

Reamy, Bill, and Martha Reamy. *Records of St. Paul's [Episcopalian] Parish Registers.* Vols. 1 and 2. Westminster, MD: Family Line, 1988.

———. *St. George's Parish Registers, 1689–1793.* Westminster, MD: Family Line, 1988.

Robert, Joseph C. *The Story of Tobacco in America.* New York: Knopf, 1949.

Romilly, Samuel. *Observations on the Criminal Law of England: As It Relates to Capital Punishments, and on the Mode in Which It Is Administered.* London: T. Cadell, 1810.

Rule, John. *Albion's People: English Society, 1714–1815.* New York: Longman, 1992.

———. *The Experience of Labour in Eighteenth-Century Industry.* London: Croom Helm, 1981.

Rule, John, and Roger Wells. *Crime, Protest and Popular Politics in Southern England, 1740–1850.* Rio Grande, OH: Hambledon, 1997.

Russell, Donna Valley. *Frederick County Wills, 1744–1794.* New Market, MD: Catoctin, 2002.

Russo, Jean, and J. Elliott Russo. "Court Treatment of Orphans and Illegitimate Children in Colonial Maryland." In *Children Bound to Labor,* edited by Ruth Wallis Herndon and John E. Murray, 151–65. Ithaca: Cornell University Press, 2009.

Scharf, John Thomas. *History of Maryland–From the Earliest Period to the Present Day.* 1879; Hatboro, PA: Tradition, 1967.

———. *History of Western Maryland: Being a History of Frederick, Montgomery, Carroll, Washington, Allegany and Garrett Counties from the Earliest Period to the Present Day, Including Biographical Sketches of Their Representative Men.* 1882; Baltimore: Regional Publishing, 1968.

Scott, Kenneth, and Janet R. Clarke. *Abstracts from the "Pennsylvania Gazette," 1748–1755.* Baltimore: Genealogical Publishing, 1977.

Semmes, Raphael. *Crime and Punishment in Early Maryland.* 1938; Baltimore: Johns Hopkins University Press, 1996.

Shackel, Paul A., Mark S. Warner, and Paul R. Mullins, eds. *Annapolis Pasts: Historical Archaeology in Annapolis, Maryland.* Knoxville: University of Tennessee Press, 1998.

Shaw, Alan George Lewers. *Convicts and the Colonies: A Study of the Penal Transportation from Great Britain and Ireland to Australia and other Parts of the British Empire.* London: Faber & Faber, 1966.

Skaggs, David Curtis. *Roots of Maryland Democracy, 1753–1776.* Westport, CT: Greenwood, 1973.

Smith, Abbot Emerson. *Colonists in Bondage: White Servitude and Convict Labor in America, 1607–1776.* 1947; New York: Norton, 1971.

Smith, Daniel Blake. *Inside the Great House: Planter Family Life in Eighteenth Century Chesapeake Society.* Ithaca: Cornell University Press, 1980.

Stevenson, John. *Popular Disturbances in England, 1700–1832.* New York: Longman, 1992.

Stuart, Sarah Elizabeth. *Abstracts of Kent County Calendar of Wills, 1738–1776.* Baltimore: Maryland Historical Society, 1933.

Styles, John. *The Dress of the People: Everyday Fashion in Eighteenth-Century England*. New Haven: Yale University Press, 2007.

Summers, Anne. *Damned Whores and God's Police*. Ringwood, Victoria: Penguin Books, 1982.

Tate, Thad W., and David L. Ammerman, eds. *The Chesapeake in the Seventeenth Century: Essays on Anglo-American Society*. Chapel Hill: University of North Carolina Press, 1979.

Thomas, Donald. *Henry Fielding*. London: Weidenfield & Nicolson, 1990.

Thomas, Hugh. *The Slave Trade: A History of the Atlantic Slave Trade, 1440–1870*. London: Picador, 1997.

Thomas, James W., and Thomas John Chew Williams. *History of Allegany County Maryland*. Cumberland, MD: L. R. Titsworth, 1923.

Thompson, Andrew C. *George II: King and Elector*. New Haven: Yale University Press, 2011.

Thompson, Edward P. *Customs in Common*. New York: New Press, 1993.

———. *Whigs and Hunters: The Origins of the Black Act*. London: Allen Lane, 1975.

Tracey, Grace L., and John Philip Dern. *Pioneers of Old Monocacy: The Early Settlement of Frederick County, Maryland, 1721–1743*. Baltimore: Genealogical Publishing, 1987.

Trevelyan, George Macaulay. *English Social History*. London: Longmans, Green, 1948.

Walsh, Lorena. "The Experiences and Status of Women in the Chesapeake, 1750–1775." In *The Web of Southern Social Relations: Women, Family, and Education*, edited by Walter J. Fraser, R. Frank Saunders Jr., and Jon L. Wakelyn. Athens: University of Georgia Press, 1985.

White, Shane, and Graham White. *Stylin': African American Expressive Culture from Its Beginnings to the Zoot Suit*. Ithaca: Cornell University Press, 1998.

Williams, Thomas John Chew. *A History of Washington County, Maryland from the Earliest Settlements to the Present Time*. 1906; Baltimore: Regional Publishing, 1968.

Williams, Thomas John Chew, and Folger McKinsey. *History of Frederick County, Maryland*. 1910; Baltimore: Regional Publishing, 1979.

Wilstach, Paul. *Tidewater Maryland*. New York: Tudor, 1945.

Wolf, Stephanie Grauman. *As Various as Their Land: The Everyday Life of Eighteenth-Century Americans*. Fayetteville: University of Arkansas Press, 1993.

Wood, George Arnold. *The Discovery of Australia*. London: Macmillan, 1922.

Wood, Gordon S. *The Radicalism of the American Revolution*. New York: Vintage Books, 1993.

Wright, F. Edward. *Anne Arundel County Church Records of the Seventeenth and Eighteenth Centuries*. Westminster: Family Line, 1989.

Wrigley, Edward A., and Roger S. Schofield. *The Population History of England, 1541–1871: A Reconstruction*. New York: Cambridge University Press, 1989.

Wulf, Karin. *Not All Wives: Women of Colonial Philadelphia*. Ithaca: Cornell University Press, 2000.

Yentsch, Anne Elizabeth. *A Chesapeake Family and Their Slaves: A Study in Historical Archaeology*. Cambridge: Cambridge University Press, 1994.

Zinn, Howard. *A People's History of the United States, 1492–Present*. London: Pearson/Longman, 2003.

Index